The
Home
Extension
Manual

Acknowledgements

SPECIAL THANKS TO
Basil Parylo, G. D. Rawlings Building Contractors, Bill Carless

PHOTOGRAPHY
David Davies, Basil Parylo, Richard Woodroofe MRICS

Thanks also to
Aylesbury Vale District Council, David Snell, UK Timber Frame Association,
Ann & Rod Smeaton @ eddystoneselfbuild.co.uk, Mark Harding @ Birmingham City Council,
Duncan & family builders, Ian MacMillan FRICS, Buildstore.co.uk, Jeremy March MRICS and Mrs Linton.
And
HeritageBathrooms.com, InStyle Products Ltd, Solalighting.com, Capitalfireplaces.co.uk, Caple Kitchens,
Roycebathrooms.co.uk, Celcon, Milbank Floors Ltd, PolarLight UK, Capel, Bristan.com, Potton Ltd, Raindance,
Hepstore.com, Designer-radiators.com, Shower-guide.com, Acantha Lifestyle Ltd, DCLG & HMSO, Savrow Stilts,
Visionhouse-software, GA fixings, Sadolin.

Published in March 2007

British Library Cataloguing in Publication Data:
A catalogue record for this book is available
from the British Library

ISBN 978 1 84425 357 9

Published by Haynes Publishing, Sparkford, Yeovil,
Somerset BA22 7JJ, UK
Tel: 01963 442030 Fax: 01963 440001
Int. tel: +44 1963 442030 Int. fax: +44 1963 440001
E-mail: sales@haynes.co.uk
Website: www.haynes.co.uk

Haynes North America Inc.
861 Lawrence Drive, Newbury Park, California 91320, USA

Printed and bound in Great Britain
by J. H. Haynes & Co. Ltd, Sparkford

By the same author

ISBN: 978 1 84425 214 5
RRP: £19.99

ISBN: 978 1 84425 213 8
RRP: £19.99

The
Home
Extension
Manual

Ian Alistair Rock MRICS

Technical consultants
Colin K. Dale FRICS, **Michael Haslam** MSc FRICS

CONTENTS

INTRODUCTION

Sooner or later, most homes can start to feel
a little crowded. So if you find yourself
hemmed in and running out of space, there
will be two possible alternatives to consider:
moving, or improving.

The problem with moving house is that it's officially one of life's all-time most stressful events, ranking somewhere alongside the joys of personal bankruptcy, death, divorce, and redundancy.

So if you're happy with the location of your present home, and your neighbours are simply the best, the ideal solution may be to make it bigger and build on. By making the most of your existing house you can avoid all the dreaded pitfalls of moving – broken chains, inexplicable delays, damning surveys and gazumping, not to mention the pleasures of dealing with dubious estate agents and frosty solicitors – all of which can conspire to send your blood pressure rocketing. Extending your home makes even better sense when you consider the small fortune you will save by not having to pay sales fees and stamp duty.

On the other hand, there are plenty of folk who can reel off spine-chilling stories of cowboy builders and breathtakingly incompetent DIY disasters. So 'getting the builders in' is unlikely to prove much of a rest-cure. There are many good reasons to extend, but the desire for a peaceful life probably isn't one of them.

It's important to be realistic about what can be achieved. TV property programmes make compulsive viewing, but they can also be highly misleading. Going from zero to 'property hero' in the space of a 45-minute programme doesn't really tell the full story. TV cameras make saints of us all. The reality is that construction projects can go horribly wrong. Even the smartest people can come unstuck, marooned in half-finished buildings nursing ruinous bills.

But do the job right and you will find the experience of getting your new home extension designed and built highly rewarding. Apart from significantly upping the value of your main asset and saving shed-loads of money, you should emerge from the project with many useful new skills (and a few good stories), well equipped to carry out future grand designs.

So whether you intend to take the conventional route by employing an architect and main contractor, or to save money by directly employing your own sub-contractors and doing some of the work yourself, this comprehensive *Home Extension Manual* explains all the tips and traps at every stage, from design through to successful completion.

WEBSITE
Further detailed information, sample plans, letters, documents and design software can be found at our website **www.home-extension.co.uk**.

Photo: H+H Celcon Ltd

1 BEFORE YOU START

There's no point going to all the expense and trouble of extending your house if it's not ultimately going to make your home-life considerably more enjoyable. By improving the practicality for everyone living there and adding to your property's value, it should be a win/win situation. But a successful outcome will only happen by thinking ahead very carefully and planning for all eventualities. So before getting up from the sofa to set off on this costly expedition into the unknown, it is well worth taking a few moments to mull-over the following issues.

What's the point?

Let's face it, building work can very easily end up being a massive intrusion.

No matter how well things are planned and managed, you won't get thanked for the inevitable dust, mud, noise and disruption. And if the builders manage to cut through your mains services (as so often happens) you will instantly be promoted to the status of household Public Enemy Number One. So it's well worth making sure at the outset that your partner and the rest of the family are as keen on the idea of extending as you are.

A quick internet search for books about 'how to build a home extension' comes up with this helpful piece of advice: 'Customers who bought this also bought: "How To Get Divorced In Ireland".' You have been warned.

Is it practical?

Before involving anyone else, it's important to first consider what you really want from the project. Reasons for wanting to extend typically revolve around the need for:

- ■ **More space** – At the end of each year, as the 'Battle of Cooking Christmas Dinner' draws to its weary close, there is an inevitable realisation in many households that 'the kitchen is just too small'. The resulting New Year's resolution may be to build a dream kitchen in a new home extension. But of course, the need for more space can occur at any time as our lifestyles continuously change – babies arriving, oldies needing a 'granny' annexe, or just somewhere to farm out teenagers.
- ■ **Greater comfort** – There was a time when clashing interests meant that the male of the species would spend half his life exiled to a cold, dank garden shed. But not any more. Now the nation's menfolk can live in peace with cigars, home brew, bass amps and drum kits, pimping the ride on that nitro-fuelled street-machine in comfort.
- ■ **Improved saleability** – This is perhaps the hardest reason to justify extending, because it's not that easy to stand back and look at your home through the impartial eyes of a property developer.

The most common reasons for extending are to create larger kitchens or add bathrooms. But before embarking on a major project, check that you've made the most of the space you've already got. That means utilising all available storage space and underused rooms. For example, it may be possible to add a small en suite bathroom without extending, just by partitioning off a corner of a bedroom. A space measuring only 1 x 2.6m is the minimum required.

If you do decide to extend, it pays to be critical about your ideas at the outset. Be harsh with yourself now, rather than discovering after all the hard work and expense that everyone detests the new layout. Ask yourself if your Grand Design will significantly improve the desirability of the property for all who live there? Or will it take up too much of the garden, drastically reducing the amount of useful 'amenity space'?

Physically your options may be quite limited, if, for example, the house already occupies most of its plot, or has already been extended. If you live in a terraced house with a small garden there may be very limited scope for expansion. Converting the loft space is often the cheapest option, but is not always possible, especially on more modern properties. In terms of cost, two storey extensions are about 20% cheaper to build per sq m than single stories, because the cost of the foundations and roof is effectively halved, being spread between two floors.

Later we'll consider the minefield of technical issues arising from the site itself. The presence of nearby drain runs, tree roots and buried pipes and cables all need to be checked. Also there may be legal nasties waiting to jump out and bite you, in the form of party walls, old rights of way, and vaguely defined boundaries.

Your freedom to design will also be restricted by things like the location of existing services, which can dictate the position of new kitchen and bathroom fittings. Of course, anything's possible if you throw enough money at it, but to keep within any realistic budget sensible planning at the outset is crucial.

Will you get your money back?

Don't automatically assume that you will make loads of money by building on to your house. Having an ugly, poorly designed and badly built monstrosity stuck on the side of your home could seriously damage its resale value.

For the majority of home-extenders the motivation behind extending is to improve lifestyle rather than to reap any immediate profit. Nonetheless, making such a massive financial investment means that it's essential to be aware of all the monetary implications before reaching for your chequebook.

It's always possible that your initial assumptions could be way out. For example, the proud owner of a small ex-

Council semi who enthusiastically transforms his entire back garden into a giant swimming pool complex may be convinced that the value of his house has sky-rocketed. But the sad truth is that for most buyers this kind of 'improvement' is a real disincentive. On the other hand, the same improvement could be perfectly appropriate for a house with larger grounds.

Of course, for each type of house there are limits as to how much value can realistically be added. There will be a maximum price anyone will be prepared to pay for a property in a particular location regardless of how superb it looks and how many aircraft carriers you can fit in the living room. Seek the opinion of an experienced local estate agent.

So what adds the most value? Basically, if your plans help overcome a seriously negative aspect of the original house then you should be onto a winner. For example, enlarging a tiny original kitchen. As a rule of thumb, things like well-planned extra bedrooms and en suite bathrooms normally add value. But be careful not to let your enthusiasm for adding new rooms actually detract from the layout of your existing house. It is not unusual for new rear extensions to blot out light to the old dining room, which then becomes a sort of murky no-man's-land that nobody uses; or for a loft conversion to require a new staircase that results in the loss of one of the original bedrooms – *ie* gaining one room, but in the process losing another.

Kitchens are best located so that you don't have to traipse through them to get somewhere else, so adding a new

Link detached house (right) would become an end terrace, if extended above garage, potentially detracting from value.

bathroom extension to a kitchen could detract from the existing layout. And adding another few metres to an already large room won't normally pay back the cost of the work.

As a nation, it seems we are becoming ever more hygienic. Current tastes demand one 'family bathroom' for every three bedrooms, plus en suites for the master bedroom and guest rooms.

As everyone knows, property values are very much influenced by 'kerb appeal'. Considering the way a property looks, and how the new extension will affect first impressions, is particularly important with older 'classic' houses – Georgian, Victorian, Edwardian, and even inter-war properties. Happily, the planners will generally welcome designs that enhance the original architecture. For listed buildings or those in conservation areas, architects may have no choice but to come up with something 'sensible', rather than being tempted to spin off into orbit with anything too outrageous.

Is it neighbourly?

It's a strange fact, but neighbours can live together in perfect harmony for decades – until relations suddenly turn sour as soon as the builders arrive. Fortunately, nine times out of ten the solution is down to simple communication. Just taking time out to talk, well in advance of the work starting, should help ease any potential conflict. A few soothing words now will be far cheaper than conducting warfare via solicitors at a later date.

So at this stage it pays to consider what effect your proposed building work is likely to have on your neighbours. Even if the extension itself is not a problem for them, the inevitable noise, mess and large trucks delivering building materials at all hours of the day, surely will be. Builders have an endearing tendency to commence work on site at the crack of dawn accompanied by much whistling, singing, swearing, thudding and crashing. This can strain even the best of relationships.

Involving the neighbours in your plans at this early stage not only helps prepare them for inconveniences to come, but may also help sweeten things a little before the

Council planners thoughtfully invite them to submit objections to your scheme.

To be fair, although you rarely hear a good word about the poor old planners, they play an essential peacekeeping role by ruling out at the design stage any overbearing, monolithic extensions that would condemn next door to a life of perpetual gloom, blocking out daylight and staring down invasively at their private property.

Ideally, to refine your plans before they get cut to ribbons by the planners, you really need to consider how you would feel if your neighbours were proposing to build a similar design.

How much should you do yourself?

Building work

Don't bite off more than you can chew. Speaking from bitter experience, it is sometimes easy to underestimate the amount of work involved whilst overestimating one's own abilities. Unless you're used to doing heavy building work, and have good experience at plumbing, bricklaying, joinery etc, make it easy on yourself and get the professionals in.

If you're determined to tackle some of the work personally, one golden rule is to never be in a position where you're under pressure to rush a job. Give yourself a break by doubling the amount of time that you first estimated that particular job would take. It's always a good idea to select jobs that aren't too time-critical. Getting to the stage where the roof is on and the building is weathertight can often be a race against time. After that you may find there is less urgency. But bear in mind that different trades need space to work without tripping over each other or you. To save money, you may find it easier to have a bash at doing some of the decoration and finishing works, such as landscaping, at the end of the project, once the contractors have completed the main works.

Design

You may find it easier to make a serious contribution by doing some of the design and planning work rather than attempting hod-carrying. This could make a significant saving on costs without crippling your back.

However, whilst there is no legal requirement to use an architect or surveyor, it usually pays to tackle things yourself that you're good at and employ others with special skills to do the rest. So it's normally a good idea to discuss your plans with an experienced professional designer at the outset – which may even avoid the need to extend at all – perhaps they'll know some ingenious way to make space-saving improvements at a fraction of the cost.

Project management

Part of the fun of TV property programmes is watching in horrified disbelief as people who haven't got the first clue about construction suddenly decide they are perfectly qualified to take on the role of 'Project Manager'. In fact, the Project Management role is a highly skilled one, the objective being to successfully steer your project to achieve a quality product, within budget and on time. This is not at all an easy task, as national newspaper headlines routinely remind us – massive delays, unfinished works and staggeringly huge cost overruns are only too familiar, even on projects managed by major award-winning firms of architects, think of Wembley Stadium, the Channel Tunnel, and The British Library, to name but a few.

The good news is that yours is not a complex mega-build, and that any decent firm of contractors will be aiming to achieve a successful completion within the agreed timescale, with or without someone standing over them. In which case you may think 'If they're so good at managing themselves, why not just let them get on with it?' One reason is that, with the best will in the world, the builder's objectives will be different from yours, and handing over total control of your home and your wallet to them is a somewhat risky strategy – see Chapter 5.

But to be a successful Project Manager you don't need to be a genius. Clear planning ahead, and applying common sense to problems as they arise, will do much to ensure a successful outcome.

Will it blend in?

To get some idea of what kind of extension is likely to be permitted, take a wander round the local area and make a note of the size and style of extensions that other people

have built. In most cases you are restricted to four basic variations: a single-storey or two-storey building which can have either a pitched roof or a flat roof. Having decided which combination works best for you, the design details can then be considered.

Your proposals will need to broadly comply with the Local Development Plan, which can be viewed at the planning department of your local Council, or online.

Taking a look around could also provide you with useful ammunition if the planners decide to resist your proposals. Identifying similar designs in the neighbourhood to the one you want to build can present a very powerful argument in your favour (assuming they weren't built illegally). Or you may be lucky and find that the size and style of extension you want to build falls within 'permitted development' rules, so you don't need to worry about getting planning consent at all. See Chapter 3.

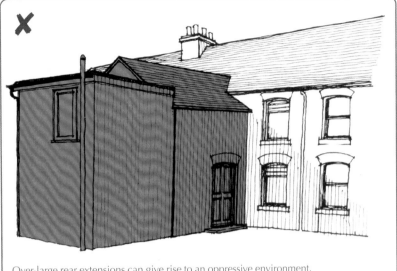

Over-large rear extensions can give rise to an oppressive environment.

Drawing: Aylesbury Vale District Council

Can you afford it?

There seems to be an unwritten rule that building projects must inevitably overshoot their budgets, usually by a substantial margin. Fortunately, newbuild projects such as constructing a typical home extension are considerably easier to cost than the equivalent refurbishment of an old building.

With a little careful planning at this stage, the total payments you'll have to make should be fairly predictable. If you want to get a rough idea of the likely costs now, run your plans past a friendly architect or surveyor, or check the 'cost calculator' on the website. In reality, builders' prices sometimes bear little relationship to the actual price of materials and labour. Like other businesses they'll be riding the waves of supply and demand, perhaps with a bit added to reflect the builder's view of 'what your area will take'. Some boast shamelessly about adding an extra 25 per cent as soon as they enter a 'posh postcode area'! On the other hand, smaller jobs can often turn out to be more difficult than large projects, generating relatively small sums in profit. So a significant mark-up is needed to make it worthwhile. Fees for a designer (not including managing the project) will probably add another five to ten per cent, and Local Authority charges for planning and building regulations can add upwards of £1,000.

That just leaves the small matter of coming up with the ready cash. It is essential to arrange funding early on, as nothing sours relationships with builders more than delayed payment.

A few money matters worth pondering at this stage are:

- Don't finance building work on your credit card – the interest rates can be ruinous. Mortgage funding is normally the cheapest option, and because banks know that building an extension means the value of your property should increase proportionately it is nearly always possible to arrange. Unsecured loans are dearer, but still better than credit cards.
- Keep a contingency sum in reserve as there will inevitably be some unforeseen extra expenses. The biggest budget breaker is not actually overspending, but producing an unrealistic budget in the first place. Probably the biggest source of unexpected expense is the need for unforeseen drainage or foundation work.
- Grants for improvements are occasionally available from Local Authorities, but don't get too excited – they're normally only obtainable if the proposed extension meets very specific criteria, like providing a missing basic amenity (if you currently have no indoor WC or bathroom) or if the extension brings the house up to a 'fitness standard' by helping to overcome serious disrepair. Grants for disabled facilities are widely available for registered disabled owner/occupiers, such as funding towards the cost of an extension for a suitably equipped shower room. The Local Authority may even assist with the design.

VAT

Whilst on the subject of finance, one of the great iniquities of life in this country is the way VAT is charged on building works. Essential maintenance, improvements and extensions to existing homes are charged at the full rate, whilst property developers building new houses pay nothing. The cost of paying VAT will add a significant amount to the price of your extension. Builders' quotes are often rather vague on this subject, so make sure it is clarified early on. There are, however, some possible small consolations. Your contractors may agree to you deferring payment of VAT to them until completion, and if you're VAT-registered you may be able to claim some of the tax back.

VAT on listed buildings is reduced to zero per cent for 'approved material alterations' when undertaken by a VAT-registered contractor. Work on houses left empty for ten years or more should be free of VAT, and those left empty for three years or more may be chargeable at only five per cent, the same reduced rate as for flat conversions.

Of course, it is always possible to save on VAT by directly employing individual subcontractors who are non-VAT registered. But main contractors are highly unlikely to have a low enough turnover to fall into this category. See Chapter 5 and www.hmce.gov.co.uk .

Is your health up to it?

Those of a nervous disposition would be well advised to consider spending their money on a relaxing holiday rather than getting the builders in. Alternatively, it would be prudent to arrange for the whole project to be professionally managed at arm's length by an experienced

firm of architects or chartered surveyors. Watching your home become transformed into a building site for months on end can be somewhat disheartening, even for the hardiest of souls.

Is it legal?

As a general rule, the less you have to do with lawyers in life the better, so it's worth considering some basic legal issues on Day One. Here are some of the more common 'legalities' to ponder:

■ Houses and bungalows are almost always Freehold, but if your property is leasehold (normally flats and

maisonettes) you'll not usually be permitted to extend or make structural alterations without the prior written consent of the Freeholder.

■ Extending your home may be legally prohibited by a 'restrictive covenant'. These are conditions sometimes written into the deeds of the property by the original developer at the time of construction. Their intention is to prevent residents 'lowering the tone of the area' by such activities as parking a fleet of kebab vans in driveways, running brothels, or erecting inappropriate structures in their gardens. Even if you have planning permission to build, you can still fall foul of the law by breaching such a condition. Fortunately, it is usually not too difficult for solicitors to overturn them.

■ Mortgage lenders like to know in advance of any proposed significant alterations to their security (ie your home).

■ Check that your buildings insurance cover remains fully valid during the works. If not, will the builder's insurance cover the cost of any damage? You'll also need to take out insurance for the works themselves.

■ Nothing cheeses neighbours off more than discovering that their boundary walls have been totally redeveloped. So check the Title Deeds and land registry documents in advance to see who owns which boundaries and if there are any rights of way over the land. If you infringe someone else's land, their lawyers will be licking their lips at the thought of embarking on costly litigation, at your expense. The bad news is that official drawings of plots on the deeds are usually such an incredibly small scale that it may be virtually impossible to pinpoint the exact dividing line on the ground, so you may need to formally agree the precise boundary line on site with the neighbour, with a surveyor present. This is particularly important if you need to build right up to the boundary line. See party walls in Chapter 3.

Personal safety

You are about to experience some of the most hazardous weeks of your entire life. Building sites are dangerous places, so it's essential to take all sensible safety precautions. There's no point building yourself a brilliant new home extension but only being able to appreciate it squinting from inside a mobile life-support system.

However, you could be forgiven for assuming that many builders welcome a spot of self-harming, since the sad reality on many sites is that health and safety is routinely ignored. Most safety advice is just common sense, like not mincing around building sites in sandals, or operating power tools whilst anorak toggles or jewellery are dangling down. You don't have to be Oliver Stone to work out how a cinematically gruesome death can result from a combination of long hair, scarves and powerful machinery.

- **Toes and feet:** Always wear steel-capped boots.
- **Eyes:** Wear goggles/eye protectors, especially when operating power tools. It just takes one tiny shard to fly into your face to blind you for life.
- **Ears:** Operating noisy machinery, especially in a confined space, means risking partial deafness in later life – like an ageing heavy metal guitarist, but without the fun. Wear ear protectors.
- **Lungs:** A dust mask is a cheap and easy way to stop you inhaling dangerous particles and developing irritable lung syndrome.
- **Back:** Back injuries are surprisingly common – from trying to lift too much or in the wrong way, or from falls. Take special care with bags of cement, plaster, heavy lintels etc. Keeping the site tidy will help avoid tripping up.

On large professionally managed housing developments, the signs are unambiguous: '*No helmet, No safety boots, No job*'. They will also insist on site staff wearing lurid, luminous, lime-coloured safety jackets (on some sites different trades wear different colours). You might wish to enforce similar safety standards on your site.

A guide to body-care on building sites would have to include:

- **Brain:** A 'Bob the Builder' safety helmet is essential anywhere you might cut your head open or where stuff could drop on you.
- **Hands:** Gloves must be worn for all work shifting materials around – especially bricks and blocks and chemicals. Even cement and concrete can burn your skin.

And finally…

If all the above hasn't completely turned you off the idea of extending your home, now is a good time to take a look in some detail at what lies beneath your feet – the ground that will need to support the new wing of your residence.

2 INVESTIGATING YOUR SITE

If you thought you knew everything there was to know about your own backyard, prepare to be surprised. Even the most tranquil of suburban gardens can conceal all manner of underground nasties awaiting the unwary builder.

Although there's a fairly good chance that your plot will turn out to be perfectly sound for development, it's just too expensive a risk to simply assume all is fine down below.

The official figures make alarming reading. 440,000 UK homes are on ground that's liable to subsidence, and another 100,000 on sites at risk from landslip. That's not counting the ones potentially at risk from flooding, radon gas, and wind damage.

It may seem obvious to check what you're likely to hit before letting the mini-diggers rip into your lawn, but the reality on many projects is that the first major disaster occurs on Day One. It's not unusual for over-enthusiastic excavators to slice through your gas, water or drainage pipes, or sever your neighbour's electricity and phone cables. Not only does this result in massive inconvenience and unnecessary expense but it is also potentially lethal.

you're building on top of. Some concerns are fairly obvious – things like springy ground (suggestive of a high water table), slopes greater than 1:25 or nearby trees. Site investigations typically begin with some initial desk research and a 'walkabout' around the site, followed by the physical digging of trial pits and taking of soil samples. Before spending a lot of time sketching out your design in any great detail, the following factors must first be considered, since they can all have a crucial impact on the design, and cost, of your extension.

And that's before the unwelcome discovery of hidden treats like unstable subsoil, old plague pits or subsiding mineshafts lying in wait. The good news is that your garden is probably virgin territory, so you shouldn't have to worry about ground contamination from old factories and petrol stations. But some modern town houses are built on old 'brownfield' sites formerly occupied by buildings with basements, which have not always been properly demolished or filled.

Things to check before designing

It's simply not possible to design a successful building without first doing a little detective work to find out what

Existing foundations

You may be shocked to discover how shallow the existing foundations of your home are. Start by digging a small trial hole with a spade next to the outside wall, at the point where the new extension will join the existing building. Taking great care to avoid any hidden pipes or cables, dig sufficiently deep to expose the old foundations and reveal their type and depth. This is not wasted effort since the hole can later be incorporated into the new foundation trenches.

What you find will depend to a large extent on the age of your home. As a general rule, the older properties are, the shallower their foundations. Footings on Victorian houses were commonly less than 450mm deep, gradually increasing throughout the next century. Make a note of the depth of your existing foundations, as both Building Control and your designer may want to take a look. In the unlikely event that old body-parts start appearing in the excavated soil from under your patio, fill it in quick!

Drainage

There are two very good reasons for taking a close interest in the precise whereabouts of your underground drains. First, so that you don't go smashing into them when the foundations are excavated, and second so that you can design an effective new connection into the existing drain run (assuming your extension includes a new kitchen, bathroom or WC).

But pinpointing the position of underground drain runs isn't always that simple. Traditionally, it was done by consulting old plans from the Council or water authority, but these were sometimes extraordinarily inaccurate. Even 'the official map of public sewers' available from your Local Authority won't include private sewers or drains running under your land. With luck, these may be recorded in your property's deeds, or if it's a more modern building the developers may have copies. So to trace them accurately, a 'drain survey' may be required. Although a set of plans is always a good starting point.

A useful course of action might be:

- Start by lifting up covers of inspection chambers (manholes), beginning with the ones nearest the house. Ideally there should be an inspection chamber at each bend in the pipe run, but in reality this is rarely the case.
- Make a note at each chamber of the depth from the cover to the bottom of the channel. Measure the precise positions of the chambers in relation to the house, noting any branch pipes, and mark these on a scale site plan.
- To check the route that waste water takes from bathrooms and kitchens, you can mix coloured dyes in each WC, bath, sink and shower and see where it appears in the chambers.
- Metal detectors may be useful in helping pinpoint any Victorian cast iron drainage pipes, although most old pipes were made of salt-glazed clay.

It isn't unusual to discover that there is a drain-run just where you want to build, and once again, the age of your house should provide some useful clues as to what to look for. For example, in Victorian houses the shared sewer often runs across the back gardens. The foul drains may run straight back from the house, connecting to this sewer at a 'T' junction.

Typical 1930s semis, on the other hand, were built with upstairs loos discharging via a soil and vent pipe on the side wall, which connects underground to a drain run parallel to the side wall, leading out to the street. Modern

post-war houses were increasingly designed with the kitchens and bathrooms to the front, so the drains could run straight out to the sewer in the road.

The most popular reason for extending is to enlarge the kitchen. For many of us this means building a simple addition onto the back wall of the old kitchen. Unfortunately, this also happens to be the most common spot for kitchen waste drainage to discharge underground, usually via a gulley. And rather inconveniently, the rainwater downpipes may also have chosen this location to disappear into the ground.

If this is the case, you can't just cover up old gullies and carry on regardless, pretending they don't exist. The waste water system in this area will need to be redesigned with new connections made to the existing underground drains. See Chapter 8.

Even if there are no downpipes directly where you plan to build, underground rainwater pipes may be crossing under the proposed site, en route to soakaways further out in the garden (soakaways are underground rubble-filled chambers used to disperse rainwater).

Sewers and pipes – who's responsible?

Did you know that you may be legally responsible for someone else's 'foul waste' without even knowing it? In such a case, ignorance may be bliss – until you need to build an extension. 'Foul waste' is the name for waste water from kitchen sinks, bathrooms and toilets etc, and there are three main parts of the underground drainage system that carry foul waste water:

Drains
A drain is the name for a pipe that carries foul waste water from just one property. This is the responsibility of the householder until it joins another person's pipe, where it officially becomes a 'sewer' (either a private or public sewer).

Public sewers
Public sewers take foul waste away to be treated, most running below the road. 'Public' means they have been 'adopted' and are now the responsibility of the water

authority, who should pay for any repairs. Note however that all *shared drains* built before October 1937 (or before April 1965 in Inner London) count as public sewers, even those running under private gardens.

Private sewers
A private sewer is any pipe which takes foul water from more than one property but which is not classed as a public sewer. Typically this would be those under a private road, or where all the underground drain pipes from a row of houses (built after 1937) join up into one shared pipe before connecting to the public sewer under the road. Just to make things more complex, private sewers don't just run under private land; they can run under the highway until physically connecting to the main public sewer. The repair and maintenance of a private sewer is the shared responsibility of all the owners of the properties that use it. So it's possible that you could have joint responsibility for the cost of clearing a pipe that you use, even where it runs beneath someone else's land. The cost should be shared between all the households that use that part of the sewer.

Services

Make a note of the position of your gas, electricity, and water meters. Then try to calculate the route of the incoming supplies to those meters, normally from the street. Water main supply pipes commonly make their first above-ground appearance below the kitchen sink or in the cloakroom, and may have to be diverted if the kitchen is being extended or relocated.

However, it is not unknown, especially on pre-war houses, for water or electricity supplies to enter not from the street at the front but underground from the side or rear. Some electricity supply cables will enter at roof level.

Your energy, water, and phone suppliers should be able to offer a free site survey using special detection equipment and provide a plan of their pipes and ducts. But location plans used alone without a site survey can often be inaccurate, so take extra care when digging.

Wells, cesspits and soakaways

Old wells, soakaways and cesspits are a surprisingly common feature of the hidden underground landscape. Build over one of these without taking suitable precautions and you risk witnessing your freshly completed extension subside into oblivion.

If you do happen to come across one, the first thing to check is that it isn't still being actively used. Septic tanks and cesspits are private drainage systems that treat foul waste where no mains sewers are connected. There are various ways of spotting a 'live' tank. One big clue is if your water bills exclude sewerage charges; in which case the existence of any private drainage should have been made clear by your solicitor and surveyor when you bought the house. Alternatively, if the mother of all foul stenches overcomes you when the cover is lifted (often a concrete slab) it would suggest that it's 'live'.

Matters become immensely more complicated when the tank is shared, with someone else's loos discharging into it. So check with the neighbours, since relocating the tank away from your building plot will not be cheap, and you may be able to share the cost.

If septic tanks or cesspits need to be relocated they'll need to be replaced with a modern system set at a suitable distance from buildings. Because potentially explosive methane ('sewer gas') may still be lingering, they need to be decommissioned by being emptied, doused with lime, then filled with hardcore and capped under reinforced concrete.

At least such private drainage systems should be fairly easily located (since there will be some kind of cover for emptying access, probably overgrown). By contrast, the precise location of soakaways serving your rainwater system may be a complete mystery. The first you may know of them will be the distinct 'crunch' when you dig into one, since soakaways are basically holes filled with a load of old stones and rocks.

To prepare the ground for construction, any deep holes should first be filled with hardcore. However, because this will settle over time the concrete for your foundations must be reinforced with steel mesh so that it can bridge over the hole and reach good load-bearing ground on either side. If the old hole is dry and shallow it can simply be filled with concrete before being bridged over. Unfortunately, the soil surrounding old pits may have become damp and soggy where foul water has seeped out over many years. Great care must therefore be taken locating adjacent firm ground. In all such cases, the foundation design must be checked by a structural engineer. Even if old pits and wells are not within the immediate footprint of the extension, they may still need to be filled, so as not to destabilise nearby foundation trenches or pose a danger to occupants. Aim for a safety zone of firm ground extending about 8m beyond the building.

Ancient history

Do you know who or what once occupied the site of your house? A good way of researching your plot is by perusing old Ordnance Survey maps, which are widely available from Victorian times onwards (1:2500 and 1:1250 scale).

These can reveal the existence of previously unknown buildings on the site. It's possible that remnants of foundations of long-demolished buildings may still exist underground. Who knows, right now you and your sofa may be perched directly over an ancient archaeological gem.

OS maps may also reveal the position of old ponds and pits, long since filled in but still a concern for the construction of sound foundations. Aerial photos of your area can also help locate any obscure ancient burial mounds or prehistoric settlements. On the plus side, unearthing a Jacobean treasure trove might go some way towards financing the project…

Where your house was built as part of a development on former 'brownfield' land, the site history can be more of a worry. The danger tends to be where heavy industries once existed, so this is more of an issue on modern housing estates where old factory sites were redeveloped. Previous uses such as gasworks, refineries, heavy manufacturing and blast furnaces mean there's a risk that toxic heavy metals, slag waste, or unstable backfill could be present in the ground. In such cases serious detective work will need to be done to clarify what remedial work, if any, was undertaken by the developers. Such work may have included removal and replacement of all topsoil down to a specified depth with a suitable membrane installed to seal potentially polluted subsoil below. So the fact that your lawn doesn't physically glow in the dark needn't necessarily mean that everything's fine and dandy down below. First stop would be the archives at the Council planning department, then a trip to Building Control to check how deep you can excavate new foundations without risk. Building Control Officers often have excellent local knowledge about ground conditions.

Photo: archaeologicalplanningconsultancy.co.uk

The strange case of the disappearing back garden, Redruth, Cornwall, 2000.

Mines

There's rarely any warning other than a brief rumbling noise: then there's a gaping abyss where your garden used to be. Disasters of this type have occurred for many years. In 1992 a 75ft deep crater suddenly appeared in the garden of a house in Woodland Way in the Cornish town of Gunnislake. In less than 30 seconds it had not only swallowed the entire back garden but also two telegraph poles and the garden shed. In another case the corner of a house disappeared down an old 1,000ft deep mineshaft.

So if your region was at some point in the past known for mining – and much of the UK was – you'll need to consider the possible existence of underground tunnels and mineshafts, even where local collieries have long been closed and their pits capped off. Land searches are supposed to flag these up when you buy a property, but they have sometimes missed them, causing whole estates to become blighted. Since it did not become a legal requirement to maintain accurate plans of underground workings until 1872, many ancient shallow mines have never been recorded.

In the 1960s it was not unknown for new housing estates to be built on top of overgrown, derelict sites which later turned out to be former mining land. If you live in a former mining area, it is therefore essential to thoroughly check local records before digging.

Subsoil

To be certain what secrets the ground below your feet may hold, you really need to dig a trial 'borehole'. This should be excavated to a depth of at least a metre (sometimes as much as 3 metres), and be about 5m away from the house and any other buildings. Using a JCB will prove a lot easier than a hand-held auger for this purpose. The objective is to reveal whether the ground is predominantly chalky, sandy, or composed of clay, gravel or peat. Of course it would be a lot simpler to find this out from a geological map of your area, but these are drawn to such a small scale that they only provide a very rough guide to what you're actually likely to discover.

Much of southern and south-east England is notoriously comprised of shrinkable clay, which in dry spells has been known to cause foundation movement to some older properties with shallow foundations. Another clue to the presence of clay is where the soil dries out quickly in summer, with evident shrinking and cracking. Look for sudden changes in vegetation that may also be indicative of unusual ground conditions, for example streaks of brown grass across an otherwise green lawn may indicate the path of pipes running close to the surface.

If, when digging your trial pit, you start unearthing bits of old china and fragments of tiles, bricks or bottles, this is a strong indication that you're into 'backfilled' ground. This is where previously excavated ground has been filled in with old earth and rubble. The problem is that backfilled ground tends to be softer than the firm surrounding earth if it wasn't properly compacted (compressed). In such cases you need to discover the depth of the backfill by digging down until you reach virgin ground underneath. Small areas can be bridged over, but larger amounts of backfill can be a problem and a structural engineer will need to advise. The worst case scenario is extensive backfill across the entire site to an indeterminable depth, in which case the cost of specialist foundations could make the project uneconomic.

The design, and therefore the cost, of your foundations will depend on what ground conditions you find. The problem is that if your architects make a simple assumption that the foundations will need to be only, say, 750mm deep, the builder will price up the work accordingly. This can cause trouble later in the project when work on site is in full flow, if the Building Control Officer instructs the builder to change the foundation depth or type (at your expense) or holds up work awaiting engineer's

calculations. It's obviously a lot less risky to dig a trial hole before designing the foundations, or at least seek the early opinion of Building Control.

It's not unknown for geological fault lines to run through sites. Cracks called 'fissures' exist where one type of subsoil collides with another, so you might have more than one type to contend with. Thankfully, however, Britain is free of major intercontinental tectonic plates, so such minor geological curiosities should pose little problem. However, if your plot is on a steeply sloping site the foundations will need to be specially designed to prevent any risk of the excavation work destabilising the hilly ground.

Trees and hedges

Make a note of all nearby trees since the foundation design will need to take account of them. Species such as oaks, poplars and willows are notorious for affecting nearby ground conditions, especially during long dry spells. Clay subsoils and sloping sites are most at risk from trees. Fast-growing species such as leylandii and eucalyptus can also cause clay to shrink and swell, which is bad news for houses with shallow foundations. See Chapter 8.

But before rushing out to do battle, clutching your favourite chainsaw, remember that there are severe penalties for removing trees and hedges protected by Preservation Orders. In conservation areas all trees are effectively protected. And it's not just their felling or removal that's forbidden – even minor lopping can get you into trouble. So if the proposed route of your extension happens to clash with existing foliage, you'd be well advised to check it out with the Council before finalising the design.

Whilst on the subject of protected species, note that animals and their habitats can also enjoy legal rights. So if you encounter bats, great crested newts or other rare wildlife be sure to consult English Nature (or the equivalent Scottish, Welsh or Irish bodies) for their considered opinion before setting about annihilating any protected habitats.

Flooding, ditches and streams

Do you live near the coast? Are there any rivers or streams in the vicinity of your home? If you can answer 'yes' to either question there's likely to be some potential risk of flooding

to your property. If you find evidence of a high water table, such as freshly excavated trenches filling with water, it should ring alarm bells. Today more than ever, this must be taken into account in the design of the foundations. With global warming high on the agenda, the risk of flood damage is increasingly real, potentially affecting more and more people. So constructing the ground floor of your extension higher than the existing property may prove to be a sound decision. The marginal cost is minimal compared to the potential benefits should flooding occur.

Take time to research this subject. If you're fairly new to an area consult your neighbours, since they may be able to recall any history of local flooding. Maps are now available online from the Environment Agency showing the location of flood plains.

If you have a ditch or stream running through your garden you'll be legally responsible for maintenance of the banks as well as the 'river bed', which might mean having to clear out debris now and again. The law also stipulates that if there are any pipes or drains that run under your property (known as 'culverts') it is down to you to keep them clear. If your land happens to border a ditch or a stream, the responsibility for maintenance is normally shared with the owner on the other side.

Whilst on the subject of ditches, it is an offence to obstruct a watercourse, so wise men are never seen chucking loads of old garden rubbish into them.

Radon gas

Sounding a little like something from *Doctor Who*, radon is a radioactive gas found naturally in some parts of the UK, most notable in Cornwall and Devon (see map on website). It is estimated that 429,000 UK homes are exposed to radon.

However, it is very difficult to detect since it is invisible and odourless, but if exposed to large enough doses over time it can be harmful. Fortunately, new buildings in high risk areas can be fairly easily radon-proofed and the occupants sealed from exposure by the use of a radon-resistant floor membrane that prevents the gas from entering the building. Some additional minor precautions are also needed, such as ensuring seals around service

Radonproof floor membrane. (eddystoneselfbuild.co.uk)

openings are fully airtight. Modern 'beam and block' concrete ground floors must be fully ventilated to allow effective dispersal.

Methane gas

When a bungalow in Loscoe, Derbyshire, suddenly exploded in 1986, the somewhat distressed occupants were surprised to discover the cause. Invisible methane gas had been seeping into their home over a number of years from a nearby refuse landfill site, its normally highly distinctive rotten smell having somehow gone unnoticed.

Methane, unlike radon, is largely a man-made threat that not only causes nausea and headaches, but is dangerously explosive when mixed with air. The government policy of disposing of much domestic waste by burying it in landfill sites – giant holes in the ground – means that increasing numbers of properties are potentially at risk. The main problems occur where organic vegetable matter such as old food, garden refuse and dead animals, rots over time, slowly decomposing to produce flammable gases that can percolate up to the surface. This is why the bin men don't like it when you sneak grass cuttings into your black bin liners.

Methane can also occur naturally in the form of 'marsh gas' or 'sewer gas', but it is unusual to find it affecting suburban gardens other than in old cesspits. Methane can enter buildings through gaps around service pipes and cracks in floor slabs, as well as through wall cavities. The danger is that it tends to accumulate in confined spaces such as voids under floors, in drains, and in cupboards, making them potentially vulnerable to explosion.

Sites most at risk are obviously those close to where landfill has taken place – the official 'risk zone' is within 250m of a landfill site. Local Authority searches should reveal the locations of existing and former landfill sites.

In such cases the design of your extension may need to incorporate extra precautions to protect against gas or contaminated substances (Part C of the Building Regulations). The design solution is pretty much as described for radon with plenty of air vents to disperse gas away from the sub-floor areas and gas-tight seals to

services etc. Use of gravel-filled shallow pits known as 'French drains' around the outside of the main walls can also help disperse gases.

Rights of way

Having to worry about invasions of backpackers exercising their 'right to roam' across your land may seem like something only rich celebrities and royalty need worry about. However, it's fairly common – in Victorian terraces, for example – to find a shared right of way running across all the back gardens, close to the rear walls just where you want to build. And such rights of way are not always visually obvious on site. Keen ramblers can become quite upset to discover their favourite route has just been obliterated by a massive new extension. So to stay on the right side of the law, it's important to check for the existence of any public footpaths or private rights of way across your plot.

These matters are normally investigated by your solicitors carrying out a local land search when you purchase a property. If you do find such rights across your land they may by now be defunct so it may be possible for them to be legally overturned. Sometimes a right of way can be legally re-routed by the Council making an order to close or divert it. The order must be advertised and anyone can object, which makes it a fairly lengthy procedure. More commonly found are legal rights for service supply cables and pipes known as 'wayleaves'.

It's important to note that even if planning permission has already been granted it doesn't mean you can then start building and interfere with a path. In fact, if you carry on regardless and obstruct a right of way the Local Authority can force you to demolish the extension or pay a crippling fine.

On that happy note, assuming you're now fully confident that the piece of land you want to build on isn't about to disappear down a mineshaft, and that death from radon poisoning or methane explosion pose no threat, the next step is the big 64,000 dollar question of all property development: will you get planning consent?

3 PLANNING PERMISSION AND BUILDING REGS

By now you probably already have a pretty good idea of how you'd like your new home extension to look. So the next step, designing it in detail, should be one of the most enjoyable parts of the process. This is where you begin to see your ideas 'come alive'.

You now have to overcome what is probably the single biggest hurdle of the entire project: getting planning permission. Without it, you may not be allowed to build much more than a glorified dog kennel. And when the planning's all sorted, you then need to satisfy the folk at Building Control. Without their approval you would find it virtually impossible to sell your house, since prospective buyers and mortgage lenders would assume it was structurally unsafe. So the purpose of drawing up detailed plans is very specific – to gain planning consent, and to show that your ideas will comply with the Building Regulations. The plans will also form the basis for working drawings to guide the builders on site.

It's important to realise that Planning and Building Regulations are two totally separate things. What the two departments normally have in common is that they're both run by the Local Authority, respectively the Development Control Department and the Building Control Department at the Council offices.

The chief concern of the planning department is essentially to balance one person's right to build against the rights of other interested parties, such as the neighbours. They'll also aim to protect the character of an area from being wrecked by hideous, overbearing new buildings, or from potentially disturbing changes of use. Which is why you can't suddenly convert your living room into a 24 hour lap-dancing establishment (the killjoys). Basically, the planners will want you to achieve a decent-looking home extension that doesn't unduly detract from other local residents' enjoyment of their homes. They will also take into account any road safety implications resulting from new driveways. The objective of Building Control, on the other hand, is to ensure compliance with basic safety standards and prevent the erection of jerry-built death traps. One thing both departments have in common is their draconian enforcement powers should anyone choose to carry out an illegal development.

Planning Permission

Until 1 July 1948 it was every British citizen's God-given right to build pretty much whatever they wanted on their land with the bare minimum of interference from government. Which was fine, until your neighbours decided to build a giant monolith in their back garden, blotting out the sun and casting a permanent shadow over your home.

So today, before you can even think about laying one brick on top of another, in most cases you'll need to apply for planning permission (a.k.a. 'consent' or 'approval').

This will either be granted or refused in accordance with the plans you submit. The process is designed to ensure fairness by requiring compliance with the Council's policies as shown in their local development plan, although the principles are to a large extent dictated by central government.

Each year there are over half a million UK planning applications, yet the system is not particularly user-friendly.

However, when you consider all the areas where the planners can fault your ideas, and that most applications are not submitted by architects, it may come as something of a surprise to learn that approximately 80 per cent of all applications are successful. It's always worth talking your plans through with a planning officer before officially submitting them. This gives you the chance to take on board any suggested changes at the design stage, thereby improving the likelihood of success. The process of submitting your planning application is explained later in this chapter. But first, there are some circumstances where you may not need to bother with all the hassle of applying for planning…

Will my new extension need planning permission?

When modern planning legislation was originally introduced in 1948 (in The Town & Country Planning Act), a certain amount of minor building work known as 'general development' was still permitted without the need for formal consent. So today, things like inconspicuous front porches, lean-tos, small single-storey extensions and conservatories can often be constructed quite freely as long as they don't go beyond specific limits.

Rather cunningly, however, Councils can choose to remove such rights where they feel the character of an area is particularly vulnerable, by slapping on an 'Article 4 Direction'. So to avoid any confusion, it's always best to run your proposals past the planners in the first instance. If it turns out that your project doesn't need consent, and you want a formal ruling to prove it, for a small fee they'll issue a Lawful Development Certificate (or give you a confirmatory letter for free!).

Permitted development rights

You're normally allowed to build without planning consent in cases where the 'permitted development' rules listed below apply. Of course, in reality every case is different and your local planners may need to advise on individual schemes. Specifically, your 'free allowance' for building without planning permission applies where:

- The volume of the 'original house' is increased by no more than 15 per cent or 70m^3, whichever is the *greater* (or by only 10 per cent or 50m^3 for terraced houses, including end terraces). This is subject to a maximum overall limit of 115m^3. (The term 'original house' means the property as it stood on 1 July 1948 or, for more modern houses, as originally built.)
- The roof of your new extension will be no higher than the highest part of the existing house.
- Any part of the new extension that will be within 2m of the garden boundary must be no more than 4m high (3m for a flat-roofed structure).
- No part of the new extension will be nearer to a public highway than the existing house (unless the whole

thing when finished will be more than 20m away from the highway, in which case it doesn't matter). A 'public highway' means not just roads but also public footpaths and bridleways.
- All the existing additions combined cover no more than half the original garden space (*ie* all those built since 1948).

Just in case you were thinking this is all surprisingly generous, there are inevitably some 'buts'. The main problem is that your 'free allowance' may have long since been eaten up by a lot of stuff added on since 1948 – such as old lean-tos, outbuildings and even loft conversions. These only count if they're bigger than 10m^3 and within 5m of your planned new extension, but even so, you may have no free allowance left. However, this isn't necessarily bad news – it may be possible to demolish an old garage and build an extension in its place without the need for planning consent. But remember that all these nice permitted development allowances are cruelly snatched away if you live in a listed building, and are severely restricted in some other locations (see below). When you're calculating volumes, always use external measurements (*ie* ones that include the walls) and don't forget to include roof spaces. Also, the height of a building is measured from the ground level next to it – so constructing a basement or semi-basement can be one way of getting more 'bang for your bucks', subject to the technical feasibility of actually building it within the available plot. And that's an important point to bear in mind at the design stage – a great design that the planners think is the cat's whiskers may not actually be financially viable or technically practical.

Listed buildings and conservation areas

Special rules apply for listed buildings and for properties in conservation areas, where your freedom to build is more tightly controlled. So an extension that might be permitted elsewhere could in such cases be unacceptable.

If your property is listed in any form, *ie* Grade I, II star or II (or Grades A, B or C in Scotland and N. Ireland), it means it has been deemed of 'special architectural or historic interest' and particular importance will be placed on retaining its character, identity and appearance. So in addition to submitting a 'normal' planning application you'll need to apply separately for special Listed Building Consent, which is required for any alterations, including internal changes that normally wouldn't interest the planners.

On the plus side, building work on listed buildings should be zero rated for VAT purposes, so you should be able to claim back VAT paid on materials. In fact, the contractors should not charge VAT at all on their labour (so you need to notify them in writing asap that it's a listed building).

Conservation areas are 'areas of special architectural or historic interest' and there are currently over 9,000 of them. It's crucial to check whether you're located within one, since the permitted development allowances are restricted to a miserly 50m³ (the same limits apply in Areas of Outstanding Natural Beauty, Areas of Special Control, National Parks, and the Norfolk and Suffolk Broads).

Here the planners have a duty to ensure that any external alterations 'preserve or enhance' the character and appearance of the area. Essentially this is intended to prevent incompetent DIYers from blighting the neighbourhood with artificial stone cladding and clumsy UPVC porches. In effect, it gives the planners carte blanche to get closely involved with the style of your design, even down to your precise choice of materials. They may, for example, stipulate that your extension's modern cavity walls are built to look like traditional Victorian 'Flemish bond' solid walls using expensive second-hand stock bricks,

'snapped headers' and traditional lime mortar pointing. Or they may insist on expensive clay tiles or natural slate for the roof. Paying for such historic detailing may well cost you more than you'd like, but it should ultimately add to the 'kerb appeal' of your property and hence boost its value. Basically, if you live in a conservation area it's safest to assume that you'll need special consent for any external changes, even down to fences, railings and trees.

Other stuff

Here's a rough guide to all those other awkward 'bits and pieces' planning questions:

Porches

Small porches are exempt from needing planning if the floor area is no more than 3m² (measured externally) and where the porch is less than 3m high and not within 2m of a public highway.

Loft conversions

Loft conversions that add less than 50m³ volume to the house (40m³ for terraces) should also be exempt, as are roof extensions such as dormer windows which do not face a highway and do not raise the overall height of the roof.

However, the front of the property is always going to be a sensitive area, so you could consider fitting skylights instead, which are more discreet and do not normally require planning consent.

Right: What a pair of front dormers! – unlikely to be approved today.

Below: Porches of similar form and materials to the house are generally acceptable.

Drawing: Aylesbury Vale District Council

Demolition

Should the fancy take you, it's entirely possible to knock down your own house and outbuildings without the tedious business of having to first tell the planners. In theory. The trouble is, it doesn't automatically follow that you'd be granted planning permission to build a suitable replacement, which could prove a trifle embarrassing. So it's always advisable to include any demolition as part of your overall application. Building Control, on the other hand, must always be notified in advance of any proposed demolition. And unless your house is detached, adjoining houses will have a mutual legal right of support.

Outbuildings and annexes

If all else fails, an alternative way to add space is to build a new structure in the garden. A new home-office, playroom or gym is always an attractive proposition. If it's more than 5m away from the house, it doesn't actually count as an extension. But you'll need to prove that it's used in association with the house (ie not run independently). The good news is that ready-made kits are available, rather like fully insulated, hi-tech, log cabins. Conservatories will often fall within your permitted development allowance, but it's always best to check first.

Storage tanks for heating oil

These need consent if they're nearer to the road/footpath than the original house (unless they're more than 20m away) or if they're taller than 3m above the ground or contain more than 3,500 litres. If the tank contains any liquid fuel other than oil (such as LPG) there are no exemptions – you'll need consent in all cases.

Fences, walls and gates

These don't need consent up to 1m high next to a road, or 2m high elsewhere. However, you're normally allowed to demolish or alter existing fences, walls and gates to your heart's content no matter how high, without getting consent (except, of course, to listed buildings and conservation areas or where Councils have imposed boundary restrictions).

Hedges

Planting hedges doesn't normally need consent, unless they could block a driver's view or are restricted by some old planning condition. But don't forget that hedges may be protected under a preservation order, or there may be a legal restriction preventing them from being cleared and uprooted. Conversely, some housing estates with 'open plan' front gardens (typically c.1970s) have restrictive covenants on the deeds that restrict new planting and fencing.

Patios, paths and driveways

It is heartening to note that British citizens are still free to do entirely as they please with their hard surfaces, without anyone from the Council having the right to stick their oar in. Although the neighbours may find your creative ideas slightly alarming, so long as the hard surfaces in question are at ground level (or near ground level) you have complete freedom to cover your private fiefdom as you see fit – with layers of tarmac, crazy-paving, decking, concrete or gravel, perhaps garnished with a tasteful sprinkling of luminous, banana-coloured stone chippings. Your call.

The obvious exception to this liberal regime is where you want to construct a new car access or driveway from the road over a pavement or verge. Clearly there are safety issues involved here, so consent will be required. Even widening your existing driveway can require permission, depending on how busy the road is.

Ex-Local Authority properties

These may have a sting in the tail – there's often a restrictive covenant on the deeds requiring you to get

Right: Front extension transforms ex local authority semi.

additional legal approval from the Council's Housing Department before extending. However, judging by the large number of ex-Local Authority properties that have been successfully extended this is unlikely to prove too draconian a restriction.

Basements and cellars

If you're going to build an extension, why not go the whole hog and build yourself an underground 'den' in the process? If the planners aren't keen on building upwards,

surely they can't object to you going underground where no one can see?

The downside of this cunning wheeze may lie with the technical challenge of excavating in close proximity to adjoining houses. Digging giant holes next to old buildings with shallow foundations can cause the opposite of underpinning – undermining. So new basements need to be very carefully and professionally designed from the word 'go'. See Chapter 7.

Alternatively, you may want to extend your existing house downwards into the ground. Converting an existing cellar doesn't require planning consent, though you're likely to confront some serious technical challenges. Most cellars have low ceilings, so to get some decent headroom the floors need to be excavated. Unfortunately, this will also involve expensive underpinning of shallow foundations – at least doubling the total cost compared to converting an existing full-height cellar. Old cellars are almost inevitably damp, requiring expensive 'tanking', and the provision of light and ventilation can prove troublesome. Consequently, the cost and complexity of such a task compared to the resulting increase in property value can often render such a project unrealistic.

Planning principles

To win consent for your extension it helps if you talk the same language as the planners. There are a number of key criteria used to judge all proposals, in order to be fair and objective, although local interpretation will inevitably play an important role. Getting planning consent has nothing to do with funny handshakes and buying generous rounds of drinks for local councillors (or so we're told!).

Should your neighbours decide to object, they'll also need to couch their arguments in planning terms rather than, say, moaning about possible noise from builders etc.

These are the kind of planning considerations your design must take into account:

Overlooking

If the planners consider that your design could seriously compromise your neighbours' privacy, it may well be sent back to the drawing board. It is for this reason that 'exotic' features like balconies, roof gardens, upstairs conservatories and windows in side walls are often resisted.

The trouble is, for most urban or suburban houses it can be difficult to come up with a design where the windows don't in some way overlook a neighbour's house or garden. One solution is to design the extension with fashionably low roof slopes so that the upstairs bedrooms are in effect 'loft rooms' with skylight windows that gaze harmlessly out into space. Or windows can be designed at high level (sills at least 1.8m above the bedroom floor),

Below left: Spot the local councillor's house!
Below: Neighbourhood surveillance.

allowing sunlight in whilst preventing the occupants from easily seeing out. For bathrooms, windows can be fitted with obscured glass.

Overdevelopment

In built-up urban areas, plot sizes may be fairly small, so extending the house could seriously eat into the available garden space. The planners will therefore want to be satisfied that your plans provide sufficient remaining amenity space, otherwise the project may be construed as 'overdevelopment'. If this looks like it could be a problem, providing evidence of similar local developments that have previously been approved should help your case.

Overshadowing and 'right to light'

Especially relevant to rear extensions, excessive overshadowing of adjoining houses can be a good enough reason alone for refusal. Obviously this is going to be more of an issue for multi-storey designs or where the back of the property happens to be south-facing. (See 'The 45-degree guideline' opposite.)

Although not specifically a planning issue, there is an ancient piece of land law dating from 1832 that still protects homeowners' 'right to light'. Basically, if you build or plant something that substantially blots out light from a neighbour's window, then the neighbour can take legal action against you for infringing their 'right to light' – as long as their window has been in existence for 20 years or more. There are exceptions to the right, such as where developers of some estates took the trouble to remove the legal 'right to light' of future occupiers of their properties.

Conversely, there is no such thing as a 'right to a view' in law, so if you happen to live at 'Ocean View' and someone decides to construct a tower block smack in

Sunlight should be considered even where extensions comply with the 45° guideline.

Drawing: Aylesbury Vale District Council

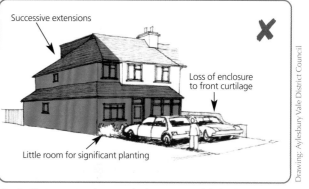

Drawing: Aylesbury Vale District Council

Successive extensions

Loss of enclosure to front curtilage

Little room for significant planting

Gradually increasing the size of a house inevitably leads to greater demands for off-street parking, often to the detriment of visual amenity.

your line of vision, thereby massively reducing the value of your house – tough.

Parking and highways

Some planning authorities set a lot of store by how many off-street parking spaces your new design will provide. They know that properties with increased numbers of bedrooms can ultimately mean more car-owning occupants, all requiring extra parking spaces. So if you want to convert your existing garage for use as living space, or you want to build over your driveway to the side of the house, you'll normally be asked to compensate.

If your house occupies a corner plot, or is near a busy road, and you want to build a front or side extension, the planners will probably refer your plans to the Highways Department for their considered opinion.

Landscaping

Attractive landscaping is more than just 'the icing on the cake'. It's a secret weapon that can be used to help swing a decision in your favour. Omitting landscaping details from the application is therefore a lost opportunity. Where landscaping isn't shown on the plans, consent is normally issued with a condition that details of planting and landscaping must be submitted before commencing any work on site. This can, of course, lead to delays further down the line.

Because building an extension inevitably means losing some of your former garden space (unless it's a loft or basement extension) there'll be less remaining land for 'amenity use'. So the environmental impact of your plans will be a serious consideration. Things like planting, surface treatments, screening and retention of existing hedgerows and trees can all influence the ultimate decision.

Where trees are protected by tree preservation orders (TPOs) you'll need the Council's consent to prune or fell them. As noted earlier, all trees in conservation areas are effectively protected.

The 45-degree guideline

The planners will normally apply 'the 45-degree guideline' to predict the likely impact of your design, preventing undue loss of daylight to neighbouring properties or excessive overshadowing of their gardens.

Rear extensions

The distance you are allowed to build back from the main house will be more restricted for two-storey or higher extensions, even if your back garden is huge. Typically you may be limited to no more than about 3m for a terraced house and 3.5m for a semi-detached.

You can calculate the effect of your proposed extension by taking a plan (ie looking from above) and drawing a line at 45° from each corner of the furthest new wall back towards the main house.

If you imagine the line casting a shadow over next door's property, then it must not engulf the window closest to your house. This only applies to windows of 'habitable rooms' ie not to utility rooms and cloakrooms etc. If the line does hit anywhere beyond the nearest part of their window, you'll have to amend the design. Or only build single storey.

Side extensions

Although building out to the side is a popular improvement, some Councils may want to resist the infilling of gaps between dwellings, particularly for two-storey extensions, in order to preserve the open character

of an area. They may also prefer you not to build within 1m of a shared boundary. However, many side extensions are designed to replace existing structures such as old garages, and are therefore less contentious.

Front extensions

The front elevation of a house is the most vulnerable to unsympathetic alterations. Large front extensions are rarely acceptable since you'll need to have regard to the original 'building line' of the street. But the more set back the property is from the street the more freedom you're likely to enjoy with your design. For a typical semi or terraced house, a porch may be about the most you could hope for, since the 45-degree principle means you'll be very restricted in what you can build without it 'overshadowing' the nearest part of next door's house.

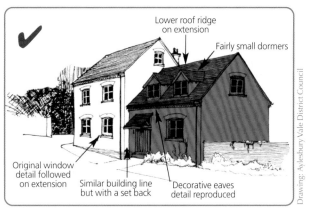

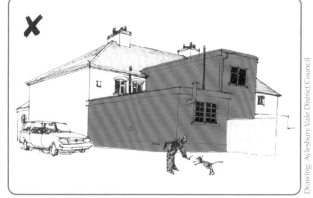

✔

Lower roof ridge
on extension

Fairly small dormers

Original window
detail followed
on extension

Similar building line
but with a set back

Decorative eaves
detail reproduced

Drawing: Aylesbury Vale District Council

✘

Drawing: Aylesbury Vale District Council

Extensions which are smaller, lower and which follow the design
of the original houses are normally acceptable.

Bulky, box-like extensions should be avoided in favour of smaller
additions which respect the form of the original building.

Design and the planners

How do you define 'good design'? One person's fabulous
home improvement is another's ghastly eyesore. The
trouble is, the planners may not agree with your opinion of
'good design', and it's the overall appearance of the
extension and how it will change the look of your property
that's probably *the* most important consideration of all.
Nonetheless, there are some good common sense general
rules which, if followed, should lead to a happy outcome.

Shape and scale

It's a matter of respect. Extensions should not overwhelm
the existing building. Once they get anywhere near the
size of the original building, the old architecture could be
swamped and lost, harming the appearance of the original
house. Flashy, eye-catching 'look-at-me' designs are often
rejected. Basically, your new extension should complement
the existing building rather than dominate it. To get a large
extension through planning is not impossible, but requires
real ingenuity, imagination and design flair to reduce its
apparent bulk. You're more likely to get a big one through
if its shape is traditional and blends in with the old place.

Planners claim that they don't rule out contemporary
designs that contrast with the original building as long as

the design also enhances it. For example, a big glazed,
timber-framed extension to a period house can appear
striking and new, and yet at the same time can be
somehow 'in keeping'. Or perhaps a neat timber-clad barn
design bolted on to a traditional yet mundane brick house.
Different and distinctive, yet complementary. This is where
a good architect can make a real difference.

Set-backs

In order to provide a visual break between old and new,
side extensions usually need to be set back a little from the
existing building. 'Set-backs' can make the extension seem
more visually pleasing by reducing apparent bulk, like a
smaller 'echo' of the main house. Technically this is also a
good trick to help disguise tricky joints between different
sized ancient and modern bricks and varying course
heights. It also helps separate the old and new eaves
details, which otherwise may be hard to match, and
minimises damage to the old brickwork on visually
important front-facing walls.

Materials

You can do everything else right, but choose the wrong
materials and your extension will stick out like a Day-Glo

Side extensions should be set back from the main building line.

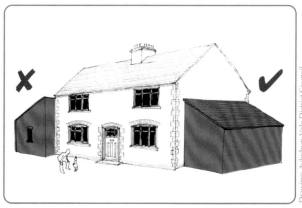

✘ ✔

Drawing: Aylesbury Vale District Council

Scottish Parliament on acid. Perhaps it was because the choice of materials didn't show up too well on old monochrome plans that some shockingly awkward designs seem to have got through the planning net in years gone by. This is a slightly contentious subject, since getting involved with the precise specification of materials is starting to go beyond the limits of planners' powers on a normal application, unless you're listed or live in a conservation area.

Happily, the chances are that you, the planners and everyone else in the street will be singing from the same hymn sheet on this one. Employing matching materials should help achieve a design that discreetly blends in with the original house, in terms of size, shape and style.

Tracking down suitable matching historic bricks and tiles etc may involve some detective work, but reintroducing original, natural materials should add to the quality and character of an older property.

Roofs

Extensions that are higher than single storey will often need roofs of a pitched design, simulating the style of the existing roof, perhaps with the new roofline a little lower than the main house. You'd normally want to match the existing roof tiles or slates, or even use better quality roof coverings than the originals. Where the original coverings have been replaced years ago with inappropriate modern ones, such as large concrete interlocking tiles on Victorian roofs, this may be a good opportunity to strip the whole lot and reinstate original natural slate or plain clay tiles throughout.

Pitched roofs are normally also preferred for single-storey extensions because they last far longer than cheap felted flat roofs, and look a lot nicer. But there may be technical obstacles, such as on many terraced houses where there simply isn't space for anything other than a flat-roofed extension.

In some circumstances a special architectural argument could be made in favour of flat roofs, for example with 1930s art deco properties when they were very much in vogue.

Roof extensions

Alterations to the height and shape of roofs will normally need planning consent. Dormer windows need to be designed quite discreetly as they are inherently rather prominent, sticking out from roof slopes. Small pitched roof dormers that match the main roof slopes can look rather cute and are often a welcome addition. But dormers are not cheap and, at around a third of the cost, skylights can be a better alternative, although planners tend to prefer them reasonably small and positioned away from the more visible roof slopes.

It has to be said, however, that you can't help noticing the occasional massive, flat-roofed monster-dormers that dominate entire streets like WW2 machine-gun

Above: Rear extensions are sometimes permitted higher than the main house.

emplacements. So it would seem that 'inappropriate' roof extensions can sometimes get through the net, even allowing for the fact that the rules are less strict for rear roofs away from the public gaze.

Small, vertically proportioned dormers designed to respect the character of the house are normally acceptable.

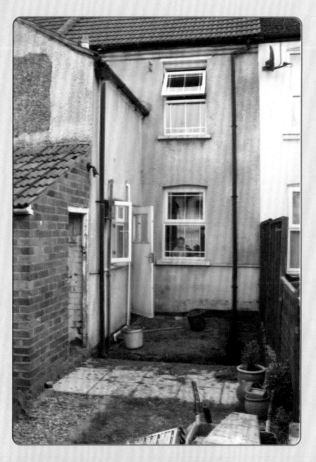

Extending a terraced house

More than a quarter of UK houses are terraced – that's nearly seven million properties. Although many have minimal space in which to extend, there's normally some scope for enlargement. But designing a successful extension with such limited options means the likely effects on adjoining properties must be very carefully considered.

Although terraces can be the most challenging of all properties for which to design a good quality extension, getting planning consent needn't be a major obstacle. For example, it may be perfectly possible to build a single storey rear extension, as well as a separate attic conversion for an extra bedroom, all quite legally under Permitted Development Rights.

Probably the most popular extension to the standard Victorian or Edwardian terraced house is to 'fill in' the small side return alley space by the kitchen, to the rear of the dining room. This is likely to involve chopping out part of the main sidewall to the kitchen, a major structural alteration.

A side return extension usually adds only 1m or 2m to the kitchen width, but this should be sufficient to transform it into an attractive family room with dining space and scope for breakfast bars and suchlike.

One challenge with this kind of project, as indeed with most home extensions, is that the new structure will inevitably reduce the amount of sunlight entering your property, often drastically darkening the dining room. This calls for the architect to utilise their complete armoury of ingenious glazing solutions to let maximum light flow in. You may also be able to compensate by moving windows and doors around, but to look right, new windows should line up with those on the original house. Single-storey extensions are easier as they can employ roof lights or glazed roofs.

In some circumstances you may be allowed to build right up to the neighbour's boundary or party wall, although planners usually like to see a gap of at least 900mm for future maintenance access.

End terrace houses normally offer more scope for extending, although where a large side extension brings you within range of a highway you may only be permitted to build up to 1m from the road. However, for a single-storey extension you may be allowed to build right up to the boundary with the pavement.

In many areas there's a maximum permitted distance that a rear extension can be built back from a terraced property, typically 2.4m, increasing to 3m on north-facing

elevations where there will be no loss of sunlight. Also, if there are other houses at the bottom of your garden the space between their windows and the rear windows on your extension must typically be no less than 18m (14m for a ground-floor extension).

One of the toughest dilemmas when extending terraces is where to put the new windows. There are minimum guideline distances you need to maintain between the side windows on your new extension and next door's existing windows – *ie* where the sides of two properties face each other. To respect the privacy of adjoining neighbours, no new windows should normally be placed within 2.4m of a boundary which they face. If this isn't possible, an acceptable compromise can be to install a wide horizontal 'clerestory' window high up the wall, above your eye level, with an internal sill height of at least 1.7m. For two-storey extensions, there should be no side windows at first floor level that can overlook neighbouring houses. But the reality for most urban properties is that space is always going to be limited, and the planners may agree to relax the guidelines, especially if there's a substantial boundary fence or garden wall between the buildings.

If rear garden space is cramped, converting the loft to provide an extra bedroom may be a more realistic option – assuming there's sufficient roof height for headroom. Loft space can be freed up by installing a new combination boiler in the kitchen so that redundant water tanks in the attic can be removed. The biggest issue is normally the location of the new staircase; usually this can be added directly above the existing staircase, sacrificing only some old cupboards or part of the first floor landing. But if it means losing a bedroom it may not be worth doing.

If all else fails you may be able to dig down – after all, you're officially the owner of all the ground down to the centre of the earth, as well as the house that sits on it.

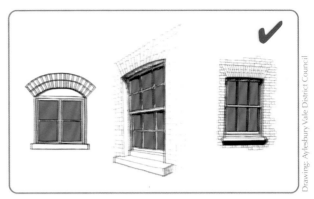

Following original designs and proportions will help relate extensions to the main building.`

Drawing: Aylesbury Vale District Council

Detailing

The devil, as they say, is in the detail. Window and door openings are especially important details to get right, as they strongly influence the look of your extension. These are a crucial architectural feature, and you'll earn extra brownie points with the planners if the new windows are appropriate to the age of the original house (even if those in the main house have long since been replaced). As well as getting their shape and size right, your design should carefully consider the alignment of all the door and window openings, and try to respect the original window pattern. Old sash windows and period doors can be duplicated with modern equivalents, custom-made to old designs. Features such as original deep stone windowsills can also be copied.

Extensions to older properties usually look best with a matching pattern of brick bonding and traditional eaves details (such as projecting decorative 'corbelled' bricks. Authentic arches above doors and windows (now available as pre-cut sets) are often more suitable than simple flat soldier courses.

Although builders who are familiar with traditional skills, such as working with lime mortar, can be hard to find, it will be worth the trouble if you're extending a historic building. But don't let the builders talk you out of doing period detailing – it is perfectly possible to echo traditional details and to still comply with current Building Regulations.

Design details can have serious practical implications. For example, your neighbour's permission will be required if your extension overhangs their property or is attached to it. They will also need to be consulted if your foundations encroach on their land, or if your builders need access through their garden. This may involve having a legal agreement drawn up, so if you're not on speaking terms right now, it's probably best to 'design-out' any such potential obstacles at this stage. Certain features can also make your house potentially more vulnerable to crime. Even a new porch or downpipe can give access to an unlocked upstairs window, and features like balconies and flat roofs need to carefully considered from this perspective at the design stage.

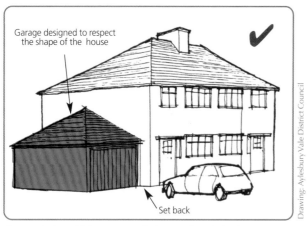

Garage designed to respect the shape of the house

Set back

Drawing: Aylesbury Vale District Council

Garage design which appears to belong to the existing home.

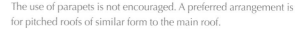

Drawing: Aylesbury Vale District Council

The use of parapets is not encouraged. A preferred arrangement is for pitched roofs of similar form to the main roof.

Garages and parking

As noted earlier, planners may take a dim view of schemes that cause a major loss of off-street parking space. New extensions tend to encourage more demand for parking at the same time as eradicating former car spaces by building over them. This can be a difficult issue to resolve, since so much UK housing was built before car ownership was commonplace. Even as late as the 1950s it was not really expected that house buyers would be able to afford to run a car as well as a mortgage.

Obviously it's important that your new extension does not impair the 'line of sight' for drivers at road junctions. Equally, any proposed new 'ingress' from the road into parking spaces (as well as 'egress' coming out of them) must satisfy the Highways people in terms of adequate visibility for drivers.

Clearly, highways issues will depend to a large extent on how busy the road is, so if your home faces straight onto the A40 don't be too surprised if concerns about parking get flagged up. Many otherwise acceptable proposals have fallen at this hurdle. Loss of turning space for cars in front gardens can also be a worry. You may be able to make

amends by offering to convert some of the front garden into car space, but it may then be viewed negatively as a 'loss of amenity space'.

If it looks like your application is headed for rejection on these grounds, you could try a pro-active approach and contact the Council Highways people direct to see if they can suggest a viable solution.

New garages don't generally belong in prominent locations, like front gardens. So designs that dramatically stick out, forward of the established building line are likely to be rejected. However, in villages and semi-rural areas permission is sometimes granted for detached freestanding garages in front gardens. This depends on local circumstances and the available space. It also helps if they're designed with a suitably traditional, appearance, perhaps 'barn style' with steeply pitched roofs and black timber cladding, or maybe 'cottagey' white render or brick and flint, reflecting local styles.

Planning conditions

When you finally receive the formal planning permission document that (hopefully) approves your plans, there will normally be a number of conditions attached. Read these carefully as, legally, the approval is conditional upon them being actioned. Don't allow the conditions to get overlooked amidst the general excitement of winning consent. Some of these may significantly affect the final appearance and cost of the building. Others may relate to fairly minor standard details. Perhaps the most common condition is the stipulation that work must be started on site within five years of the date of the consent or the permission will lapse. Ignore this, and it could prove to be an expensive mistake. Note, however, that it refers to *starting* work, not finishing it, so getting some foundation work under way in time may be sufficient to secure the consent.

If you're really unlucky, your humble garden may suddenly be deemed to be of 'archaeological interest', with a condition imposed requiring you to give 6 weeks' notice prior to construction. A further 18 weeks delay may then be imposed, sufficient for a swarm of archaeologists to descend on your property and start painstakingly sifting through the ground with teaspoons. On the plus side, you may become the lucky owner of some interesting fossils or shards of ancient pottery!

Penalties

If, after due consideration, you've concluded that you prefer the pre-1948 planning rules better (*ie* no rules), and if the temptation to build without the inconvenience of getting official consent is overwhelming, then it's worth noting that the planners have *extreme* enforcement powers. They can force you to demolish and remove any unauthorised building work at your own expense, or do it on your behalf and fine you. Or even, as a last resort, impose a jail term.

If a structure has been built illegally, it is possible to apply retrospectively for consent, but if it's refused you'll be watching it come down at demolition time. So it's generally better to co-operate.

There is such a thing, however, as the 'ten-year rule', which basically means that if an unapproved building has managed to stay hidden from the disapproving gaze of the planners for ten whole years, and you can prove the date of construction, any enforcement action may be void. But attempting anything like this is a mad gamble – it just takes one phone call from a disgruntled neighbour….

Building regulations

Your extension will need Building Regulations consent regardless of whether you've got planning permission. It's very much in your own interest to comply with the Building Regs so that the resulting structure can be shown as being safe, and will therefore be mortgageable and sellable. Only if the work has been carried out to the satisfaction of the Building Control Officer (formerly known as the 'Building Inspector' or 'District Surveyor') will you receive official Building Regs approval, in the form of a 'final certificate' upon completion of the build.

The primary responsibility for making sure your

extension complies with the regulations rests with the person doing the building work, so if you're employing a firm of builders it's important to remind them of this at the outset. Be clear about whose job it is to liaise with Building Control.

The 'approved documents'

Practical guidance showing how to comply with the Building Regulations is contained in 'approved documents' issued by the Government. As far as your build is concerned, these are the bible, and are legally enforceable. The full documents can be accessed on the website.

Approved documents
A   Structure
B   Fire safety
C   Site preparation and resistance to moisture
D   Toxic substances
E   Resistance to the passage of sound
F   Ventilation and condensation
G   Hygiene
H   Drainage and waste disposal
J   Heat-producing appliances and fuel storage systems
K   Stairs, ramps and guards (protection from falling, collision and impact)
L   Conservation of fuel and power
M   Access and facilities for disabled people
N   Glazing – materials and safety
P   Electrical safety
Q   Electronic communications

If you live in Scotland or Northern Ireland, guidance is instead provided in the form of technical handbooks. However, the nitty-gritty areas of concern are largely the same as those for England and Wales. The main difference is that in Scotland you'll require permission in the form of a 'building warrant' before work can start.

The Building Regs are essentially about health and safety – stuff you'd want to get right anyway, like sanitary fittings that don't leak and wiring that doesn't kill. Their objective is to enforce minimum standards for such things as fire protection, safe access and drainage, as well as to make sure buildings are structurally sound and weathertight. Increasingly, however, the emphasis is on meeting insulation standards in order to conserve fuel and power. Their aim is also to ensure that building work is undertaken safely, without risking the lives of the workers on site, as well as minimising danger to visitors and passers-by.

Site inspections

Inspections are carried out by the Building Control Officer at several important stages. They carry out spot checks to enforce minimum standards but do not supervise the works on your behalf. For that you'd need to privately appoint your own surveyor or architect.

The builder is required to notify Building Control in advance at key stages, and leave the work exposed for

It is possible to echo traditional details and comply with current building regulations.

Drawing: Aylesbury Vale District Council

inspection before covering it up and continuing. Should they fail to do this, they may later be required to break open and expose parts of the structure for inspection, which in the case of concrete floors and foundations can prove a trifle messy.

Stages for inspection	Notice required
1 Start on site	2 days
2 Excavation of foundations	1 day
3 Concreting of foundations	1 day
4 Damp-proof course laid	1 day
5 Oversite concrete	1 day
6 Drainage commencement	1 day
7 Drainage completion – ready for testing	1 day
8 Completion of the whole job	2 days

This list is the bare minimum, the stages where you must legally provide notice. Check the precise stages with your local authority as they are subject to local interpretation. More than one inspection may be carried out for each stage, and additional inspections are often required. For example, the following works would also normally need to be checked:

- All major structural work – new lintels etc.
- At damp-proof membrane stage to ground floors.
- At wall plate level (when the walls are finished and the roof about to start).
- New connections or alterations to drains, soil pipes etc.
- New boilers, flue liners, heating appliances, hot water cylinders.
- New water supply and waste pipes.
- Fire and sound insulation, fire escapes, fire doors, stairs etc.
- Thermal insulation and ventilation.

Notice is usually required to be submitted in writing by your builders, using a 'commencement notice' form for stage 1. Subsequent stages can normally be notified by phone, but check whether your Authority prefers notification by email, fax or phone. If the Officer doesn't arrive within the time limit don't be tempted to cover up and press on regardless – make contact!

Building Control Officers are busy people, so site inspections often tend to be fairly brief affairs. This is normally the case where they judge that the extension is not too challenging technically, and where they know the builder to be competent, an opinion possibly formed from working on previous projects with the same contractor. Don't be horribly offended personally if Officers choose to discuss construction issues directly with the builders. It's just quicker that way, but they'll gladly involve clients in the debate if desired.

Only when the final inspection has been carried out will the completion certificate be issued, but you will need to specifically request it. This is a valuable certificate, so keep it safe along with the planning consent documents, since it will be required when you come to sell or remortgage.

Policing and penalties

If you contravene the Building Regulations or obstruct Building Control Officers from doing their job then you could be fined, or even sent for a short holiday care of HM Prisons. Officers have the right to enter sites at all reasonable hours to check if the rules have been contravened. Action is normally taken against the main building contractor, but the Local Authority can alternatively serve an enforcement notice against owners, demanding the taking down and removal (or rebuilding) of anything that contravenes a regulation, or they may force you to finish the works so that they fully comply. If you refuse, they can employ other builders to take down non-conforming parts of your extension, for which they will send you the bill.

There are only a few areas of building work where you don't need to apply for consent. Things like small porches may be exempt, and even some conservatories, car ports and detached garages (up to 30m² floor area), but it depends on the specific design, since details like the electrics will always have to comply. It's therefore best to assume that all structures require consent unless officially notified otherwise.

Local Authorities do have the legal right to relax any part of the Building Regulations (known as 'varying the provisions') if they believe that the requirement is unreasonable in a particular situation. Just don't bank on them being too keen to do this!

Conservatories & glazing

Conservatories have traditionally been something of a grey area. A conservatory is an extension with at least 50% of its walls and 75% of its roof area glazed (or made of translucent material). But the Building Regs make a crucial distinction between conservatories which are 'thermally separated' from the rest of the house, and open-plan ones. The division must be done with 'proper' main walls and doors for minimal heat loss. If they're not fully thermally separated, then they count as normal extensions, albeit 'highly glazed' ones.

To qualify as exempt, their ground floor area only needs

to be less than a whopping 30m² (most conservatories are smaller than about 12m²). But unless yours is going to be used exclusively for growing marrows it's probably best to assume it will need to comply, at the very least in terms of glazing (Part N) and electrics (Part P). It's also very much in your interest to ensure compliance in other important aspects of construction, such as foundation depths.

To make the most of a small conservatory, it might be tempting to integrate it into the main house with no dividing wall or doors, turning it into a 'substantially glazed extension' built to normal newbuild standards. But first check this isn't going to scupper your plans for windows elsewhere by eating up your extension's 'door and window allowance'. The combined area of doors, windows and roof windows allowed in extensions should not exceed 25% of the floor area of the extension. If that sounds a bit mean, the good news is you can also add to this amount the area of any old windows and doors that got blocked off, or filled in, as a result of your extension being built onto the house. See Chapter 10.

Structural calculations

The chances are that Building Control will ask you to provide structural calculations for your proposed new extension from a qualified structural engineer. These will prove that all the structural elements such as beams, lintels, floor joists, roof timbers and foundations are up to the job, and that the structural stability of the extension as a whole is adequate. Any structural alterations you plan to make to the existing house, such as knocking through new openings into the extension, are also likely to need accompanying calculations. In Scotland you have to submit a special 'Structural Design Certificate' that confirms the stability of the proposed new structure.

Choosing materials

The materials used to build your extension obviously need to be safe and fit for their purpose, as well as looking good. Your designer and builders should be familiar with the materials available, and the specification for the works will normally state the quality required (*eg* 'plywood shall be in accordance with BS 1455').

Products should normally carry a recognised quality branding such as the BSI (British Standard Institute) kite-mark or BBA (British Board of Agreement) approval. Products with 'CE' marks are also acceptable as it means they comply with European standards. If in doubt, ask

Building Control what they'll accept.

The biggest problems with materials usually relate to the way they've been installed. If a dispute arises with the builders, the manufacturers normally have product advisers available who should be able to clarify matters.

Building over (or near) drains

Most extensions are built to the side or rear of the house, which, rather inconveniently, is often just where the drains are located. Having previously identified your underground drain runs, it may now be possible to revise the design so as to avoid building over them (thereby saving a lot of expense and hassle). Maybe you can shift the extension over a bit, or make it slightly smaller. If not, then the first thing to check is whether the drains are private or public.

A quick rewind back to the previous chapter tells us that private drains are the ones nearest the house that only serve your property and are therefore entirely your responsibility. These often join up with other people's drain runs to become shared drains (a.k.a. private sewers) with ownership shared between the various users. Here, all owners are jointly responsible for repair costs (regardless of whose land a blockage occurs in). This will then connect to a public sewer, normally found under the road. Some older

sewers run across a whole series of back gardens very close to the houses. Drains may even run underneath some Victorian or period houses.

To build over a shared drain or private sewer you'll need to obtain the prior consent of all the joint owners by demonstrating that it will be suitably protected from damage.

But building over a public sewer can be a major undertaking. If you choose to ignore the rules, the water company has the legal right to stop your building works. They can take down any buildings erected without prior agreement. Even building within 3m of a sewer normally requires official consent (the precise distance will depend on local water company requirements). This is because constructing new buildings near sewers increases the pressure on underground pipes, potentially causing the sewer to collapse. Not only will this block everyone's drainage but it can in turn cause structural damage to your new building. To prevent this nightmare situation arising, there are three options:

- *Avoid the sewer*: as noted earlier, the easiest and cheapest solution is to modify your plans so the extension will be at least 3m away from the sewer.
- *Divert the sewer*: where practical you could divert the sewer away from where you want to build. Most pipes should be less than 160mm diameter, which means the water company may allow your builder to do this work (subject to written consent).
- *Go ahead and build over it* (or within 3m). But before work starts you must enter into a legal 'building-over agreement' with the water utility company. There will naturally be additional charges to budget for, and until the sewer agreement is completed Building Control cannot formally approve your plans, which could hold up your entire development. A 'building-over agreement' often requires a preliminary CCTV scan inside the sewer by the water authority to check its condition. Any defects should then be repaired prior to building work, and in most cases you should not be charged for this work. Once your extension is

completed, a follow-up CCTV scan is carried out to tell if your construction works have damaged the pipes. Any repairs at this stage will be charged to you. The agreement will also go into some detail about the water company's rights of access for future maintenance and will record exactly what building works you're proposing to undertake and the methods you'll employ to protect their pipes.

First-floor extensions/ building over a garage

Extending the house by building over an existing single-storey extension or over an old attached garage is a good use of space, but it involves adding large loadings to foundations that may already be barely adequate for their purpose.

The first consideration must be to dig trial holes to expose the foundations to see if they're up to the job. If they need underpinning the cost could well blow the entire project out of the water. Invite your Building Control Officer to take a peak down the trial hole. If it looks promising then they'll probably request engineer's calculations. These will clearly need to take into account the extra loadings to be imposed (which can be as much as three tonnes per metre run of foundation for a first-floor extension). The quality, depth and thickness of the existing foundations must be considered together with the type of subsoil and any risks from nearby trees. Any existing hidden weaknesses in the structure will be amplified by such works, so lintels and beams subject to increased loads should also be checked.

One option may be to construct a lightweight first-floor structure, perhaps of timber frame and cladding, although you'll still need to provide structural calculations. Fortunately, most single-storey extensions built in the last 25 years or so should have been constructed with sufficiently deep foundations to take account of the possible need for extending upwards at a later date. This can be checked with Building Control.

If you've got a garage next to your house then building over it can also raise a number of tricky issues. Garages are usually built to a very basic standard. The walls may only be the width of a single brick, strengthened every couple of metres with brick piers. And that's the posh end of the market. Plenty of garages are little more than asbestos-ridden shacks made of old breeze blocks and rotten timber. Even if your garage has any foundations at all (many are built straight onto a dodgy concrete floor slab) they probably won't be sufficient to take much additional loading. So to extend over the garage you may actually be better off demolishing and starting again.

But there is another way. It may be possible to strengthen the old structure, or bypass it entirely, using steel posts bedded in concrete pad footings to support the new loadings above. The downside is that you'll need to excavate small foundation points in a confined space, possibly through an old concrete slab.

If you want to convert an integral or attached garage to living space, even without structural changes you'll still need Building Regs consent, to ensure things like heat, fire and sound insulation are suitably upgraded. Any new structural openings to create windows etc, as well as glazing, electrics, and plumbing, will need consent, and they'll want proper foundations for infill walls where the garage door used to be.

So what now?

The next step is to get serious about having detailed plans drawn up, so you can formally submit your applications to the Council…

4 DESIGNING IT AND SUBMITTING YOUR APPLICATIONS

This is the stage where you'll need to make a real commitment to the project, in terms of both time and money. Getting plans professionally drawn up is not cheap, but careful design at this stage can save a lot of unnecessary expense later.

NORTH - EAST ELEVATION

SOUTH - WEST ELEVATION

The Design

Design details

One of the most important considerations at this stage is precisely how the new extension will join onto the existing house.

Roof detailing

The biggest weak point on extension roofs is normally where they join up with the main house. Single-storey extensions often have simple flat roofs, but they rarely look good and the coverings tend to have a short life. So for a single-storey addition, a simple lean-to (monopitched) roof may be a better option, where space permits. A 2 storey or higher extension will need a more expensive pitched roof, which means a number of design features can be explored, such as whether to opt for gable ends or a hipped roof.

Let there be light

Many otherwise brilliant designs have never left the drawing board because the extension would have made an existing room too dark. So it's important to consider which windows and doors will be covered up by the extension. The Building Regs are more concerned with ventilation than light, so the risk of inadvertently making

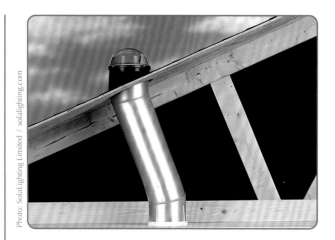

Photo: SolaLighting Limited / solalighting.com

your existing rooms unbearably gloomy may actually not be noticed until after the build is complete.

As noted in the previous chapter, adding a new window or skylight in the roof can sometimes compensate for any resulting darkness, but this is not always practical. One solution may be to fit a discreet 'light tube'. As the name suggests, these are metal tubes through which daylight from the roof surface is channelled. These are typically positioned within the loft space connected to the ceiling of the room or landing below, utilising a prism and reflector arrangement to bring daylight into areas where it would otherwise be difficult to admit natural light. Best of all, they still work on cloudy days and have no maintenance requirements.

Downpipes
Wouldn't you know it – there's a downpipe exactly in the place you want to build. The reality for most extensions is that you're probably going to have to rearrange the guttering to the main house anyway, so this shouldn't be a major obstacle. But it will probably mean having to install at least one new downpipe, and its position will need careful consideration.

New downpipes should disperse into an underground rainwater system rather than into an overflowing water butt purchased from the local Garden Centre. At worst this will mean budgeting for excavation and laying new pipework out to a soakaway in the garden via a new gulley. Downpipes obviously need to be located away from window and door openings and not too close to boiler flues.

Corridors
Adding more rooms means considering how each room should be accessed internally. This is not always as easy as it sounds and can be more of a challenge when extending bungalows. If you're not careful this can result in long, dark corridors and passageways.

Windows
One of the chief design issues that will determine whether the final product looks right is the position of the

windows. Visually it's very important to align window openings at their tops, not at the sills. It just looks better that way! Also, it's easy to overlook the impact that windows can have internally – for example, the height of the sills above floor level can clash with fittings in kitchens and bathrooms. Secure burglar-proof lockable windows are fine, but make sure you're still able to escape quickly in the event of a fire.

Neighbours
Your work may fully comply with the Building Regs, but if your design obstructs next door's extractor fans, air vents or boiler flue, causing them to malfunction, the neighbours won't be too amused. Also, if you can avoid covering existing gas and electric meter boxes it could save a small fortune having them relocated.

DIY (Drawing It Yourself)
If you're prepared to devote the time, and you're not too bad at drawing, this is one area where significant savings can be made. Even if you came bottom of the class at school for artistic merit don't despair. You may be blessed with IT skills, in which case the CAD software available for drawing simple plans may be of interest. Most architects now design on PCs using CAD programmes so you'll be in good company. See website for downloads.

Don't be intimidated by the thought that all professional designers' drawings are masterpieces – they aren't. So it may well be worth having a go yourself. Naturally there are limits to how far you can go first time around and there is a large chasm of knowledge between doing your own sketches and getting all the construction details right. Most DIY designers employ an experienced pro at some stage, at least to make sure they satisfy all the specification details for the Building Regs, although much of this tends to be fairly standard stuff.

But whether you choose to pay a professional designer or go the DIY route, there are some key quality points to check in the finished plans. A badly drawn set of plans will not only be confusing and misleading for the builders on site, but it won't present your proposals in the best possible light, crucially failing to 'sell' your ideas to the planners.

What to look for in a decent set of drawings

The right scale: Unlike a sketch, scale drawings don't use perspective, although submitting an additional sketch or photo-mock-up of the finished building can help demonstrate to cynical planners just how attractive it will look. (See 'Submitting your applications' on page 49.)

Clarity: Accompanying text and notes should be easy to read, so avoid the use of fancy handwriting or bizarre fonts. The design details should be clear and the ground levels should look realistic.

Separate drawings are needed for each of the required elevations, floor plans, cross-sections etc. The use of some artistic flair on the 'proposed elevation' drawings, showing how it will look when built, can help promote the design.

Plenty of measurements, usually in millimetres, marking the dimensions of external walls and the positions of doors and window openings.

Sufficient detail: In particular, the drawings for Building Regs need a considerable amount of text explaining how the design will comply with the regulations in key areas. This may be explained in detail on the drawings, perhaps in addition to a separate 'specification' document. If you just write something lazy like 'work to comply with Building Regulations' it may well get sent back for clarification.

Finally, there's the question of the physical size of the plans. Traditionally they've been produced on whopping great folded A1 or A0-sized sheets. But in practical terms, A2 may be more convenient and easier to refer to. On site, smaller A3 copies can be pinned up on walls and are more easily photocopied and distributed to different trades.

Finding a designer
Choosing a designer to draw up your plans doesn't necessarily mean having to appoint an architect. Anyone

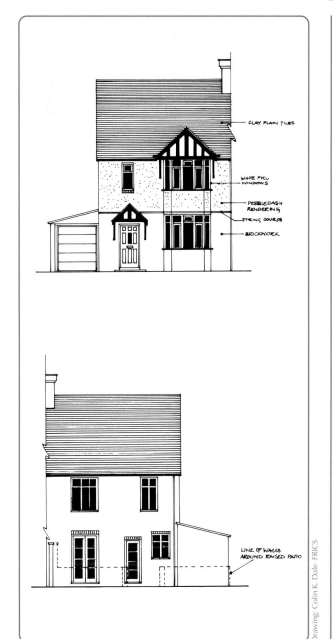

CLAY PLAIN TILES
WHITE PVCU WINDOWS
PEBBLEDASH RENDERING
STRING COURSE
BRICKWORK

LINE OF WALLS AROUND RAISED PATIO

Drawing: Colin K. Dale FRICS

Photo: UK Timber Frame Association

with a good reputation for designing residential extensions could be considered. That said, most people tend to select architects (qualification ARIBA) or chartered surveyors (MRICS or FRICS) experienced in architectural services. It's always a good idea to talk through your ideas with a professional right at the very start.

What matters most is finding someone with the right experience and knowledge to do a good job. So a warmly recommended local person with plenty of experience of similar projects but with no formal qualifications would normally be a better choice than an eminent firm of architects renowned for their groundbreaking retail mega-complexes in Abu Dhabi. A list of local architects and designers may be available from the Council (but they're not allowed to make recommendations).

Ideally choose someone who is already familiar with your Council's planning policies and how to overcome technical queries. A 'free consultation' visit should normally be offered to discuss your ideas. Note that designers have a legal responsibility for their designs to minimise safety risks on site associated with building work. Some may also be able to fulfil the Project Manager role, if required. Although local recommendations are a good start, you'll also want to see examples of previous work, drawings and completed buildings, and check they have the necessary indemnity insurance. It's surprising how much the style of drawings can vary between different designers, so compare several before confirming the appointment.

Architects traditionally work on a fee basis charging 3% of the contract value to prepare plans and another 3% for working drawings and tendering. If you want project management and an 'architect's certificate' upon completion, you'll need to budget at least another 3%. But these days many are happy to submit quotations instead.

What does the price include?

It's important to be clear about the terms of engagement and to be sure exactly what you're getting for your money. Agree a fixed fee with your designer only once the following points have been clarified:

■ Does the price include all drawings needed to get planning permission and building regulations consent?

■ Are all fees included? Legally it's the homeowner who's responsible for paying the fees for the Planning and Building Regs applications, so they may well not be included in the price. The designer should be able to confirm how much the fees will be (alternatively check on your Local Council website). It's normally a good idea to give the designer cheques for these fees made payable to the Council. Don't forget any additional fees that may arise, such as for building over a sewer.

■ Are minor amendments included? The price should always include the need for small revisions to the plans required

by the Council. If amendments are due to the designer omitting information on the original drawings, the cost of revisions shouldn't be down to you. Small amendments shouldn't be too difficult, particularly if plans are drawn on a computer. If a total 're-draw' is required because the plans were fundamentally unacceptable to the Council, an experienced local designer should have detected the warning signs early on and pointed out the likely risk to the client. If you accepted this risk, they may now be justified in charging extra.

Always be sure to get fresh copies of any amended plans. To avoid later confusion, the first drawings are usually numbered version 'A' and each revised version 'B', then 'C', etc. To be on the safe side it's best to mark all old plans very clearly as 'superseded'.

■ Are fees for structural engineers' calculations included in the price? If not, the designer should at least be able to provide a rough idea of the likely cost.

It is with the structural engineers that the buck finally stops, since everyone else is relying on their structural calculations to prove that the finished building is going to stand up soberly and not wobble or

collapse. Architects may love giant expanses of glass, and doors in weird places, but engineers tend to regard window and door openings as annoying interruptions that weaken the walls.

At the design stage it may help to bear in mind some structural facts of life. Your main walls will not only need to support vertical loadings, such as those from the rest of the building (the roof and upstairs floors etc) as well as from the occupants, but they also have to be strong enough to withstand extreme sideways forces and suction from storms or freak winds. The designer has to assume the worst possible combination of such circumstances – a Sumo wrestlers' convention upstairs whilst a Force 10 gale rages outside.

Walls can only be safely built to a certain length between main supports (such as the corners of a house). Lots of openings for windows and doors can only reduce the strength of the structure, and must normally be designed no closer than 550mm to a corner.

■ Is project management included? Project management is a major task involving frequent site visits, approving stage payments, and ultimately signing any necessary certificate upon completion. If you intend to employ your designer to oversee the whole project on site through to completion, how much will it cost and what will it include? If you drew your own plans, you may wish to employ someone just to project manage the job (although architects may not be too keen on implementing someone else's design).

Design and Build

An alternative but fairly unusual option is to go down the 'Design and Build' route. This is an all-in-one package deal where specialist building contractors can prepare the drawings in-house to your requirements, obtain all the necessary Local Authority consents, and then build the extension. The problem is, you need to be extremely sure that the contractor has the appropriate experience and isn't just being over-confident. Builders sometimes regard the 'white collar' part of the job as a bit of a doddle, perhaps not fully appreciating the sometimes confusing array of formalities and rigorous regulations you need to satisfy with the Council before getting anywhere near starting on site. You'll also need to trust the builders implicitly since the designer won't be 'on your side' if things go wrong. In such cases good communication about exactly what you want is paramount from the outset, as is a watertight legal contract.

Builders' drawings

For the more complex parts of the work (such as where the new extension meets the main house, and for any new service connections, structural alterations or stairs) the builders should be provided with additional large-scale drawings that clearly explain the details. This will help

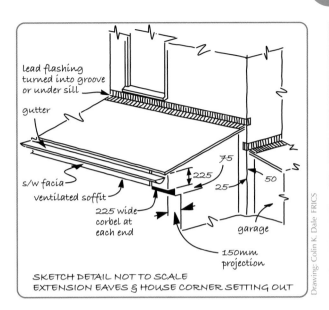

lead flashing turned into groove or under sill

gutter

s/w facia

ventilated soffit

225 wide corbel at each end

75

225

25

50

garage

150mm projection

SKETCH DETAIL NOT TO SCALE
EXTENSION EAVES & HOUSE CORNER SETTING OUT

Drawing: Colin K. Dale FRICS

ensure it all gets built right first time. If you don't, the builders will always 'know better' and will do it their way – which may be fine with an experienced contractor, but could be a disaster if they're unaware of some important element at a later stage that depends on getting this part exactly right. Without guidance, they may get hacked off and be tempted to do it cheaply and badly.

As you will see, the drawings will later form part of your legal contract with the builders, so they need to be 100 per cent accurate.

At this stage the contractors don't need to know the precise location of every switch, power point and radiator in order to quote for the job. But don't neglect this information for too long. Soon after work starts on site you'll need to provide modified drawings showing exactly where the various pipes and sockets are to be placed. Otherwise things will inevitably get positioned in the wrong place (and you may be charged handsomely for the trouble of repositioning them later). Finally, because drawings tend to get rather mashed up on site it may be worth laminating a couple of copies of the approved plans in an attempt to make them builder-proof.

Excavation risks foundation collapse – not recommended.

A load of party walls

The Party Wall Act 1996 may sound like a lot of unnecessary hassle, but its objective is to prevent serious disputes arising between neighbours. It's nothing to do with Planning or Building Regs, but is a totally separate piece of legislation based on the old London Building Acts, which proved so effective that they were extended to the rest of England and Wales. For home-extension builders, the Party Wall Act is important because it can affect the way your foundations have to be excavated.

You can understand neighbours not being overjoyed at the prospect of having their home's foundations undermined by reckless builders in mini-diggers excavating alongside them. They may need some reassurance that their property isn't about to keel over, crack, or subside from under them. On the other hand, you want to get on with

your building work without being hindered by unreasonable neighbours. The Act is designed to assist both sides.

What boundary?

The official boundary line between terraced and semi-detached properties will run through the middle of the party wall. Strange as it may sound, both owners legally have rights to the whole wall. This is because both properties rely on it structurally as well as for protection from fire and from noise intrusion. So each side needs to know in advance if the other is planning to muck about with it.

But the legislation also applies to your overall plot, including the boundary lines between gardens, which may correspond to the position of the new side wall that you want to build. Most garden boundaries are defined on the ground with well-established fences or walls separating neighbours. But the mere thought that your extension could cause the loss of a single square inch of garden can outrage some homeowners. Pinpointing the precise legal division between adjoining gardens isn't always easy. Land registry plans are not much bigger than a postage stamp and may have thick red pencil lines daubed over them. Not exactly satellite precision.

When does the Act apply?

- ▪ where work is proposed to an existing shared wall.
- ▪ if you build a new wall across the legal boundary line, such as a garden wall.

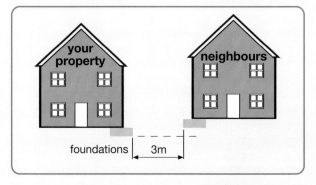

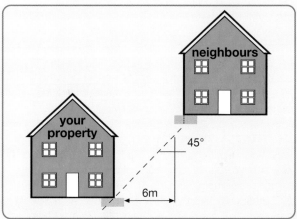

- when excavating foundations within 3m of an adjoining property, if your trenches are deeper than next door's foundations – which they normally will be. It can also apply within 6m of next door if your new foundations are deeper than a line drawn at 45° from the bottom of next door's foundations.

What needs to be done?
Before any work starts, you'll need to serve a formal notice on the owner of the adjoining property so you can reach agreement. If you're unlucky enough to live next to a block of flats, you'll have to entreat with each occupier individually. This can sometimes be done with an informal exchange of letters, but it's normally best to appoint a Party Wall Surveyor to manage the whole process from the outset.

- A written notice must be served explaining what building work is proposed.
- It must be served at least one month before starting excavating, or two months before doing any work to an existing party wall/fence.
- It needn't be on an official form, but must include drawings and details of the work.

The catch is that unless they write back within 14 days the law will assume that they do *not* consent, in which case you have to appoint a surveyor to draw up a legal agreement describing your proposed works and confirming that you'll pay for any damage caused by your digging and building activities.

If you want to build your extension right on the boundary itself, your underground foundations are normally allowed to cross underneath the boundary line, subject to the neighbour's consent and agreeing to compensate them for any damage caused to their property as a consequence.

But what if your neighbours have already built an extension up to, or on, the boundary? In such cases you'll probably need to build right up to their extension, so that it becomes your new party wall. But, again, you must give them notice and hope they agree to you going ahead. You could try 'selling' the idea by explaining how it would make their extension warmer (by their external wall becoming an internal wall), but if they object you cannot proceed, and you have no rights to construct a new party wall. All you can do then is change the design so that it is set back a bit onto your land. See also Chapter 7.

Submitting your applications

Right now, you'd probably like to get cracking with physically building your extension, rather than having to spend time getting your ideas approved by a bunch of meddling bureaucrats. But unfortunately you have no option other than to make sure your application is well enough organised to sail swiftly through the system. There is, however, one possible shortcut you could take. Because planning applications normally have a timeframe of eight weeks, and a 'full plans' application for Building Regs can take five weeks, you can save time by applying for both simultaneously rather than wait until planning is granted.

The downside is that if you steam ahead on both fronts, should things go pear-shaped with the planners there will then be a lot more expense and delay getting rehashed Building Regs drawings submitted.

Submitting a planning application
You can make two types of planning application: Detailed and Outline. 'Detailed' (a.k.a. 'a full application') is by far the more common route, but for a complex or controversial development it may make sense to first get outline consent for the general principle, leaving design details such as choice of materials etc for a later application. But for home extensions it's normally best to do it all in one go, and apply for 'full' planning consent.

Having discussed your initial ideas with the Council planners, and assuming they're generally happy and don't foresee any major difficulties, you should now be in a position to submit the required drawings with any necessary amendments already in place.

What drawings to submit
You need to submit a full set of scale drawings in metric measurements, clearly showing the work you propose to carry out. Some Councils prefer the proposed extensions and alterations to be shown in colour so that the new works are immediately distinct from the existing building. Drawings must clearly show all openings such as windows and doors. Elevation plans should also show architectural details such as timber cladding. Each drawing needs to be clearly labelled with its title (*eg* 'Existing Front Elevation'), the number (001 A etc), the scale, and the address of the property, not forgetting to include contact details. You will need to run off at least six sets of drawings, plus a few spares for yourself. See website for sample drawings. The exact requirements vary from council to council, but the drawings normally required are shown on the following pages.

NORTH - WEST ELEVATION

Drawing: Colin K. Dale FRICS

■ **Existing elevations** 1:50 or 1:100 scale, showing
the relevant front, side and rear elevations *before* any
work is carried out.

NORTH - WEST ELEVATION

Drawing: Colin K. Dale FRICS

■ **Proposed elevations** 1:50 or 1:100 scale, front,
side and rear elevations showing what the property will
look like *after* the work is completed.

◼ Existing Layout plan
1:50 scale, showing the existing floor layout of each level (*ie* ground floor and first floor, shown from above) with the name of each room clearly marked.

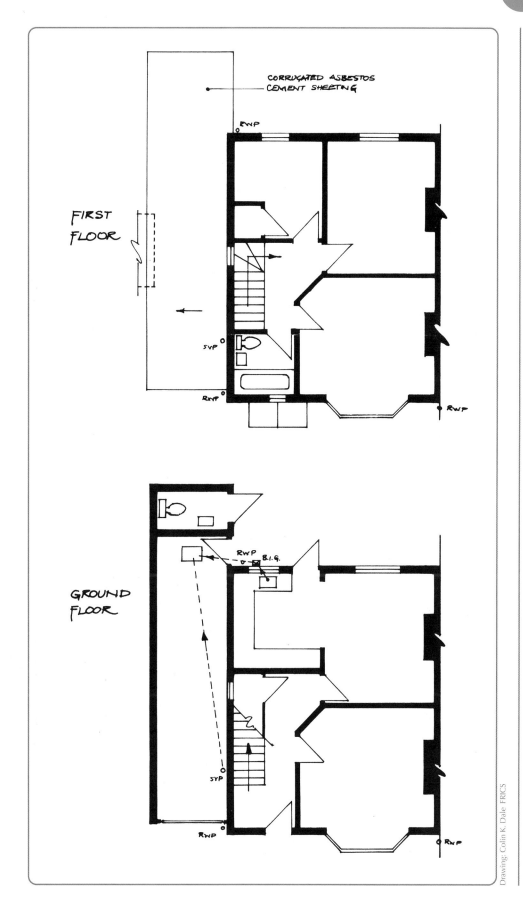

FIRST FLOOR

CORRUGATED ASBESTOS CEMENT SHEETING

RWP

SVP

RWP

RWP

GROUND FLOOR

RWP B.I.G.

SVP

RWP

RWP

Drawing: Colin K. Dale FRICS

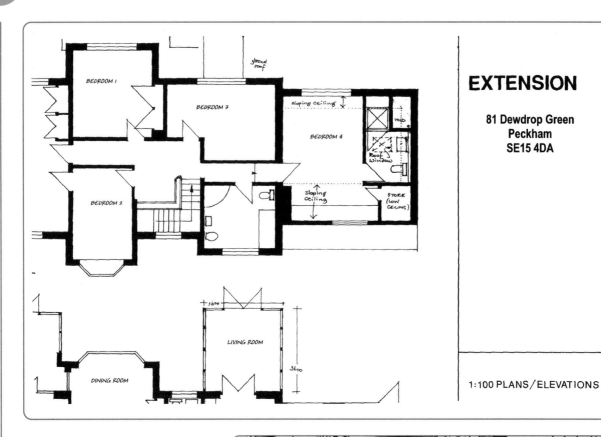

EXTENSION

**81 Dewdrop Green
Peckham
SE15 4DA**

1:100 PLANS / ELEVATIONS

Drawing: Colin K. Dale FRICS

■ **Proposed Layout plan** 1:50 scale, showing the proposed floor layout of each level including the completed extension, with the name of each room clearly marked.

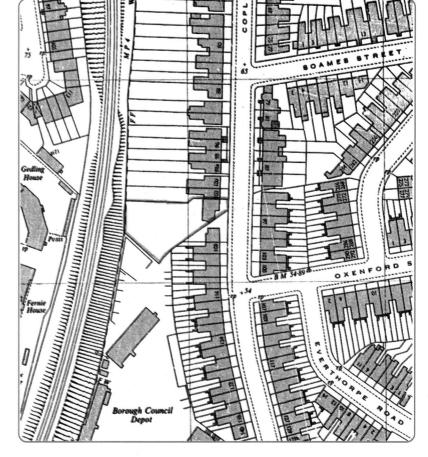

■ **Location plan** 1:1250 scale (not less than), a copy of the Ordnance Survey plan of your street, available from the Council for a smallish fee. Your site must be outlined in red.

■ **Site or 'Block' plan** 1:500 or 1:200 scale. Often combined with the location plan, this is a 'close-up' plan of your plot showing where the extension is going to be built. The site boundaries should be outlined in red, and the positions of drives, roads, drains, trees, garages and outbuildings clearly marked. It shows how the proposed extension will fit into the plot and how it relates to your immediate neighbours and the boundaries. Mark the orientation compass points.

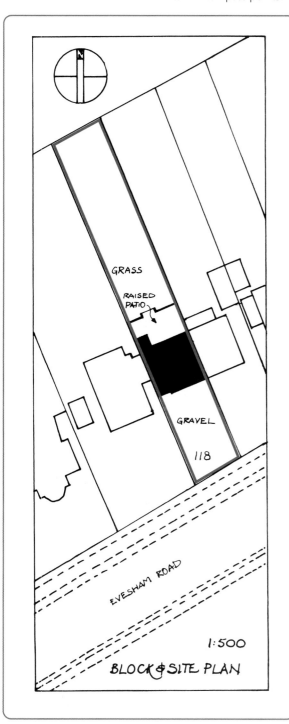

The 'Section' plan is the only drawing not included in this list. This is the key additional one you'll need for the Building Regs application. It shows a cross-section through the new building and is normally the most technically detailed of all the plans. See 'Submitting a Building Regulations application' on page 52.

Registering new applications

With all the drawings now prepared, you should be in a position to formally apply for planning permission. The only remaining task is to complete the Council application form, which can be done on paper or online. If some of the questions seem a bit odd, it's best to phone the Council planners for assistance rather than guess, otherwise it will only get sent back. You can then submit your completed application form to the planning department, together with the various sets of drawings and site plans, not forgetting to include the appropriate fee.

Within a few days, the Council should acknowledge receipt of your application in writing, confirming the name of your case officer. Having checked all the right documents are enclosed they'll then place your application on the 'planning register', which means that anyone can wander in to their offices and take a look. Small laminated notices (often coloured yellow) may be physically posted on (or near) your site and the application may also be advertised in the local press and listed on the Council website. The Council may additionally write to your neighbours alerting them to your intentions by giving them two or three weeks to lodge any objections, which is why it's always advisable to consult them personally at an earlier stage, in order to soften the blow. Other interested parties may also be consulted, notably the highways authority, the environmental health department, and the parish council. The case officer will normally visit the site within 31 weeks of the registration.

The Council should decide your application within eight weeks but they may write to you requesting more time. You can either agree to this or you can appeal to the Secretary of State, but since such appeals can take several months this doesn't usually get you very far!

Your case officer has to decide whether there are any good planning reasons for refusing permission, always remembering that there's a positive presumption in favour of development (not that you'd ever guess this by talking to some planners). The Council cannot reject a proposal just because lots of people oppose it. It will look at whether it's consistent with the local development plan, and assess its impact on the surrounding area, including any associated loss of amenity or possible traffic problems. It's worth phoning periodically to find out what's happening to your application. If the feedback is totally hostile, it may be wise to withdraw the application and start again. If minor changes are needed to resolve a difficulty, they may ask you to amend the design and resubmit it so that a decision can still be made within eight weeks.

Eventually, after considering the various consultations

and objections, and having completed their site visit, the case officer will prepare a report with a recommendation either for approval or refusal. This will then be submitted to the planning committee (made up of elected councillors) and in about 80% of cases, the official recommendation wins the day. In more straightforward cases senior officers will make the decision under 'delegated authority' without involving the committee.

Planning approval is normally granted with conditions, some of which are standard clauses, such as the condition that work on site must commence within five years. But for more sensitive developments (conservation areas etc), approval is sometimes subject to more onerous restrictions, such as a requirement that samples of your choice of materials (typically bricks and roof tiles) be submitted for the planners to have a good look at and, hopefully, approve prior to commencement of any building works.

Refusals and appeals

A refusal will be accompanied by specific reasons for the decision. Frustrating though refusal is, it may leave the door open for the resubmission of modified plans which the planners would be prepared to accept. The reasons tend to be expressed in planning jargon with references to policy numbers, so it's best to have a chat with the case officer to understand in plain English how you can best revise your design to get it approved. You're normally allowed to submit another application free of charge within 12 months of a refusal and are entitled to see background papers such as comments from highways, objectors and supporters that may have influenced the final decision.

If you feel the reasons for refusal aren't valid you can appeal within six months of the decision, to the planning inspectorate. They are an independent body, but your chances of success are fairly slim – less than one third of appeals are successful. Although there's no great expense in submitting a written appeal if you put it together yourself, it can be very time consuming. Employing a planning consultant to handle your appeal means having to pay fees, but it could be money well spent if they know the ropes. Appeals can also be made against individual planning conditions if they're unreasonable.

The basic procedure is to submit evidence that proves the council's refusal was inconsistent with its relevant policies and with Government planning guidance. What can help clinch a result is being able to demonstrate that similar local developments have recently been permitted. Above all, it's essential to stick to the facts and avoid emotional arguments. The inspector's site visits take place once both sides have made their written submissions, normally after four or five months, and it then takes another couple of months for a decision. The decision is final unless you want to take it all the way to the High Court.

Another reason for thinking very hard before appealing is that it can actually make matters worse. For example, a design that would have been accepted if modified to a smaller scale with windows not overlooking the neighbours, could now be totally rejected by the inspector as unacceptable.

In cases where you think the Council has been guilty of maladministration and hasn't followed the correct procedures, you can instead appeal to the local authority Ombudsman, but it's extremely hard to prove that the way a decision was reached was mishandled.

Submitting a Building Regulations application

Before submitting your application to the Local Authority Building Control Department you may wish to consider an alternative method that bypasses them, in the interests of consumer 'choice'. If you wish, you're allowed to submit your application via an independent 'approved inspector' instead. Approved inspectors are private firms approved by the Council to do basically the same job as in-house Building Control staff. They will process your plans, carry out spot checks on site as the building work progresses, and ultimately arrange for the final certificate once the works are completed to their satisfaction. In other words, it's all pretty much the same, but may suit those who prefer a bit of private-sector involvement.

For simplicity we will here assume that you're going to apply in the time-honoured manner, direct to your Local Authority. You now have to make an important choice,

whether to submit your application by the 'full plans' method or as a 'building notice'.

Building notice

For most home extensions, a full plans application is advisable (see below). But there's a useful short-cut. If you have unshakeable faith in the skill and knowledge of your designer and builders, you may wish to save time by skipping the full plans application. Instead you can submit a simple building notice. Here you're basically making a promise that you'll comply with the Building Regs on site, rather than submitting detailed drawings to prove it.

You'll still need to complete a form giving details of the extension and this should be submitted together with a 'block plan' (showing the position of the extended building in relation to boundaries, and the provision for drainage), and you may still be asked to provide additional information, such as design calculations. The fee is the same as for a full plans application but is paid in advance when you submit the notice. Only one fee is payable no matter how many site visits are later needed.

Once the building notice has been checked and accepted, the next stage is simply to give the Building Control Officer a minimum of two working days' notice of your intention to start work on site. The Officer will then inspect the work at key stages, just as with a full plans application.

The big risk with this method is that because your plans haven't been fully approved in advance, a site inspection could uncover something that contravenes the regulations while it's being built. Obviously this could prove highly disruptive not to say expensive.

A building notice is valid for three years, after which it will automatically lapse. Strictly speaking a Local Authority is not required to issue a final completion certificate under the building notice procedure, but they'll normally do so upon request.

Full plans application

Here, the applicant demonstrates by way of detailed drawings that the construction will comply with the regulations. If you're proposing to build some or all of your extension yourself, it's best to go this route so that you'll have an approved set of plans to work to. Also, if you're proposing to build over, or close to, a public sewer this is the only kind of application allowed.

What drawings to submit

You'll need to submit a revised version of the planning drawings with additional detailed information written on them, along with a completed application form and fee. The drawings must clearly show the proposed building works and explain the details of construction. Specifically:

■ **A location plan** showing the new building relative to neighbouring streets, houses and boundaries.

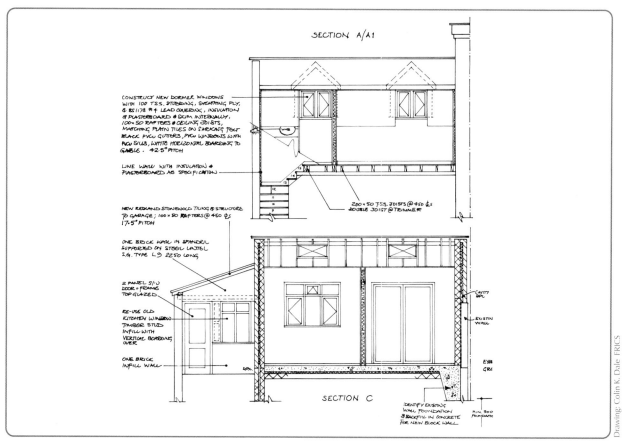

SECTION A/A1

CONSTRUCT NEW DORMER WINDOWS WITH 100 T.S.S. STUDDING, SHEATHING PLY, & BS 1178 #4 LEAD COVERING, INSULATION & PLASTERBOARD & SKIM INTERNALLY, 100 x 50 RAFTERS & CEILING JOISTS, MATCHING PLAIN TILES ON SARKING FELT BLACK PVCu GUTTERS, PVCu WINDOWS WITH PVCu SILLS, WHITE HORIZONTAL BOARDING TO GABLE. 42.5° PITCH

LINE WALL WITH INSULATION & PLASTERBOARD AS SPECIFICATION

NEW REDLAND STONEWOLD TILING & STRUCTURE TO GARAGE; 100 x 50 RAFTERS @ 450 ¢S 17.5° PITCH

ONE BRICK WALL IN SPANDREL SUPPORTED ON STEEL LINTEL I.G. TYPE L9 2250 LONG

2 PANEL S/O DOOR + FRAMES TOP GLAZED

RE-USE OLD KITCHEN WINDOW TIMBER STUD INFILL WITH VERTICAL BOARDING OVER

ONE BRICK INFILL WALL

200 x 50 T.S.S. JOISTS @ 450 ¢S DOUBLE JOIST @ TRIMMER

SECTION C

IDENTIFY EXISTING WALL FOUNDATION & BACKFILL IN CONCRETE FOR NEW BLOCK WALL

MIN 900 FOUNDATE

CAVITY DPC

EXISTIN WALL

EXIS GRC

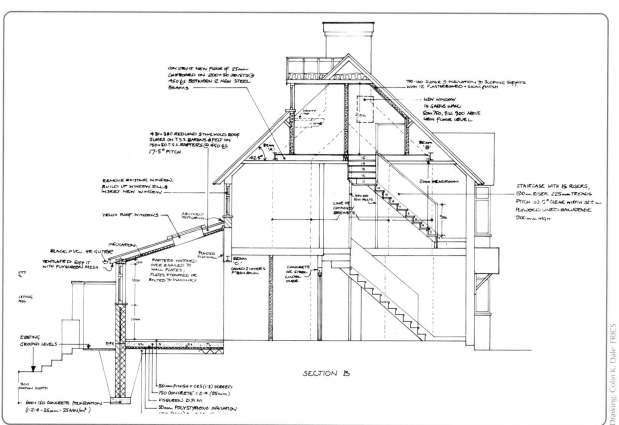

CONSTRUCT NEW FLOOR OF 25mm CHIPBOARD ON 200 x 50 JOISTS @ 450 ¢S BETWEEN 2 NEW STEEL BEAMS

TR0-130 SUPER 9 INSULATION TO SLOPING SOFFITS WITH 12 PLASTERBOARD + SKIM FINISH

NEW WINDOW IN GABLE WALL 500 x 750, SILL 900 ABOVE NEW FLOOR LEVEL

430 x 380 REDLAND STONEWOLD ROOF SLATES ON T.S.S. BATTENS & FELT ON 150 x 50 T.S.S. RAFTERS @ 450 ¢S 17.5° PITCH

REMOVE EXISTING WINDOW, BUILD UP WINDOW SILL & INSERT NEW WINDOW

VELUX ROOF WINDOWS

BLACK PVCu HR GUTTER

VENTILATED SOFFIT WITH POLYSCREEN MESH

RAFTERS NOTCHED OVER & NAILED TO WALL PLATES; PLATES STRAPPED OR BOLTED TO MASONRY

ABUTMENT VENTILATION

INSULATION

PLASTER OLD WALL

BEAM C

CASED 2 LAYERS P'BD + SKIM

CONCRETE OR STEEL LINTEL OVER

2000 HEADROOM

STAIRCASE WITH 15 RISERS, 190mm RISER 225mm TREADS PITCH 53.5° CLEAR WIDTH 800mm PLYWOOD LINED BALUSTRADE 900mm HIGH

LINE OF CHIMNEY BREASTS

EXISTING GROUND LEVELS

DPC

900 DATION DEPTH

600 x 150 CONCRETE FOUNDATION (1:2:4 - 25mm - 25 MN/m²)

50 mm FINISH + CES (1:3) SCREED
150 CONCRETE 1:2:4 (25mm)
VISQUEEN D.P.M.
50mm POLYSTYRENE INSULATION

SECTION B

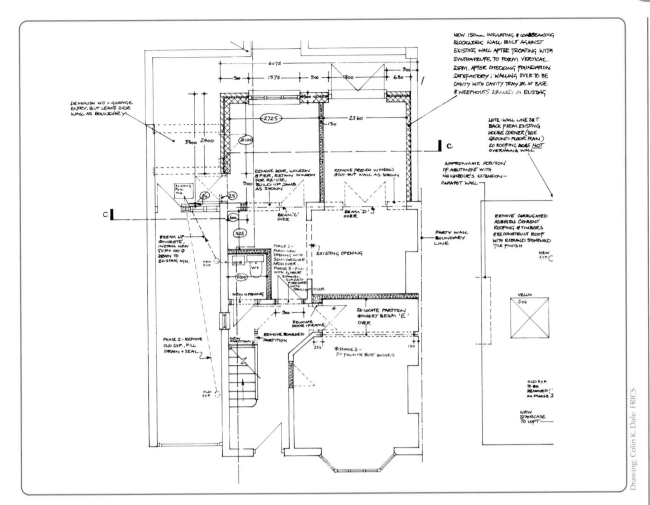

The drawing contains handwritten annotations including:

- NEW 150mm INSULATING & LOADBEARING BLOCKWORK WALL BUILT AGAINST EXISTING WALL AFTER TREATING WITH SYNTHAPRUFE, TO FORM VERTICAL DPM. AFTER CHECKING FOUNDATION SATISFACTORY; WALLING OVER TO BE CAVITY WITH CAVITY TRAY &c AT BASE & WEEPHOLES DRILLED IN EXISTING
- NOTE: WALL LINE SET BACK FROM EXISTING HOUSE CORNER (SEE GROUND FLOOR PLAN) SO ROOFING DOES NOT OVERHANG WALL
- DEMOLISH WC + GARAGE ENTRY, BUT LEAVE SIDE WALL AS BOUNDARY
- APPROXIMATE POSITION OF ABUTMENT WITH NEIGHBOUR'S EXTENSION — PARAPET WALL
- REMOVE CORRUGATED ASBESTOS CEMENT ROOFING & TIMBERS & RECONSTRUCT ROOF WITH REBAND STONEWOLD TILE FINISH
- REMOVE DOOR, WINDOW & PIER, RETAIN WINDOW FOR RE-USE, BUILD UP JAMB AS SHOWN
- REMOVE FRENCH WINDOW & CUT OUT WALL AS SHOWN
- PARTY WALL BOUNDARY LINE
- BEAM 'C' OVER
- BEAM 'D' OVER
- BREAK UP CONCRETE, INSTALL NEW SVP + 100 Ø DRAIN TO EXISTING MH.
- PHASE 1 — FORM NEW OPENING WITH SEMI-CIRCULAR ARCH OVER. PHASE 3 - FILL WITH ½ HOUSE & PANELLED GLAZED FIRE DOORS WITH FANLIGHT OVER
- NEW OPENING
- EXISTING OPENING
- RE-LOCATE PARTITION & INSERT BEAM 'E' OVER
- PHASE 2 - REMOVE OLD SVP., FILL DRAIN + SEAL
- RELOCATE DOOR + FRAME
- REMOVE BOARDED PARTITION
- PHASE 3 - FT FALLING BUTT HINGES
- OLD S.V.P. TO BE REMOVED IN PHASE 2
- VELUX S06
- NEW S.V.P.
- NEW STAIRCASE TO LOFT
- NEW PARTITION

Dimensions shown: 6075, 1575, 900, 1800, 680, 2725, 2560, 130, 3300, 2400, 2100, 900, 250, 150, 1200, 1125, 600

Drawing: Colin K. Dale FRICS

■ **A section plan** drawing showing a cross-section 'sliced through' the middle of the proposed new extension, paying particular attention to details of wall construction, joist depths, floor levels, room heights, and any stairs (typically drawn to 1:20 or 1:25 scale, and preferably no smaller than 1:50). These are the most informative of building plans since they expose the details of the new building's construction, showing materials and thicknesses as well as heights and dimensions. This is often the plan that has most of the specification written on it.

■ **Plan and elevation drawings** together with technical notes that fully describe the proposed works.

■ **Structural calculations** for new or altered load-bearing elements, and details of any proposals to build over or near sewers.

You'll normally need to print about four copies of your drawings, plus a few more for builders to quote from and some to keep spare. There are two payments you'll need to make: a 'plans fee' paid up front and an 'inspection fee' paid at start-on-site.

Having submitted your full plans application, Building Control should write confirming who'll be dealing with your case. Your application should normally be passed or rejected within five weeks, although this can be extended with your consent for up to two months.

Ultimately you should receive a 'plans approved' notice to confirm that the plans comply with Building Regulations.

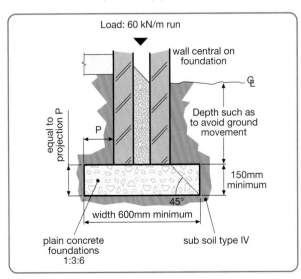

Diagram labels: Load: 60 kN/m run; wall central on foundation; GL; equal to projection P; P; Depth such as to avoid ground movement; 150mm minimum; 45°; width 600mm minimum; plain concrete foundations 1:3:6; sub soil type IV

The Building Control Officer will then inspect the work on site at key stages as it progresses. A 'plans approved' notice is valid for three years, and will then expire unless building work has commenced. It's not the same as a final certificate (a.k.a. completion certificate), which should be issued once all the work is satisfactorily completed.

Approval or rejection
There are basically three possible outcomes to your Building Regs application:

Approval
If you receive a 'plans approval notice', congratulations! But even drawings submitted by professional designers are rarely perfect first time, so it's unlikely that you'll get

everything 100 per cent right if you submit your own plans. Unless you're already familiar with current Building Regulations don't be shy of asking for a little professional input.

What information to write on the plans

On simple projects, the construction details can all be fitted onto the plans on 2 sheets of A1 (840 x 592mm). On the section drawing and the elevation plans you need to show:

Levels

■ Ground levels: Outside ground levels are rarely perfectly level, so show them true-to-life on the drawings.

■ The levels of new drains: Show the 'invert levels' (depths) where new drainage is to be connected, at inspection chambers. You can take your own levels from the existing drains by measuring the depth between the manhole cover and the bottom of the channel.

■ Floor levels: The new floor levels of the extension can be shown in relation to the existing floor level of the main house.

The specification

The specification describes the types and thicknesses of materials – see page 57. This should clearly state:

■ The dimensions of all the main components of the building (foundations, floors, joist layouts, walls, windows, doors, roof structure etc), also explaining their type and their position in the building.

■ The type and size of insulation to be used (to floors, walls and roofs etc).

■ The drains: their routes (layouts), falls (angle of slope), the position of junctions and inspection chambers, and access points for rodding, should all be described or shown, and details of how pipes are protected, *eg* where they pass under the building.

See website for samples.

Conditional approval

It's more likely that Building Control will write back to you with an 'amendments letter' asking for clarification on various points or requiring additional information, such as engineer's calculations.

Being bombarded with highly detailed questions about your design at this stage can seem rather irritating. But remember it's a whole lot easier sorting out problems on paper than it would be trying to rebuild walls on site. And you can be sure that if Building Control aren't entirely clear about what you mean, the builders certainly won't be. If you haven't got a clue what they're on about just phone or visit your BC Officer, who'll normally be pleased to explain matters in plain English.

Alternatively, they may issue approval on a conditional basis. In both cases it means that the design requires some amendment. Conditional approvals normally have the conditions listed as an attached document (*eg* stating required modifications) or they may simply request further plans to be submitted. It's important that your designer resolves these conditions in good time before the start-on-site date.

Rejection

A rejection notice needn't be as bad as it sounds. It can usually be overcome by resubmitting amended plans, for which no additional fee should be charged. Fees should also not apply for giving advice and for work that benefits people with disabilities, *eg* where extensions are being built specifically for this purpose.

5 MEET THE BUILDERS

If there's one decision that can really make or break your project it's selecting the right builder. You may have the finest drawings and the most eloquent specifications in the world, all beautifully tied up with watertight legal contracts. But a dodgy builder can, at a stroke, turn your dream extension into a traumatic nightmare. This chapter should help you avoid vexed relationships with builders.

Even the best builders need a tea break (4 sugars!).

There are basically three ways you can run your project:

- **Employ a main contractor** to carry out all the building works.
- **Directly employ your own specialist trades** (subcontractors) for each stage of the works and project manage it yourself.
- **Self-build the whole thing**, with a bit of extra help here and there.

For the vast majority of home extensions, the favoured route is the simplest one – method 1. This still leaves room for you to help project manage and to cherry-pick a few jobs where your skills are strongest, though the extent of your involvement should be agreed with the contractor at the outset. Methods 2 and 3 are only suitable for more experienced home-extenders.

Finding the right builder

Anyone with zero qualifications, lacking even the most rudimentary experience, is perfectly entitled to set up in business calling themselves 'building contractors'. This may explain why TV schedules are packed with grim tales of builders from hell preying mercilessly on vulnerable homeowners. If it's roof work, plumbing, or a new driveway that you need, it seems there's no shortage of dodgy tradesmen out there to choose from.

Perhaps because of all the negative media coverage, the general public's perception of the building trade is somewhat negative. Admittedly there's no smoke without fire – over 100,000 complaints about cowboy builders are registered with trading standards officers each year – but the plain fact is, cowboy builders are in the minority. Most builders will try to do a difficult job well. Remember that the builder is only

one part of the equation. Architects are fond of using the expression 'a good client', because it greatly helps when clients are clear about what they require from the outset. Builders, too, have to deal with their fair share of 'cowboy clients' who constantly change their minds, demand extra work free of charge, play tricks and make excuses for non payment, and then don't have any money. Good clients, tend to get good building work done for them.

Like anything, there's a right way and a wrong way to approach a job, and the golden rules for running a successful building project are explained later.

But first, how do you choose a decent builder? What you *don't* do is pick the first nice-looking advertisement you come across in *Yellow Pages* or the local paper. A glossy, professional looking ad doesn't mean the firm advertising is professional. Neither is it true that 'the posher the van, the better the builder' – it simply means he's good at spending money on vans.

The best place to start is with a personal recommendation, or by speaking to previous customers.

From a shortlist of four or five firms you should be able to find one that fits the bill in terms of price, quality, and availability to start the job within a reasonable timescale.

The criteria for selecting a builder

Recommendations
Ask people you know locally if they can recommend someone. Architects and surveyors are particularly well placed to make recommendations. Best placed of all to provide sensible advice are Building Control Officers, but regrettably they may not be at liberty to make recommendations. Citizens Advice Bureaux often keep lists of local contractors, such as those with a good track record working for senior citizens.

Trade association membership
Builders sometimes belong to trade federations, but these exist primarily to represent the interests of their members, not the customers, and the requirements for joining are not always terribly demanding. It's not unknown for unscrupulous builders to 'borrow' logos to make their ads look nicer, or even to make up their own 'guilds', 'leagues' and 'federations', of which they're the only member! So proceed with caution and check that your chosen firm's membership is still current.

Membership of 'proper' trade associations with their own codes of practice can, however, be a useful way to identify good firms. And there may be additional benefits, such as dispute resolution services and complaints procedures, or even insurance-backed warranties. But don't automatically reject a builder because of their lack of 'badges' – many excellent individual tradesmen may work entirely from local references and feel that they don't need to belong to an organisation.

Photo: H+H Celcon Ltd

Membership of trade bodies is no guarantee of site quality, but federations that offer additional insurance if you employ one of their members are a definite bonus. To be of any real value, insurance backed warranties need to cover you for a period of up to ten years after completion, for defects caused by poor workmanship or materials, or if the builder goes bust during the job.

Perhaps the best-known trade association is the Federation of Master Builders, but each trade has its own professional body. All the leading 'logos' are listed on the website.

There are also Government-funded schemes such as 'TrustMark' which claim to be able to provide consumers with a list of reliable firms. Thousands of 'pre-qualified' contractors, including many sole traders and small specialist firms, are registered with www.constructiononline.co.uk.

Quality Assurance

ISO 9001/2 and BS 5750 may sound familiar. These are widely held Quality Assurance accreditations, but although they might appear to be some kind of guarantee of quality for site work, they are not. They simply prove that a firm is able to reproduce the same standard of work time and time again. And some builders have absolutely no problem faithfully reproducing poor work! Nonetheless, they do indicate a general intention by a firm to deliver a good quality job.

Previous work

This is where a little detective work can really pay off. Although you should always obtain written references, bear in mind that they may sometimes be of limited value. A builder who's a crook will have written them himself, and the referee will turn out to be his mum or one of his mates! All decent contractors should be able to easily

Above: Space is limited on many sites.
Below: Did they get round to finishing the last job?

provide a list of recently completed jobs, and a list of customers (such as Housing Associations) to whom you can write.

Go and take a look at the work, and ideally speak to the homeowners – most people will be happy to help. Asking some fairly detailed questions will help ensure they're genuine, for example:

- Did the builders turn up when agreed?
- Did they clear away their rubbish and use dust sheets to protect furniture?
- What was the quality of work like?
- How was their attention to detail?
- Did they price extra work reasonably?
- Did the job start and finish on time?
- Were they considerate?
- Would you employ them again?

If all the referees sound the same and can't give much detail except to say the firm is 'really great', forget it.

Also, visit one of the builders' current sites to see work in progress. Note how tidy the site is, and whether materials are protected and stored neatly, or just chaotically littered about. Is it a rushed or badly planned job? Running the name of your chosen firms past Trading Standards isn't a bad idea either.

Bankers' references

Ask for a banker's reference. A firm with insufficient funds to finance the work without demanding a cash deposit for materials up front will be trouble.

Insurance

Suppose your builder accidentally drops some tiles off the scaffolding, injuring a passer-by. Or the milkman falls down an unprotected hole in the ground. If it turns out your builder isn't fully insured you could be held jointly liable to pay compensation as owner of the property. More likely some irritating minor damage will occur, like next door's fence getting dented or their phone cable being cut through. So it's important to cover yourself by asking the builder to produce his current certificate of public liability insurance, which must provide cover to a minimum of £1 million. This is a reasonable request, and any bona fide builder will have no trouble co-operating.

However, if you employ subcontractors directly, you are deemed to be an employer at least from an insurance angle. This means you will need two policies – public liability, covering risk to the public, and employer's liability which covers you should someone working for you have an accident and promptly sue you. Most employers' policies now cover you up to £10 million, and public liability for £2 million.

It also would be advisable to get 'all risks insurance' which covers theft of plant and materials from the site, as well as fire and structural damage to the buildings you're working on. In total, you might have to cough up about 0.5% of the contract sum to get a project comprehensively insured.

VAT registered?

Unfortunately, VAT is chargeable on home extensions. Even if your builder only undertakes a few small extensions in a year, his turnover will almost certainly place him above the VAT registration threshold, so he'll need to be VAT registered. It's wise to assume that VAT has to be added to the quotation, unless it is clearly shown. You should obtain proper VAT receipts for all payments, so check the builder has a valid VAT number and isn't just pocketing it. Cash deals are best avoided.

Guarantees

Defects in major components such as foundations, floors and double glazing can take several years to appear. For extensions there is no direct equivalent to the NHBC warranty for new houses, but fortunately with most standard contracts like the JCT Minor Works (see below) six-year warranties are included. In any case, guarantees are only as good as the firms offering them, so to have any meaning they need to be insurance-backed.

Quotation or estimate?

Quotations and estimates are two very different things. A quotation is a firm price which is legally binding. It's a fixed sum for a fixed amount of work. An estimate, on the other hand, is the builder's best guess at what the cost might eventually be. It's not legally binding, and allows the

builder to present a higher (or lower) final bill, and is far too risky for a big project like an extension.

If you insist on a firm quotation you'll need to provide sufficient information for the builder to understand exactly what you want built. To judge how good a quotation is, consider the amount of care and detail that's gone into it (*eg* references to your drawing numbers etc) and check that the builder actually went to the trouble of visiting the site before quoting.

This is important, because having provided a quotation your builder must stick to it. If you're presented with a larger final bill, you're only obliged to pay the agreed quotation price unless you've requested 'extras' or agreed to 'changes' (for 'Extras and changes' see Chapter 6). Most contractors will increase their price to cover the risk that the job may turn out to be more complicated than it seems.

You'll need to obtain four or five quotations in writing. Quotations are normally presented in terms of a firm price for the completed job which is what you actually pay, or in terms of a 'metreage rate' known as 'pricework'. This is where you're given a price expressed either per square metre (tiling, brickwork, plasterwork etc) or per metre run (for laying pipes etc). Quotes based on a price per day ('day rate') are best avoided because of the obvious temptation to sit around and string the job out indefinitely.

The information you send to contractors for pricing can be in the form of a letter and a set of detailed plans. It's worth confirming in your covering letter that you've already got your Local Authority consents, otherwise they may consider it a waste of time replying! But the best way to get a job priced is to tender it (see page 67).

Small builders

A smaller firm of builders will have less labour available to share between competing jobs, so you should have more chance of getting their undivided attention for the full project. If you're very lucky they may even finish one job at a time rather than juggling resources between different jobs, as larger firms invariably do. But avoid small firms that don't have enough funding to pay for materials up front. That said, the builder is in a vulnerable position, effectively extending you credit, and will be as wary of potential clients as they are of him.

Contingency sums

The chances are that as you watch your extension take shape there'll be something that will occur to you (or your partner) that 'would look nice'. Something you wish you'd included in the specification. You're not alone. It's not unknown for architects and surveyors to omit things from specifications. It's therefore always wise to budget five to ten per cent more than the quoted cost, to allow for the inevitable 'human error'.

The contract

A building contract is simply an agreement between you and your builders, for them to undertake a list of specified

tasks to a certain standard, for an agreed sum of money. Although, strictly speaking, accepting a verbal offer could form a contract in law, to run the job properly it's advisable to use a written contract, signed by both parties.

Dodgy builders have been known to quote for a job but never actually start on site, and then try to claim compensation when your patience is finally exhausted and you tell them to sling their hook. They may claim that you entered into a verbal contract. So if you do accept a builder's offer to do a job without a formal contract, always make your acceptance conditional upon them confirming in writing that they agree to a specific start date and completion date.

By providing a quotation from your plans or where a contract can be proved to exist, there are two key implied conditions – that 'the work shall be performed within a reasonable time' and 'with reasonable care and skill'.

Using a written contract is always advisable because it shows that both sides are serious, and gives you both certain rights and duties which are enforceable in court. Without something written down it's your word against theirs. If things all go horribly wrong later, your case will be a lot stronger if you can produce a contract, signed by the builder, saying that he agreed to finish by the end of September, when your roof's still not on in October.

Rather than sitting there feeling a complete berk, it allows you (the innocent party) to seek compensation ('damages') for any losses incurred, or to withhold payment, or even to terminate the contract and employ someone else.

But which contract to use? There's nothing to stop you writing your own if you want, but it's a lot easier to use a ready-made 'off the shelf' variety, such as a suitable JCT (Joint Contracts Tribunal) contract. The JCT 'Building Contract for a Home Owner/Occupier' can be used for straightforward or lower-price jobs (costing below about £20,000). Or for more complex or expensive projects there's the JCT 'Minor Works' contract. Alternatively, the Federation of Master Builders have a free one you can download from the website.

Don't be too gobsmacked when you first read the contract. It's basically a collection of all the things that could ever go wrong with a property development, based on other people's bad experiences over many years. It clarifies who's responsible for what, thereby reducing the risk of a major dispute messing up the job. All the important stuff is there, including how frequently you pay the builders, and who's responsible if the extension is only half finished by the completion date.

There's nothing to stop you adding your own specific conditions if you wish. For example, you might want the builder not to start work until after 7.45 am, not to work at weekends, and not to entertain the neighbours by blasting out Def Leppard's greatest hits all day long. You might also want to stipulate that they take all reasonable measures to protect your newly paved drive from damage.

Before you sign the contract, remember it's your last chance to ensure you'll be getting exactly what you want: any changes from now could cost you more money.

Specifications

Most disputes with builders are (surprise, surprise) about money. This is often down to misunderstandings about what work was meant to be done for the quoted price. This may be because the client or architect didn't clearly specify the required work at the outset. Builders aren't psychic. The key to a smoothly run scheme is, above all, to specify clearly what you want, so you know exactly what you'll be paying for. This, of course, is easier said than done.

An architect or surveyor can write a specification of the work, often referred to as 'the spec' (pronounced 'spess'). This is basically a long shopping list stating each separate piece of work required which is sent to the contractor to work out how much the job will cost. If anything, having a professionally drawn up specification is of more value than a formal contract, because it should prevent a lot of misunderstandings arising in the first place. More upmarket jobs tend to have the spec written separately from the drawings. Together, the spec and drawings should make it clear exactly how many square metres of plastering, roof slates, tiling etc are needed, so the contractor can simply write a price next to each separate component of the job. The whole lot is then totted up to produce a grand total.

This is especially useful later on when it comes to paying the builders, since you can pay them the price they've quoted for each piece of work. It also helps in avoiding overpaying for any 'extras', as you can base the price on the figures quoted here for similar work.

Much of this information will already have been written down on your Building Control drawings, which, if adequately detailed, may alone be sufficient for the builder to price from. It's a good idea in any case to write down your own detailed list of requirements because it helps focus on exactly what you want, reducing the risk of misunderstandings later. See website for examples.

Briefs

If it's your first time attempting to write a specification, it would be a good idea to first run it past someone with good construction knowledge, because if you miss stuff out that later needs to be done on site it will count as an 'extra', which could prove expensive. So if you're going to do a DIY spec it may be better to refer to it as a 'detailed brief' when you submit it to the contractor. Whereas a spec is regarded as a definitive list, a brief is simply 'your best attempt' to convey your requirements. A brief doesn't exempt the contractor from his responsibility to use his expertise to interpret your desires, and to employ suitable methods and materials. In the event of a later dispute, a brief can be a little more forgiving.

Start by writing down a general outline of the work and then list specific requirements, explaining what you want and the standards you expect. You need to research the available sizes and quality of materials such as bricks, tiles and lintels (available on manufacturers' websites).

Using the phrase 'allow for all necessary work in connection with…' covers a multitude of sins and will reduce the risk of the contractor trying to charge extra for something which is obviously needed but which you might have forgotten to include in the brief.

Workmanship

So much for accurately describing the job and defining the required materials. But there's one thing that's a lot harder to nail down, and that's the standard of workmanship. Under the terms of the contract, the builder will normally be required to 'use reasonable care and skill', which is obviously open to some interpretation. One solution is to specify 'British Standard BS8000' on the plans, and to make sure the plans are included as contract documents so that, if push comes to shove, they are legally enforceable (so staple a set of plans to the contract and have each party jointly sign all pages and drawings). Then if the workmanship becomes unsatisfactory at any stage, your builder will be in breach of contract and you'll be able to terminate the contract or to give notice to correct defective work.

Design detail – choosing materials

Never assume that the builder will automatically do everything just the way you like it. This may sound obvious but many disputes grow out of misunderstandings over tiny details. For example, you might have visualised Victorian-style ogee architraves and 'torus' skirting that beautifully complement your new bathroom fittings, but unless instructed otherwise the builder may just stick on the cheapest bit of wood he can find. And unless you clearly specify that roll-top, claw-foot cast iron bath you've always dreamed of, the contractor will be perfectly entitled to plonk in a cheapo plastic jobby. So think carefully about

the details – the precise kind of light switches, sockets, taps and basins that you want – or you'll inevitably find they've fitted ones left over from the last job.

On the other hand, your builders may well come up with helpful ideas as the job progresses, which can sometimes reduce the cost. Most builders know their stuff and have seen it all before, so don't be too proud or suspicious and reject all their ideas out of hand. Just be aware that some suggestions come with a price tag. If your builder suggests that something 'might as well be done', don't assume he'll do it out of the kindness of his heart.

Now is the time to do your homework. There'll be less room for mistakes if you quote details and catalogue numbers. If you intend to supply some fittings or materials yourself make sure that your specification or brief states that the contractor is to 'allow for fitting only'. This means that you're solely responsible for ensuring these items are available on site exactly when the fitter needs them. If they're delivered too soon there'll be more risk of theft or damage – too late, and the plumber or chippie may not be on site again for another month.

The responsibility for supplying materials and fittings must be made very clear at the start, or it can very easily flare up into a major issue later. Rather than supplying things yourself, it's usually simpler to specify exactly what materials you want by writing 'allow price of £X to supply 1 no. pair *Pegler* bath taps ref: ABC123' (*ie* quote the order number). This will save a whole lot of your time fetching and delivering things.

Provisional sums

Most of us like to take our time mulling over the precise choice of visually important things like taps, worktops and tiles. After all, rushing such key design decisions could result in catastrophic style errors that haunt us for the rest of our days. On the other hand, you don't want to hold up the entire project whilst umming and ahhing over samples and colour swatches for months on end. And you certainly don't want to keep changing your mind about exactly what styles you really want as work progresses on site.

Thankfully there's a convenient solution. Using 'PC

sums' or 'provisional sums' in your specification allows you to have your cake and eat it, so you can get on with the job whilst postponing such tough decisions.

Photo: Royce Bathrooms

PC sums allow clients the freedom to select the precise product at a later date. So you might write in your specification '*allow the PC sum of £500 for supply only of bathroom suite*' as an estimate of what you think it's likely to end up costing. The contractor will have to include

this amount in his quotation, but the actual figure you pay will be down to which suite you actually choose. The builder then quotes only for the labour to fit it and adopts your stated 'guide price' for the materials. Similarly, provisional sums are 'an allowance for unknown items of work or goods, including labour costs, overheads and profit'. They are useful where there is some doubt about the likely extent of work to be carried out, such as for underground drainage works.

These are only estimates, not firm prices, so the actual costs (which could be higher or lower than estimated) will need to be sorted out later. Adjustments will normally be made in the final bill. The downside is they can introduce an element of uncertainty, a potential cause of disputes, and should be avoided if at all possible.

Preliminaries

The 'prelims' are your way of explaining to the contractor the arrangements for all those important little things that make a job run smoothly – such as provision of toilets for the lads on site, rubbish collection, site security, scaffolding, temporary power supplies, and arrangements for storage of materials. If you skip this, it may only be when you notice rubble-filled wheelbarrows being carted through your expensively wallpapered entrance hall that you realise you should have agreed site access arrangements in advance.

Another crucial prelim is to arrange for a convenient water supply, such as from an outdoor tap, or perhaps from a large water butt, since running a hose from your kitchen all day long will drive you bananas. Not unreasonably the builder will expect free access to the site for the duration of the contract, so if you suddenly jet off on holiday half-way through the project leaving the house locked up, the builders may well disappear off to another job and may never be seen again. Indeed, if the client causes delays to the work the builder can submit a claim for losses and expenses incurred as a result, which would make it rather an expensive holiday.

Prelims are also important because there are a lot of potential costs involved – things like hiring port-a-loos,

security fencing, and massive storage containers. If things are not spelled out clearly, family mealtimes may be enlivened by builders trekking through the house to use the loo. Or you may wake up one day trapped in your home by mountains of concrete blocks deposited outside the front door.

Tendering

A tender is a sort of super-detailed competitive quotation. There are two good reasons for tendering a job. First, it immediately weeds out dodgy builders, who won't want to go to all the trouble of completing and replying to tenders. And second, it lets you easily compare rival firm's prices for the same job.

Start by phoning or emailing your shortlisted building firms to ask whether they'd like to tender for your extension. This saves wasting time sending out documents to firms who are either too busy or just not interested. Next, send out your tender documents and wait for the reply.

The tender documents together amount to a written list explaining exactly what you want built, against which the builder can offer a price:

- The latest version of the drawings used for Building Control, plus any additional builders' drawings illustrating key construction details.
- A detailed brief or specification.
- Preliminaries (or you could list these in your covering letter instead).
- A completed form of tender (see website).
- A photocopy of any contract you propose to use, left blank.
- A covering letter clearly stating the precise deadline by which completed tenders should be submitted. If you allow any less than four weeks they may not have time to obtain prices from subcontractors and suppliers, and will 'guesstimate' with inflated prices to allow for risk.

You may also wish to provide a list of any special items you require (like a specific brand of bathroom fittings). It's worth

asking the contractors to quote their rates per square metre for works such as plastering and pointing, or per metre run for jobs like laying pipes. This may come in useful if you later need to ask for additions to the quoted job.

Comparing offers

Come the stated deadline you should have at least three completed tenders to choose from, but no matter how many weeks' notice you've given you can be fairly sure one will arrive at the last minute in the hands of a motorcycle messenger or you'll get an urgent phone call asking for more time. Take a deep breath, open the envelopes, and check the bottom lines.

If it transpires that all the prices submitted significantly exceed your budget, don't despair. There may be ways to reduce the costs by agreeing to omit some parts of the work that weren't essential.

Unfortunately, selecting the best tender is not as simple as just choosing the lowest bid. The cheapest price is not necessarily the best one. This is where you need to get smart and read between the lines. One builder may have undercut the others because he's just totally inept at estimating. Another may have underpriced part of the job, and may need to recover that loss by cutting corners as the work proceeds. But sometimes, wide variations in quoted prices for the same job may simply be down to each builder assessing the risk of the job differently, and loading prices accordingly.

Just to get you really paranoid, it's not unknown for a builder to deliberately submit a super-cheap price as a strategy to secure the job, and then pile on lots of expensive 'extras' later. An unscrupulous firm may be quite skilled in spotting loopholes in your specification, knowing they can later charge you premium prices. So it's worth spending some time comparing all your tenders, section by section, since this may reveal surprising differences in quoted prices for the same works.

Suppose you have five tenders and you're looking at all the prices for the same roof job. Naturally, the cheapest price will always appear very attractive – who can resist a bargain? But take a minute to consider why it's that cheap. Is it because they're desperate for the work? Or it could be that roofing work is that firm's speciality, their area of expertise. Fair enough, but if it's absurdly cheap compared to the others it may be that they've forgotten to include some materials or labour. This means you'll either end up with a badly done job or paying for lots of hugely profitable extras. Unless the firm has been highly recommended, it may be cheaper in the long run to select another, rather than risk them scrimping on materials and labour to recoup losses. High standards don't tend to go with low prices.

Then there's the important matter of the start-on-site date. It's unlikely that a good small firm would be so in need of work that it could start tomorrow. But on the other hand, a firm that can't begin for another 11 months may not be ideal either.

Finally, use a little intuition about the people themselves. Are they people you can do business with?

Or is there something about their attitude that makes you feel uneasy. If in doubt, go for the good communicator, or the one you get on with best, as they'll be more likely to understand your requirements.

13 Subsidence Street *new rear extension*

PROGRAMME OF WORKS	Date
1 Start on site	3 March
2 Demolish old garage/patio	7 March
3 Groundwork: excavate foundations & pour concrete	14 March
4 Excavate and lay drainage	
5 Ground floor slab	
6 Construct main walls up to DPC	
7 Build main walls to first lift	
8 Complete main walls	
9 Roof structure	
10 Roof coverings	
11 Windows & doors	
12 Knocking through	
13 Plumbing, heating & electrics 1st fix	
14 Floor screed and plastering	
15 Internal joinery	
16 Kitchen and sanitary fittings, connect drainage	
17 Plumbing, heating & electrics 2nd fix	
18 Decorations	
19 Practical completion	
Bodgit & Scarper Building Contractors, Old Nick Lane, Dartmoor DN1	00/00/00

And the winner is...

Having made your choice, you'll then need to set up a meeting to go through your drawings and specification in some detail prior to signing the contract. If you're employing an architect, they should also be present so that any complex parts of the design can be discussed.

Run through key things like the depth of foundations, the type of bricks (stone, render, cladding etc), the sizes of roof timbers, types of windows and doors, and the number of coats of paint on external timbers.

If the builder's face turns a peculiar shade of ghostly white at any stage it means he's just realised something's been seriously underpriced. If his pricing is very low for one particular part of the job compared to the others, mention this by saying 'Your price for the [whatever] seems to be a lot less than the average for this work. Would you like to check your price before signing the contract?' It's always better to agree a revised price at this stage than to have a dispute later on site, but it must be agreed in writing since it changes the tendered sum. Legally you could hold them to their tendered price, but this would only encourage a cheap job to save money.

This is the honeymoon stage, and everything is sweetness and light as the contractor basks in the warm afterglow of winning the tender. It's therefore as well to bring things sharply down to earth and remind them about all the important issues – the agreed start date and completion date, arrangements for storage of materials on site, the welfare facilities (loos etc), health and safety matters, frequency of site meetings, and the agreed method for dealing with any changes you might later require to the work (*ie* written instructions).

Although as a rule they don't like doing this, ask the contractor to provide a detailed week-by-week programme, so that you can monitor progress. Even a simple 'milestone programme' would be useful, as shown left.

Having satisfied yourself that the builders are fully aware of what's required of them and are happy to deliver it, the next step is to fill in all the important parts of the contract. These will include the start and completion dates, any damages (penalties) for overrunning, the dates you'll make payments, and the amount of retention you plan to keep (see 'Payments and retentions', page 79).

As far as the agreed timescales are concerned, it's not unknown for contractors to be prone to bouts of over-optimism at this stage, which will only cause problems later if you have to apply damages for their non-completion. So it may be worth asking them to think twice about the projected time to finish the job. If necessary they might want to agree an extra couple of weeks, just in case. They are, of course, perfectly at liberty to finish the job earlier if they wish (but they won't). All contract documents, including the drawings and the form of tender, now need to be signed by both parties and stapled together with the contract itself. Hang on to the originals, and provide photocopies to the contractor.

If you're not using a ready-printed legal form of agreement, you can complete the deal by writing to the contractor to formally accept his offer. Your 'letter of acceptance' is a legally binding contract document and should include a list of the drawings and documents on which he based his quote, together with confirmation of the agreed price (the 'contract sum'), the agreed timescales, and the stages of payment etc. You must also request that the builder formally replies and acknowledges receipt of your letter.

Site safety

The designer has a legal duty to minimise safety risks by drawing up a health & safety plan which is administered by the main contractor. Failure to comply with these 'CDM regulations' can result in criminal prosecution. If you are the client this should not be your responsibility, but if you are managing your own build, then you could be regarded as a contractor – see next chapter.

Either way, it's a good idea to specify aspects of site safety in the prelims and to encourage the builder to keep the site as tidy a possible at all times. For example, 240v power supplies are prohibited on building sites so contractors must only use 110v power tools, and it wouldn't do any harm to include a reminder of this in the documentation. You must also ensure that children are physically excluded from entering sites at all times by erecting suitable child-proof barriers.

Building sites are renowned for serious accidents. Approximately half of all construction fatalities are due to falls, hence the recently introduced 'Working at Height Regulations' which, amongst other things, restricts the use of ladders. Where ladders are essential, their tops must be anchored to something secure. But these aren't the only worry. The risks from such routine objects as power tools, sharp blades, holes in the ground, bricks dropped from scaffolding, flame guns, toxic or flammable sprays and live electric cables are very real and need to be treated with respect.

It's never worth taking chances on site. Always wear a hard hat, steel capped boots and a safety jacket. Look where you're stepping, and if you really must ascend the scaffolding notify the contractor first.

Employing your own subcontractors

If you've always wanted to manage your own team, now's your chance. Of course you can't expect to instantly become the Jose Mourinho of the home extension world without a little prior experience, so only take this role on if you know your headers from your stretchers. Otherwise, there is always going to be the risk that if some less scrupulous subcontractors figure they're working for a novice, they could be tempted to cut corners.

Strictly speaking, subcontractors are tradesmen employed by a main contractor. If they work directly for you then they aren't actually subbies at all, just plain old contractors. They tend to operate either as one man bands or as small firms – but everyone still calls them subbies. It's important to note that if you become the main contractor, then you're suddenly responsible for policing your subbies' tax affairs. If your project is construed as being connected to running a business or trade, then you could be deemed to be a 'professional developer', getting lumbered with all the main contractor tax and insurance liabilities. But if you are a client, you don't have to worry. The definition of a domestic client is 'a client for whom a project is carried out'.

It's unusual to sign written contracts with subbies, and the work is normally described with reference to the plans. But the clearer and more specific you are about what you

want, the less chance of expensive misunderstandings. If you're acting as a client who has chosen to do some of the building work yourself, and to employ some trades direct, you will still need to adopt some of the responsibilities of a main contractor, and to budget for increased overheads, especially phone bills and mileage.

Your mission is to achieve nothing less than the smooth running of the project, which means having to co-ordinate all the various materials and trades on site at each stage of the build. Easy to say, hard to deliver.

The team

Like any team, yours will only be as strong as its weakest link. Select only those who you know to be skilled and experienced at their particular trade. You need to ensure that each 'subbie' knows exactly what's expected of them,

or the job will be done the way that's easiest for them rather than the way you want it. Earlier, we described how to go about getting quotations. Now, as client and main contractor rolled into one, you'll need to apply this 'get a quote' process to each trade in turn, to be clear about what exactly is included in each subbie's price.

Each trade has its own quirks and particular ways of working:

- **Brickies** often work in gangs of two, plus a labourer and do not usually supply materials. Quotations tend to 'measure through openings' on the walls for both brick and blockwork. *ie* they don't deduct anything for the air spaces that are window & door openings (perhaps 25% of the surface area). This compensates for all the 'fiddly bits at reveals, and window templates etc.
- **Chippies** often work in pairs, and don't supply materials.
- **Roofers** may be hired in gangs who supply and fix, sometimes also organising scaffolding.
- **Plasterers, plumbers, electricians** are usually one man bands or small firms

Subbies who supply materials as well as labour ('supply & fix') typically include **roofers, plumbers, electricians and kitchen fitters**. They make a markup on the materials they buy on your behalf.

Ordering materials

Managing the logistics of getting the right materials delivered to the right place at the right time can be a demanding task, one that clients using main contractors often take for granted. If work on site grinds to a halt due to lack of materials, it will now be you who'll personally carry the can for non-completion. So if you decide to source your own stuff, start by writing out a detailed shopping list of all your materials (known as a 'bill of quantities'). This is based on the information in your specification document, or on the plans, from which all the areas and volumes can be calculated with the help of a scale rule (*eg* 1:50). Your specification should be clear about whether you want the trades to provide their own materials or just supply 'labour only'.

When ordering materials you often have to accept the nearest pack quantity size. Bricks for example are delivered in packs of 410, which may prove inconvenient if you only need a few. And don't forget to add an allowance for the materials that get wasted, or are surplus, perhaps to the tune of around 10%. Ordering more than you need may be expensive, but buying too little is probably more so.

Having worked out exactly how much of what you need to order, next select two or three major suppliers (usually builders' merchants) and give them your shopping list together with a copy of your drawings. Ideally show them samples of the specific bricks and tiles you require.

Most small builders expect to pay about 30% less than the list prices shown in catalogues, so there's no reason you shouldn't be able to negotiate a sizeable discount for such a large order. But you first need to open a trade account. You will be quoted keener prices if they know you're serious about buying, rather than just researching prices for estimating a job, and it always helps to persuade them that you are a good payer.

You should qualify for at least a month's credit. By postponing a purchase beyond the end of the month you can often qualify for an extra 30 days' credit. Haggling over prices is standard practice at builders' merchants, but not of course at the big DIY sheds like Wickes and B&Q, where some prices can be as competitive as trade prices elsewhere. To compare quotes from rival suppliers, ensure that you're actually comparing like with like and that the materials are the same. Also check that VAT is included, and that quantities and delivery dates are all clearly stated.

A single large supplier should be able to provide all of the

Keep your materials safe and secure.

big stuff you'll need, from cement and aggregates to roof tiles – one well-known firm's brochure even promises 'no unpleasant surprises'! Builders' merchants are normally most competitive on price when supplying timber, mass produced joinery, sand and cement, drainage and plastering materials. However, some components, such as double-glazed windows, bathroom fittings and kitchen units, may need to be ordered from specialist suppliers well in advance.

A useful alternative if you have implicit trust in your builder and his trade connections and you don't fancy your chances haggling with the stony-faced hardmen of the building supply world, is to strike an enterprising deal closer to home. You could offer to pay your builder to source the same materials at perhaps 10 per cent below your best supplier's quote. The attraction for the builder is that if he can then obtain the materials for a lower price through his contacts, he gets to keep the difference.

Plant hire

Just when you're starting to appreciate how much the main contractor does for his money, there's a third dimension to add to the equation: the curious world of plant hire. Just about everything can be hired, from JCBs, scaffold towers and cement mixers to angle grinders, power breakers and tarpaulins, normally on a daily or weekly basis. But hiring only really makes sense over short

periods. Hire for more than a few weeks often means you could have bought the tools for the same money. Be clear about who's job it is to arrange plant hire – there's a limit to how many excavators you can make use of at one time.

If you're employing subbies, it's a good idea to discuss each trade's requirements beforehand. Whereas some subbies tend to arrive fully tooled up (eg electricians, plumbers and carpenters) others, such as brickies, may only possess spirit levels and trowels, leaving you to fork out for cement mixers and scaffolding.

Scaffolding is normally priced for a hire period of 8 to 10 weeks, with a small surcharge levied for each extra week. The price should include scaffolders making return site visits at different stages to erect the next storey ('lift') when needed. Prices are quoted in terms of £x per metre run for each lift.

Yee-haa! Dangerman delivers bricks.

Deliveries

Delivery dates are crucial. But it's an unfortunate fact of life that materials sometimes arrive later than promised. Get this wrong and you could end up paying trades to sit around idle on site, and then have trouble getting them to turn up again next time. It's not unknown for crucial deliveries, like the concrete wagon, to somehow get mysteriously cancelled by suppliers despite having been paid for in advance, which can obviously mess up your programme. Correct ordering and punctual delivery of joinery, especially the windows, is always a critical element in any build. So if speed is of the essence, you'd be better off only ordering readily available products.

Never leave things to chance – it's best to double check with a quick call to your supplier a day or so in advance to confirm the delivery date. When deliveries do arrive, always check the materials for damage before signing them off. If in doubt write 'unchecked' next to your signature.

To avoid access problems, allow about 3m width for vehicular access, and make allowances for turning circles, parking, and space for off-loading from trucks.

Storing materials and site security

There's an art to managing incoming materials. The key is to plan ahead by considering which materials will need to be specially protected from the weather with covers, and to avoid blocking access routes. Then there's the matter of security, and of course the timing of deliveries – the longer you leave stuff piled up on site the more temptation there is for thieves to liberate it. Your site will need to be fenced off to deter intruders, using steel mesh fencing equipment. This can be hired.

delivered fresh, just prior to use. Materials made of timber are especially vulnerable to distortion and warping, especially if allowed to get damp. Roof trusses must be stacked on a level base kept clear of the ground and covered.

Driveways and anything likely to be damaged should be protected. It may be useful to take photos before the work starts as evidence of prior condition. Don't forget, it's essential for builders to have sufficient room to work, so be sure to leave plenty of clear space around the footprint of the proposed extension. A tidy site is a safe site, so it may be worth hiring a giant container to save a lot of storage and security headaches.

Staggering delivery times can help avoid overcrowding the site with mountains of materials. Try to get deliveries stored away swiftly, covered up, and distributed around the site to where they'll be needed. Make full use of lockable garages and garden sheds.

Of course, it helps greatly if you've got a generously sized site with plenty of space for storage, so that materials requiring protection can be delivered days before they're needed. Things like bricks, blocks, and roof tiles can be stored for quite a long time, subject to being protected from the weather (heat can be as damaging as cold, wet, and frost). Particular care should be taken with piles of sand – the local cat and dog populations will be just itching to make full use of them! Tarpaulins or plastic sheets weighed down with blocks should do the trick.

Materials like plaster and cement powder need to be

Programming

To keep control of things, you'll need to prepare a written programme showing week-by-week what's supposed to be happening at each stage in the project. Obviously it's essential to co-ordinate the delivery of materials with the scheduled arrival of different trades on site – which is why it's vital you check the availability of stocks well in advance, particularly of materials like bricks and roof tiles which can be subject to shortages.

Having researched your material supplies and the availability of labour, you can then complete the various times and dates. Allow some flexibility for bad weather and the inevitable unexpected delays. Remember, these dates and times are only your best guess – they're not set in stone and you may need to fine tune things as the project develops.

Cleanliness and protection

Never underestimate the amount of dust and mess that building a simple extension can create. Power sanders, demolition works, and angle grinders cutting chases in plasterwork, can swiftly create an unpleasant swirl of gritty smog that rapidly engulfs your living space, clothes, food, children etc. If you're employing subbies direct, they have a reputation for being rather messy, regarding clearing up as the client's problem. But if they are supplying their own materials they should also be prepared to clear their waste away after they finish.

For many homeowners, this is the most disheartening part of the whole home extension process. But the problem can be minimised by good planning – keeping the newbuild separate from the main house for as long as you can by postponing 'breaking through' until as late as possible. It's also well worth stocking up on dustsheets to protect existing surfaces.

6 PROJECT MANAGEMENT

'Project management' is probably one of the most abused and misunderstood terms in the English language. There's considerably more to successful project management than many aspiring TV property developers might imagine. It's not just a matter of donning a brightly coloured hard hat and goose-stepping around the site barking orders at anyone who'll listen.

Overseeing the works

The objective of the Project Manager is nothing less than successfully achieving the holy grail – a *quality* building, delivered *on time* and *within budget*. On a day-to-day level, the job is about ensuring that everything is proceeding according to plan and that when problems do arise, they're dealt with swiftly.

If you decide to personally take on this responsibility, think of yourself as the hub of a large wheel. It's your job to ensure clear communications between all the various parties – which includes you (wearing your client hat), the contractors, the designer, Building Control, and your suppliers. One secret to successful outcome is to 'build the house in your head' first, identifying who is going to do what, when and with what.

Every hour spent planning the job can save 3 or more hours sorting out problems later on site.

Attitude

It's generally agreed that the appropriate attitude to adopt when managing a building project is one of 'friendly formality', but it can be a difficult balance to get right. If you get too matey it may become hard to maintain authority, but if you strut around treating builders as an inferior sub-species they may be tempted to seek payback (weeing down your cavity walls is one well-known method, but there are others…)

Just checking

It's surprisingly easy to unnerve builders on the job. Despite their hard reputation, all a client needs to do to psychologically antagonise the workforce is to continually walk about wearing a gravely worried expression, peering over shoulders whilst waving around sets of drawings. Checking everything very obviously with a spirit level and tape measure every couple of hours is also guaranteed to disturb the peace. Since it doesn't pay to irritate the hell out of your workforce, it's best to wait until work has finished for the day before doing routine checks.

It's important to take a close interest in the work on site so you're aware of what's going on, but you must do it

Routine checks

- **Check the site**: A site unnecessarily littered with old materials and tools is a badly run site and a safety hazard.
- **Check the 'setting out'**: The position of the walls and doorways etc should correspond to the drawings.
- **Check DPMs** are continuous and that there are no gaps to the insulation.
- **Check with a spirit level** that all vertical and horizontal surfaces are true.
- **Check details** like the height of wall switches and sockets.

without constantly getting in the way. Checking work as it progresses means you can nip problems in the bud – otherwise you risk only noticing that the walls have peculiar bumps in them weeks after moving in. Just like buying something in a shop, before handing over your cash you want to be happy with the quality. So if you see anything that looks a bit dubious, don't be shy about mentioning it to the contractor. If you think he's fobbing you off, seek the opinion of a surveyor or architect, or have a friendly chat with your Building Control Officer (they don't *have* to give an opinion, but it's always worth asking).

A firm of building contractors is basically just a bunch of guys with different skills. It's when they stray from the trade they know best, tackling something unfamiliar, that jobs tend to get botched. Specialist materials like lead, zinc, stone slates and marble normally require specialist skills, not a 'jack of all trades' learning on the job.

Progress

Don't expect everything to run like clockwork all the time. Even the best builder in the world can be the victim of last minute 'no show' deliveries or subbies going AWOL. So the occasional day with no one on site is to be expected, and a bit of slack needs to be built into the programme to take account of this. You need to allow your contractor some degree of freedom to manage the workload, so give him a little room to breathe. Larger firms will have several jobs running simultaneously, which can require skilled juggling of manpower. Inevitably an electrician or plumber will be urgently needed at two sites at the same time, just when he's disappeared for a week's holiday.

As Project Manager, you'll want to regularly compare progress on site to your original programme. But you need to be reasonable, as some things are not foreseeable. Delays due to severe weather aren't the contractor's fault (although they aren't necessarily an acceptable contractual reason for a project overrunning). It's therefore possible that the completion date may need to be extended. However, a site that remains spookily silent for days on end will soon mess up your programme, and you'll need to formally request that progress is restored. If the builders fail to respond then the matter may need to be treated as a dispute (see below).

Communication

The hardest part of a successful build is achieving good communication. Holding a brief site meeting with the main contractor perhaps every couple of weeks is essential. This means all parties, including yourself, can be regularly updated, thereby answering queries and preventing minor disputes from becoming major. Much as builders instinctively dislike 'wasting time' by turning up to tedious meetings, in the long run it will actually save time by minimising the chances of costly time-consuming mistakes.

Agents

If you're employing a property professional such as an architect or chartered surveyor to manage your project, legally they are your 'agent' and all communications and instructions to the builder should go via them. The builder will get totally confused if you start telling him some things and the agent tells him other stuff, in which case he'll probably end up ignoring you both.

Fresh drawings

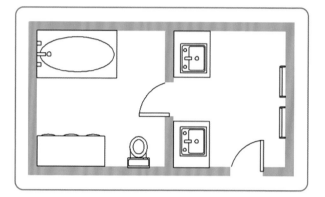

It may seem obvious, but everyone working on the project – client, architect, contractor, subcontractors etc – should be singing from the same hymn-sheet. That means having the latest version of all drawings distributed and available for those working at the coal face.

Mark revisions clearly with the appropriate revision identification, such as 'Drawing No.005/REVISION C', and be sure to remove all earlier drawings from circulation.

Keeping records

When the completion date finally arrives there are always going to be a few loose ends to sort out with the contractor. If the project runs late, the contractor will immediately give you ten good reasons why it wasn't his fault. Typically these relate to things like bad weather and undelivered materials, but a whole raft of personal problems may also be cited.

By the end of the project, everyone will have forgotten exactly what happened, or didn't happen, weeks ago on site. It's therefore worth keeping a simple daily site log of things like weather conditions (at least for the external work stages) and what labour and materials were present on site each day. Ideally take dated photos to prove it.

Instructions

Another area shrouded in mystery and collective amnesia by the end of a project is 'who said what to whom'. For example, when you realise in horror that the kitchen walls have been painted a vile shade of slime green, the builder quite reasonably points out 'that's what it says in the specification, boss'. Your claim to have told his mate Dave to change it to magnolia some weeks ago is greeted with utter disbelief. The moral of this tale, of course, is *keep a written record of every instruction and change agreed*, with dates and details. Send a copy to the contractor, and if possible keep a folder on site that everyone can refer to. Any changes proposed by the contractor, such as substituting your first choice of parquet flooring because it's no longer available, should also be agreed in writing. Any cost implications should be made clear, ideally in the form of a 'change order' (see example below).

AGREED CHANGES		
Date	Instruction	Contact
2 Feb	Paint colour to kitchen walls changed to magnolia	Dave Amnesiac
1 Mar	Change main external door to 'Malton Glazed' hardwood 78x33in, ref 208-243	Mad Jack MacMad

Extras and changes

As noted earlier, if there's one golden rule above all it is to think through your plans very carefully at the design stage so that you don't keep changing your mind as the build progresses. If you do have to alter the design after the job has started, or you need to request some 'extras', always broach the subject first with your main contractor. Avoid making direct arrangements with subbies as this is outside the terms of the contract, and will seriously dismay your main man, resulting in a bad atmosphere and a lack of future co-operation.

In an ideal world, it shouldn't be necessary to vary the work as it progresses. But in reality there are five situations where this may happen:

You request additional work – As you watch your extension take shape, something will occur to you that you wish had been included but wasn't. Some builders make nearly half their profits from customers requesting extra works, because very often the client forgets to ask about the cost implications. You may therefore notice hands being rubbed with glee when you saunter up and ask your builder 'Could you just tile the basin splashback'. So, always be sure to get an estimate of the cost of any additional work before it's carried out, and then note how long the work takes and the materials used. It's very easy to underestimate extra costs and, as time goes by, to lose track, resulting in an unpleasant surprise when all the costs are finally totted up at completion. What can really cause trouble is issuing belated 'surprise' instructions, such as for extra roof work long after the scaffolding's all been taken down, or for an extra radiator once the system's already up and running.

The builders suggest extra work – Most builders have considerable experience of similar projects to yours, and as a result may have some genuinely smart ideas about how to improve the design, even saving you money by doing it another way. On the other hand, many are also highly skilled at the art of 'soft selling'. Friendly, casual suggestions, such as 'While we're at it we may as well replace those old ceilings', or 'It's no problem to just replaster the walls' may be perfectly pitched to illicit the required client response. It's fatal to assume there'll be no charge. Always ask how much it will cost.

Unforeseen circumstances – The builders stumble across something unexpected – a rotten timber lintel in the wall of the old house when breaking through, or dodgy electric wiring in an unexpected position. This requires extra work that wasn't specified. But who pays the

Left: "Looks like you need a new bathroom mate!"

additional costs? It depends on whether such work was reasonably foreseeable and should have been built into the contractor's tender price. Or perhaps it should have been clearly specified by the client.

Items not specified – Basically, you expect to get what you asked for. If you specified 'guttering' but didn't specifically mention the extruded aluminium ogee style guttering that you really wanted, the contractor will price for fitting cheaper standard half-round black plastic guttering. If your architect leaves 'holes' in the specification that end up costing you extra cash, you may be entitled to claim a proportionate reduction in their fees.

Change orders

It's always better to hammer out a price at the time that the required extra works are requested. Then, to eliminate any possible doubt, a form known as a 'change order' (formerly known as 'variation orders') can be submitted, listing all the agreed changes. Change orders are written instructions from the client to the builder that authorise him either to omit work that was previously agreed, or to carry out additional work, together with the appropriate increase or reduction in costs (see below, and see website for sample forms). It's also very much in the builder's interest for any extras to be confirmed in writing, since there's no legal obligation to pay for them unless they were formally agreed. It's surprising how memories can fade, so written evidence is important.

ref	Change Order	£
JB 1 20.7.08	Omit: external lighting system	(1,250)
BG 3 30.7.08	Add: Supply and fit 1 no. shower screen (B&Q ref 12345) to bath	105.00

Where the cost isn't known, providing a written 'instruction' as described earlier can allow the work to proceed without holding things up, by kicking the cost implications into the future – to the 'final account' stage. But this is obviously risky. So that you don't get fleeced for extra works, try to ensure that the builder sticks to the same profit margin for the extra works as tendered for the original job. Of course it helps greatly if the builder's original quotation or tender clearly spelt out the rates charged, for example 'brickwork charged @ £X per square metre', so that additional work can be priced at the same rates. Similarly, you can base the cost of extra materials on the original prices pro rata.

An alternative method is for extra work to be priced using hourly labour rates. It's best to agree such 'daywork' rates with your builder at the outset. Labour charges can be verified with trade associations, and the prices of material researched online. You can then monitor roughly how long the extra jobs take. But bear in mind that the cost to a main contractor of bringing a subcontracted electrician back just to fit one socket will be disproportionately expensive. The total cost would need to also include materials and allow a profit margin. The obvious snag with daywork is that some less saintly builders could be tempted to devote excessive time to chatting, whistling and singing – time for which the client is paying.

Changes to the contract period

Requesting additional work not only means a bigger bill, but is also likely to have a knock-on effect on your completion date. The job may therefore need to run over a bit, and the delays to your programme should be agreed along with the costs. Confirm the revised completion date in writing so that the builder won't be hit with any penalty clause for missing the original completion date. The builder may also incur extra hidden costs, such as hiring security fencing for a few more weeks, which he will have to pass on.

Money matters

Payments and retentions

The stages at which you pay your builder should be agreed in advance. For small projects that take 2 to 4 weeks or less he may accept one payment on completion, but for a typical home extension job 'interim payments' are made, often every four weeks, and certainly no more than once a fortnight. It's obviously important to keep clear records of each payment you make. To avoid 'double counting', each consecutive payment starts by totalling up all the work completed to date, and then deducting all previous amounts paid.

It's customary on all but the smallest jobs for the client to hold back a sum of money during the works, which must be agreed at the outset. The main purpose of this is to provide an incentive that will encourage the builders to return at later stages to fix any minor defects. Normally the contract permits the deduction of a small retention (say five per cent) from each payment. Half the retained money is released to the builder at the end of the build, at 'practical completion', and the remaining half is paid after a further three months, the 'defects liability period' (sometimes six months on larger projects).

If you insist on keeping too large a retention, the contractor will simply price the job higher. But if the retention is too small, they might consider it easier to lose the money than to physically come back and carry out any minor finishing tasks. If you're dealing with a trusted local firm you may not need to keep a retention.

There are two golden rules when it comes to payments:

Never pay for work in advance
If the builder goes bust half way through the job, or if he's a rubbish builder and you want to terminate the contract, you'll be in a far stronger position. Also, if you pay for work that hasn't yet been done it removes much of the incentive for good quality workmanship to be completed on time.

Pay contractors promptly
Failure to pay is a breach of contract. You're normally obliged to pay within 14 days of the due date (or within 30 days of practical completion). No one is going to do their best work if they're not paid on time. Typically, builders are at their most financially vulnerable towards the end of a job, and paying promptly is an easy way to create a positive atmosphere of trust and co-operation.

Making a payment

Normally you make a payment to the contractor for the value of work completed by each agreed date, say, on the last day of every month. The amount you pay is based on the price the builder quoted for each piece of work that's actually been completed. If a job is only half complete,

then you simply pay a pro-rata amount of the price quoted for the full job. Valuing partially completed works is always going to be a bit of a guess, so it's not worth quibbling about the odd £50 here or there.

In addition you must include the value of any substantial materials stored on site, such as bulk deliveries of 'unfixed' bricks, blocks, tiles etc. Note that once you've paid for materials they are legally yours, so check they don't later mysteriously disappear.

Next, add any extras or changes that you've agreed – if you don't have a firm price, estimate it approximately. Finally, you should add VAT (unless you've persuaded the contractor to generously accept that the VAT can be left until completion). After deducting the agreed amount of retention, you'll arrive at the actual sum due to be paid.

Note that large quantities of bank notes and building sites don't make good bedfellows, so it's not wise to pay in cash. A cheque or debit card should be perfectly acceptable, for which a receipt should be forthcoming.

The contractor may want to submit his own version listing the work that's been done, but to ensure you're not paying too much always carry out your own valuation.

An alternative method of payment is by making simple 'staged payments'. This is the way mortgage lenders like to release funds on self-build properties. Banks will normally advance moneys to you as each major element of the work is completed, once it's been verified by their valuer (and guess who pays their fees?). So you can then pay the builders a previously agreed amount for work completed to key stages, for example upon completion of foundations, at DPC level, at completion of the main roof etc.

If you later need to withhold payment because of problems with workmanship or materials, it's essential to notify the builder in writing immediately, stating your reasons. If you fail to notify them and still withhold payment, you'll be in breach of contract and the builder can give you seven days' notice of his intention to stop work.

Final payments

Towards completion, the contractor will submit his bill, the dreaded 'final account'. It's at this point that many a client has required the assistance of a stiff drink.

"Of course the price we quoted doesn't include skips …"

If you're a savvy client, here's what you do. Try to plan your payment dates so that the final payment is going to be a substantial amount. This means there'll be a real incentive for the builders to fully complete the job.

It's worth remembering that after a long project, final accounts are frequently something of a negotiating matter. Whether the figures look a little high or not, you'll need to run through them to compare them with your own records, especially things like extras, changes, and provisional sums. You may want to request copies of suppliers' invoices to help analyse the cost of materials that you're being charged for. If you haven't done so already, endeavour to agree the correct (fair) price for any additional work. But ultimately some degree of compromise will be necessary from both sides.

Penalties

Most contracts include a penalty clause, requiring the contractor to fork out money (known as 'liquidated damages') if the job isn't completed on time. This is stated in the contract as a maximum sum in pounds per week, agreed by both parties at the outset, for each week that the job overruns without a good reason. The client is in theory entitled to deduct this money from the builder's final payment. In reality, however, it can be hard to justify legally unless you can prove you've suffered real financial loss as a result, or that the delays were excessive and unjustifiable. Only larger firms of contractors are likely to accept such clauses. Nonetheless, this is a useful piece of ammunition in the event of delays and slow progress.

Practical completion

This is the stage at which the client obtains full use of the building, although some very minor finishing works may still be outstanding. If you're not keeping a retention, it may be possible to delay the final payment until any minor snags are sorted. At the very least wait for the 'completion certificate' from Building Control before releasing the final payment. (See Chapter 16.)

Guarantees

Construction work is traditionally guaranteed for a minimum period of 12 months against material and workmanship defects. Insurance-backed guarantees are preferred, since they'll still be valid if the contractor goes bust. But it's not just the building that's covered. Should your gleaming new oven promptly catch fire or the boiler conk out, it's worth noting that legally it's the responsibility of the supplier of the equipment to deal with the problem – which may be your contractor, unless you supplied it yourself. Always insist that contractors provide test certificates for fitting appliances as well as for all electrical, gas and heating work, to prove it all works safely.

Your have a legal right as the customer for the work to be carried out 'with reasonable care and skill'. If a significant defect becomes apparent soon after completion, you may reasonably claim that the workmanship was negligent. If a contractor fails to honour the guarantee, you must write informing them that you intend to appoint another firm, at his expense, and give him a final opportunity to sort it out himself. But talk to Trading Standards or a solicitor first.

Latent defects

In some parts of the structure, such as foundations and roofs, it may take quite a while for defects to become apparent, often long after the 'defects liability period' has expired. Only after the first heavy snowfall or severe storm might stresses cause structural cracking due to errors in the design or construction. Contracts normally allow you to take legal action for such 'latent defects' within 6 years of the appearance of problems. In some circumstances this can be extended to 12 years (such as where company directors sign the contract as a 'deed').

Dealing with problems

There's always a chance that your project will run super-smoothly all the way through. But the reality is that problems and misunderstandings of one kind or another will inevitably arise, and when they do there's a right way and a wrong way to deal with them. Depending on how this is done the problems will either be amicably resolved or will enter the dangerously expensive orbit of lawyers and tribunals.

On a personal level, avoid getting too emotionally wound up and resorting to angry outbursts. Take a deep breath and try to look at things objectively. Avoid the blame game, and instead focus on solutions and improving communications for the rest of the project.

To avoid frayed nerves and wrecked bank balances, the first step is to define the type of problem you're dealing

"It's just a bit of shrinkage cracking mate."

with, and then take the appropriate measures to solve it. There are basically two types of problem: practical problems on site (*ie* unforeseen technical difficulties), and dissatisfaction with the builders' performance.

Practical problems

The first step is to identify the problem, for example the kitchen base units don't fit, as the available space is too short. Then consider alternative solutions, such as using shorter units, or cutting back the plaster on the walls. Contractors have a lot of experience at solving such problems, so don't automatically dismiss their suggestions. Finally, you need to agree a solution, and confirm it in writing, which should allow work to proceed subject to reaching agreement about cost. But defining who is responsible can often be tricky. Were the plans badly drawn? Should the contractor have noticed this detail? Hopefully it should be clear from the specification or brief who was responsible. Often small problems where responsibility isn't clear can be settled by agreeing to split the cost 50:50.

Dissatisfaction with the contractor

You may be unhappy with the contractor's rate of progress, or quality of work. Or both.

If so, don't waste time discussing it with tradesmen or subbies – arrange a meeting with the main contractor. If there's no improvement write a formal, but not unfriendly, letter requesting that the matter is rectified. Most disagreements with builders boil down to one of four things:

Poor quality workmanship

Any decent builder will know very well whether work is sub-standard or not, and should rectify it when requested. If not, the obvious answer is to simply say you're not paying for poor work. You may find keeping photos a useful record. Ultimately an independent contractor may need to be paid to make good the defective work (remember some builders love nothing better than to 'slag off' other builders, so surveyors are a more impartial source of advice).

Prolonged delays

The work has not been completed, or is way behind schedule. First check the contract and advise the builder that his inaction will put him in breach of contract, and that the breach must be remedied by him getting off his backside. Quote the relevant contract clause. If there's no response within a week, you may then need to go into 'dispute mode' (see below).

Charges for additional work

As noted earlier, to calculate reasonable charges for extra work they should be broadly comparable to the originally tendered work, or at least 'the going rate' in that trade. If all else fails you could refuse to pay any more than you think reasonable.

The extent of works required in the specification

You think a piece of work should have been included in the original price. The contractor does not. So that the entire project doesn't grind to a shuddering halt, for the time being you may have to 'agree to disagree', and later go with the opinion of a mutually acceptable third party professional.

Disputes

If you find yourself bogged down with a disagreement that can't be resolved, you may have a legal dispute on your hands. This means an independent third party capable of providing an objective professional opinion will need to be appointed to adjudicate, normally an experienced chartered surveyor or architect – but not the person who designed your extension, in case it turns out that some problems are due to bad design. Disputes should always be dealt with promptly, as they only get worse if ignored. If the problem is due to building work that's below par, and the builder has refused to rectify it, then a good first course of action is to ask the Building Control Officer's opinion. A site meeting will need to be held to discuss matters. The final option of terminating the builder's contract is Big Potatoes, requiring legal advice. Once the dust has settled you'll need to appoint another builder to finish the job, for which they may well charge a premium. See website for further advice.

And finally...

If all this makes you feel a little queasy about going anywhere near a firm of builders, it shouldn't. The vast majority of projects succeed perfectly well, sometimes in spite of less than brilliant project management. Remember that what all the parties involved want most, is a successful outcome. It's mainly just about applying a little common sense. So with no further delay, let's crack on and get that home extension built.

7 START ON SITE

Groundwork – foundations and ground floor

You've spent months preparing for this day, yet not a single brick has so far been laid. But the good news is that all the trouble taken preparing for the build should now really start to pay off, by helping avoid all those nasty mistakes, expensive conflicts and hidden dangers that are lying in wait to trap the unwary.

The site itself should now be as clear as possible, with obstructions like paving slabs removed and perhaps fences temporarily set aside (best tell the neighbours first!). Access routes need to be as clear as possible. The location of services such as electricity cables, gas, water and underground drainage pipes should have been identified and marked. Now it's simply a matter of transforming those carefully drawn plans into a 3D building.

NOTIFY BUILDING CONTROL 1
Start on site – two days' notice

Day One. Start on site is usually a fairly harmonious occasion. Everyone is full of the best intentions and wants to crack on and make it happen. The first phase, known as 'groundwork', comprises excavation for foundations, and usually also for the drainage. This is followed by construction of the below-ground footings and the main walls built up to damp-proof course (DPC) level together with the ground floor. The basic rule is 'the sooner out of the ground the better'. Once this essential phase is satisfactorily completed you'll be able to proceed with confidence onto the above-ground superstructure of your extension.

Disposing of waste

The first job is for all vegetation, shrubs, roots and topsoil to be removed from the whole area that's to be built on. This must be carried out to a depth that will prevent later growth. But before enthusiastically ploughing into the ground with your JCB, it's important to consider what arrangements are in place for getting rid of the piles of muck that even a small building project will inevitably generate. The smaller the site, the more critical this is, as work will soon grind to a halt once you become inundated in your own excavated earth and rubbish.

All the excavated waste will need to be removed from the site at regular intervals. Not only is this essential from a practical viewpoint, but keeping the area tidy will also encourage tradesmen to be tidy and to do a good job.

Some waste can normally be recycled, saving money. Things like broken bricks, blocks and tiles can be set aside for later use, perhaps for drainage in soakaways. You may also be able to disperse some of the excavated topsoil around the garden.

Skips and grab trucks
The time-honoured method of waste disposal is, of course, our old friend the skip. So much are skips part of our modern urban culture that economists have devised theories that measure the nation's economic growth rate by the number of skips present at any one time in a city's streets!

Think where you want your skips positioned, which should be in as convenient a location as possible for the builders to access them, ideally within your garden.

Otherwise it may be necessary to park a skip on the road, for which the supplier should have a Local Authority licence. Note that you could be liable to prosecution if a skip is left overnight on a highway without appropriate lighting.

But be warned that weird nocturnal phenomena can sometimes occur when a skip is left empty overnight in the street. Next morning you may discover it filled with ancient sofas and old mattresses, which have mysteriously appeared out of thin air. To avoid this, it's best to arrange for skips to be delivered early in the morning, thereby giving you a good chance of using them before nightfall. Otherwise, take the precaution of covering them with a tarpaulin to reduce the temptation to flytippers.

Skips come in 3 sizes – large (6.2m^3), medium (3m^3) and mini (1.5m^3) but calculating how many you'll need can be tricky. Excavated subsoil expands in volume once dug (as it is no longer compacted) and 1 cubic metre can weigh up to 2 tonnes. There always seems to be massively more of the stuff than you'd reasonably expect. To calculate the amount of excavated waste, work out the volume of the trenches being excavated and then add 50 per cent.

Alternatively it may be worth hiring a tipper lorry with a 'grab' which can be used to take soil and rubble to the local tip. These trucks can handle a large quantity of waste and can also be used to deliver bulk supplies such as ballast and sand.

Digging the foundations

As everyone knows, foundations have a very simple purpose in life – to transmit the load of the building safely down into firm ground. They need to provide a strong, level base for the new structure, spreading the load of the walls built on them. But they work the other way too: any movement in the ground gets transmitted back up to the building, and the foundations have to allow for this.

Before the long dry summers of 1975 and 1976 foundation depths weren't given a great deal of consideration. Victorian houses might have been built with brick or stone footings down to about 450mm or less. Over time, depths gradually increased as concrete trenches became widely used from the 1930s.

Many pre-1980s buildings have remarkably shallow foundations by today's standards. Only when massive subsidence claims started to hit the insurance companies in the late 1970s was it finally accepted that to resist ground movement foundations needed to reach down to ground of adequate 'bearing strength'.

The type of foundations your new extension needs will depend on your local ground conditions, which vary greatly around the UK, each having different strength or 'bearing' characteristics. Some, like chalk, are excellent for building on and require relatively shallow foundations, perhaps only 500–750mm deep, to protect against frost which can damage buildings with very shallow foundations.

Others, like sand and clay, have good load-bearing capabilities but also have a worrying tendency to move about and cause subsidence. Your Building Control Officer will be familiar with the ground conditions in your area and will dictate the required depth.

Excavating to a decent depth should prevent your new walls cracking as a result of movement caused by seasonal ground changes, or the impact of nearby trees, or 'slope creep' if you're building on a hill. A required depth of about 1.2m is fairly typical in clay areas, although the minimum recommended depth for clay is actually only 900mm. Elsewhere in Britain, on non-clay ground, the absolute minimum depth of any foundations is 450mm.

Good trees, bad trees

Because of their large size, oaks, willows and poplars are notorious for causing damage to buildings. These thirsty broadleaf species are the bad guys of the tree world. Their thirst is legendary, at least compared to well-behaved evergreens. But these aren't the only trees that deserve an ASBO.

Because trees, such as plane, lime, and ash are more frequently planted close to buildings, they too have a bad record. Perhaps most notorious of all is leylandii which, along with eucalyptus, is a super-fast grower that can dry out the ground.

As a rule of thumb, damage can usually be avoided if the tree is no closer to the foundation than its mature height. Less thirsty trees should be no closer to the building than half their mature height.

Tree	Height[1]	Distance[2]
Very thirsty		
Oak	16–23m	13–25m
Poplar	15–24m	15–30m
Willow	15–20m	11–25m
Elm	20–25m	12–30m
Hawthorn	10m	4–12 m
Leylandii / cypress	20–25m	8–13m
Fairly thirsty		
Plane	25–30m	15–25m
Lime	16–24m	8–18m
Chestnut	20	15m
Beech	20	10–15m
Ash	20–23m	10–20m
Sycamore / maple	17–24m	10–16m
Apple	10m	5m
Pear	12m	6m
Cherry & plum	8m	8m
Conifers	20m	8m
Not too thirsty		
Hornbeam	17	8
Birch	14	7
Elder	10	5
Hazel	8	4

[1] Typical mature height
[2] Typical minimum recommended distance from buildings with non-specialist foundations

The problem with clay soil is that it's very susceptible to volume changes – first violently shrinking, then swelling up as moisture content changes with the weather. The soil near the surface swiftly dries during the summer and becomes wet again in the winter, shrinking and swelling. The effect of this can extend to around 900mm below the grass. Not surprisingly, the soil is driest towards the end of summer and wettest in early spring and the amount of ground movement will be greater in unusually dry years.

The presence of some notorious species of trees can require the digging of deeper foundation trenches or the use of special heavy-duty foundation types. But if you think cutting down such trees prior to construction will solve the problem, think again. Once thirsty trees are removed the clay ground may become freshly invigorated with all the water no longer sucked out by the trees, causing it to expand and 'heave'. Predicting the likely effects of trees on ground conditions is a specialised job. Because each site is different, Building Control should be consulted as to whether your foundations will need to be dug deeper to compensate. In more complex cases it's worth seeking the opinion of an arboriculturalist (a tree expert), but as a rough guide the NHBC's foundation depth calculator can be a useful tool: by simply lining up a tree's height and distance from a building you can work out the required foundation depth (see website).

Of course, the great irony with home extensions is that while your main house may be sitting happily on its quaintly shallow original foundations, your extension will have to be built with virtually nuclear-blast-proof boots deep underground. And having two such wildly different foundation depths on the same building means there's a real risk of cracking taking place at the point where the new extension and the old house meet. This is due to 'differential movement', a factor we consider later when building the walls.

It's generally a good idea to get all the excavation done at the same time, whilst you've got diggers and labour available on site (see 'drainage'). So check your plans to see if any additional foundations are required for any new chimney breasts or load-bearing internal walls. Or perhaps your design has a suspended ground floor (rather than a solid concrete floor slab). If the floor size is very large, then the beams may require extra support at mid-span from mini 'sleeper walls' under the floor, which will also need foundations.

Basements

If you have a sloping site, or one requiring piles or rafts, then the addition of a basement can make sense, since some of the excavation work may already be required. Although conventional blockwork can be employed, there are various alternative means of construction, such as using pre-formed 'ThermoneX' concrete panels craned into place onto a raft foundation, or hollow styrofoam blocks that you put in place and then fill with poured concrete. The walls need to be reinforced and integrated with the flooring.

The Achilles heel of basements is, of course, the risk of damp either penetrating through the walls and floor or pouring down the cold underground walls in the form of condensation. Great care must therefore be taken with waterproofing the structure, normally achieved by incorporating overlapping layers of thick waterproof membranes. Special care must also be taken to ensure floors and walls are well insulated, and that there's sufficient natural light and ventilation.

Setting out trenches

It's not unknown for a bloke with a shovel to take a bit of a guess and start digging roughly where the plans suggest the walls might be built. That's if anyone bothered to give him a set of plans in the first place.

Supervision of this crucial stage is often minimal since one muddy patch of land can look pretty much like another. It's all too easy for mistakes to occur, especially if everything's been left up to a harassed digger driver.

Trying to change the position of foundations once the concrete has been poured is obviously going to be both troublesome and expensive. So accuracy is crucial at this stage to ensure the walls are built in the right place, are square and structurally sound, which in turn depends on precise measuring. Having double-checked all dimensions on site with those shown on your approved plans, the position of the trenches should be clearly marked out. The traditional method used for setting out trenches is one that Bob The Builder's great-grandfather would have recognised.

Tools required for setting out
- A large spirit level
- Some string line
- A datum peg
- 4 profile boards
- A builder's square

A 'datum peg' is nothing more exotic than a chunk of wood (roughly 400mm long and 50mm square) hammered

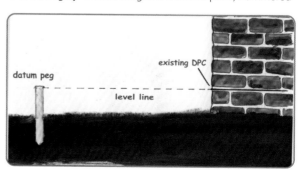

datum peg   existing DPC   level line

will normally be parallel to (or in line with) those of the main house. Additional boards and lines can be installed, one pair for each new wall. A builder's square is used to ensure adjoining walls meet at a perfect 90° right angle.

into the mud to mark levels on site. Its top must be level with an agreed point on the existing house, usually the DPC or ground floor level. Place the datum peg into the ground at the far side of the proposed new extension, about 1.5m further out than the position of the new wall (so it doesn't get booted over). Getting it level with the existing DPC or floor is done by running a string line from the DPC on the main house and checking it with a spirit level. Additional pegs can then be positioned around the site as required, and should be regularly checked.

'Profile boards' are used to mark the positions of the trenches and walls. A profile board is basically a horizontal strip of wood about 1m wide with four nails or screws lined up along the top. The space between the two outermost nails (about 600mm) represents the total width of the trench to be dug, and the narrower space between the inner pair of nails shows the planned wall width (about 300mm).

Each board has two vertical stakes for legs so it can be hammered straight into the ground. The tops of the boards must be level with the tops of the datum pegs. There should be one board at each end of the planned foundation trench. To actually mark the position of the trenches, run some builders' line between the two boards at either end of the trench (outer nail to corresponding outer nail etc), thereby creating 'tramlines' with the two inner string lines showing the finished wall positions and the two outer string lines the foundations. The new walls

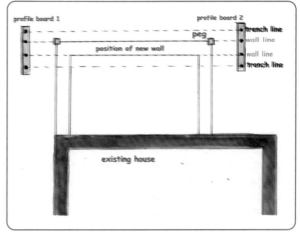

Having double-checked all measurements so that the string lines perfectly correspond to the position of the new walls shown on your drawings, they should then be marked on the ground. Starting with the outer line, this was traditionally done by sprinkling a line of sand directly over the strings, although a can of spray marker paint may prove more robust. When a clear outline is marked on the ground, all the string lines can be removed. But the boards should remain in place, so that the inner wall lines can be put back once again after the concrete foundations have been laid, in order to guide the bricklayers up to DPC level. The profile boards can then finally be removed.

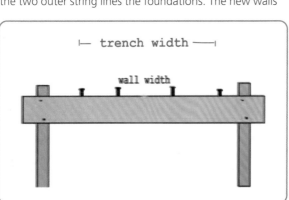

Excavation

At least two days before work begins, you must formally notify Building Control. True, they may sometimes choose not to visit at this stage, waiting instead until the foundations have been excavated, but that's their call, not yours. Failure to notify them is an offence for which you can be prosecuted.

NOTIFY BUILDING CONTROL 2
Excavation of foundations – one day's notice

Digging foundations by hand is about as close as you're ever likely to get to the true meaning of 'hard labour'. Unless you were a gravedigger in a previous incarnation, leave it to the experts. Indeed, so arduous can this activity be that the nineteenth-century Russian mystic Gurdjieff actually sought out work digging foundations – having discovered that the sheer strain of the job was very effective at sending him into a stress-induced trance (history does not record whether the resulting foundations were straight).

If handling pickaxes, shovels and wheelbarrows really isn't your thing, then the alternative for all but the smallest jobs is to hire a JCB or mini-digger. Select the 600mm width bucket (rather than the narrower 450mm one) and you're away. But just when you're making rapid progress doing the work of ten men at the push of a lever, *crunch!* – the time you've gained is lost by chopping through someone's electricity supply, or severing a gas or water pipe or fracturing the drains. Which is why a lot of fuss was made earlier about locating the routes of underground services. Armed with such advanced information you can carefully excavate by hand around the sensitive pipe and cable areas, and use the digger for everything else. Of course, before deciding to employ giant mechanical diggers you'll obviously need to check there's sufficient space on site, which may rule out their use for some terraced house extensions.

With conventional foundations, the base of the trenches should be left as level as possible (to avoid all the wet concrete sliding down to one end). Trench sides should be cut square with the base. On sloping sites small steps can be cut at intervals to maintain some consistency of depth, but don't make them too big or the walls may later settle and crack due to the different depths. Several small steps are better than a few big ones, with the height of each step no deeper than about 200mm (check on site with Building Control), and overlapped horizontally by the concrete above by about 1m.

A common dilemma when excavating is what to do with protruding tree roots. Slicing through live roots more than 50mm thick can destabilise the tree, with potentially lethal consequences. If you have to build close to a tree, it may be possible to bridge over roots, but you'll need to seek advice from an arboriculturalist.

Whilst on the subject of fatalities, it's worth noting that the second most common cause of injury on building sites (after falls) is from unguarded holes and trenches. Any left unattended must be covered or cordoned off. Trenches should be left unfilled only for the shortest possible time, to minimise the risk of accidents and problems like trench collapse and filling with water. Health & Safety 'CDM' regulations require contractors to erect barriers around any open trenches or holes more than 2m deep, and to lay stout boards over the top of them, or make similar 'protection from falling' arrangements. Trench work is usually fairly safe down to about waist height (1 metre) but any deeper and there is an increasing risk of trench collapse, so it is wise to shore up deeper trenches. To help resist ground movement, it's a common precaution in clay areas to fit special flexible polystyrene 'claymaster' or 'clayboard' sheets made of compressible material against the sides of the trench, which allow the clay some degree of 'heave' without affecting the concrete foundations.

Once you've finished excavating, it's essential that Building Control are invited to inspect the trenches before the concrete is laid. Apart from checking whether they've been dug to the appropriate depth, the Officer will also want to be sure that the trench base is firm and secure and that the sides aren't about to collapse. You may be asked to provide temporary support to the trench sides or they may want you to dig a little deeper. Building Control have the right to request such modifications even if it means going beyond the foundation depths shown on your plans that they've already approved. This is in order to make sure the foundations are compatible with the actual ground conditions on site. But this only works one way – you're allowed to increase foundation depths, but not to reduce them. Of course, this might well throw out your careful calculations for ordering the correct volume of concrete, so it's best not to finalise your ready-mix order until after the inspection.

At this stage, a little thinking ahead can pay off big-time, so before filling the trenches with concrete take a few moments to calculate where you want the level of the concrete surface to stop. The general idea is to fit an even number of courses of bricks or blocks between the top of the new concrete foundation and DPC level, which is normally at least 2 courses of brickwork (150mm) above the finished external ground level. This will be marked by your datum peg and builder's lines. Foundation blocks are normally either laid vertically in courses of 225mm, or laid flat in courses of 110m, so ideally you need to stop the concrete at 225, 450 or 675mm below DPC level. The trench-fill method (see below) is

Celcon cavity foundation blocks.

widely used in clay soil areas and most builders pour right up to the 225mm level.

Alternatively, to help calculate the number of courses of bricks or blocks, you can make a simple tool called a 'gauge rod'. This is basically a giant ruler, a length of wood about 2m long marked with the heights of brick or block courses, including the 10mm mortar joints.

Measuring downwards from your DPC line you can calculate the ideal place where the top of the concrete strip should finish. One way to mark this is to drive wooden stakes into the bottom of the trench about every 2m with their tops level with the desired surface of the concrete.

Foundation types

So far we've assumed you'll be using conventional 'strip' or 'trench-fill' foundations, which are by far the most common types of foundation, being used in around 75 per cent of new housing. Both require the same sort of trench to be excavated, as described above.

But trenches have their limits. Any deeper than about 2.5m is not normally acceptable, whereupon special types of foundation designed for use on difficult terrain may then be needed (such as on filled ground or where there's a serious threat from large trees). The downside is that special 'raft', 'piled' or 'pad and beam' foundations will always cost significantly more than traditional trenches, plus they usually require a specialist engineer to design them.

Hopefully the foundation method best suited to your site will have already been determined from a survey of the ground conditions. In reality, however, ground conditions can be very localised. Everyone else in your street may have been perfectly OK using traditional foundations, but sod's law dictates that there'll be a localised soft-spot just where you want to build. And bang goes that contingency budget.

Strip foundations

In many cases, a simple strip footing is all that's required. Also known as 'deep strip' foundations, these are the least expensive type and traditionally the most widely used

where ground conditions are normal. A trench is dug, normally to at least 1m depth and a width of about 600mm (sometimes 850mm wide on sand, silt or soft clay). Concrete is poured into the bottom of this to create a concrete strip, sometimes reinforced with steel mesh. The concrete should normally have a depth (thickness) of about 300mm, certainly never less than 150mm.

This means you'll then need to build several courses of brick or blockwork on the foundation strip to reach above ground level (calculating how many courses are required as described above). Where underground drainage pipes have to pass through, it's often easier to build around the pipes in brick or blockwork (see 'footings' below).

Trench-fill foundations

Trench-fill foundations are similar to deep-strip, except the excavated trench is filled almost to the top with concrete (normally to about 100–150mm below ground level). Although more expensive than strip foundations in terms of using more concrete, this method gets you out of the ground quicker and is widely favoured because it avoids the labour costs of building awkward brick or block walls in trenches below ground. This form of construction has become increasingly economic as labour costs have increased, and as mechanical excavators and ready-mixed concrete have become widely available.

Trench-fill is often used where soil is loose or where the water table is high, and in areas with heavy clay soil with trees nearby, because such foundations can be taken deeper than strip.

Whereas for strip foundations the minimum practical width is at least 600mm because of the difficulty laying bricks or blocks in a very narrow trench, with this method trench widths can be 600mm or narrower (say 450mm) in normal ground conditions.

For additional strength, mesh reinforcement may be required and the trench sides might need to be lined with a slip membrane, unless the soil is firm.

Where drainage pipes have to pass through trench-fill foundations of pure concrete, the pipes have to be positioned when the concrete is poured and protected by being wrapped, creating space to allow for future settlement without fracturing the pipes.

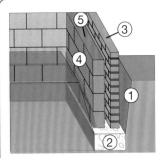

Deep Strip Foundation Construction
1 Foundation trench
2 'Deep strip' foundation
3 Outer wall
4 Inner wall
5 Damp-proof course

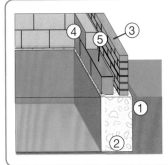

Trench-fill Foundation Construction
1 Foundation trench
2 'Trenchfill' foundation
3 Outer wall
4 Inner wall
5 Damp-proof course

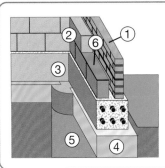

Piled Foundation Construction

1 Outside wall
2 Inner wall
3 Reinforced concrete groundbeam
4 Compressible material
5 Concrete pile
6 Damp-proof course

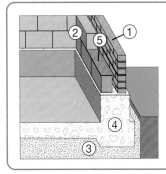

Raft Foundation Construction

1 Outside wall
2 Inner wall
3 Hardcore infill
4 Raft foundation
5 Damp-proof course

Pile foundations

Pile foundations are used in unstable ground where good support can only be found at very deep levels, or where physical site restrictions (such as in crowded town centres) make other forms of foundation impossible. They're only likely to be cost-effective where the foundations would otherwise have to be dug deeper than 2m.

Piled foundations are usually designed and installed by specialist contractors using pre-cast concrete piles. These are dug, bored or driven down into the ground using a crane-like piledriver. The piles are placed about every 2.5m under main walls, each one going down until solid ground is reached. They support concrete beams that span from pile to pile, upon which the house is built.

This method has become more common in house-building since the advent of mini-pile systems. Around 15 per cent of new houses are now built this way, making them the most common type after strip and trench. However, for a one-off home extension they're unlikely to prove cost effective.

Raft foundations

If you've dug your trench down more than about 1.2m and the ground is still very soft and muddy, it's probably time to phone Building Control. They may want you to dig a little deeper, or they may decide that a reinforced concrete raft is called for. Nearly one in ten new houses are built with raft foundations.

Rafts are basically large reinforced concrete slabs, rather like thick, super-strong solid concrete floors. Because they spread the load over a larger area, they're used in poor quality soft or made-up ground that may be prone to subsidence, or where there's groundwater on site.

They require a level site, but because they can 'bridge across' weak areas they're often appropriate on clay that's prone to excessive shrinking and swelling, or where there are unpredictable conditions deep below the surface that might lead to future ground movement, such as underground streams or old mineshafts. If subsidence occurs, the raft should absorb the movement.

Rafts have the advantage of needing only a relatively shallow depth of excavation (except that you may have already dug down to a great depth before discovering the trenches were unsuitable). Construction may entail excavating to about 650mm across the whole floor area,

and then laying a bed of consolidated hardcore, with the foundation concrete being poured on top, together with the floor slab concrete. The structure is reinforced with steel mesh laid in sheets and the process repeated with a final top layer of concrete. This consumes large amounts of concrete of a relatively high strength mix. The edges, upon which both leaves of the main walls are built, are constructed thicker and deeper and are reinforced with metal 'cages'. These are stepped down and are known as 'edge beams'. Any areas that have to support the internal walls of the building are also stiffened in this way.

When the extension is finally finished the only visible difference is where the slab projects out about an inch or so at the sides beyond the brickwork, or it may be buried entirely so no one will ever know all the extra trouble and expense you went to.

Pad and beam foundations

You can design a building so it rests on reinforced concrete beams spanning like lintels between a series of concrete pads. This is similar to piles, but instead of being hammered into the ground, large holes are dug and filled with concrete. Pads may be circular, square or rectangular. They avoid problems with piledriving such as damage from ground vibration. Pad and beam is especially good for using a lightweight structure like timber frame.

Concrete mix

Having concrete delivered ready-mixed and poured directly into your trenches from a mixer truck will take a lot of the hard work out of the job. One person struggling with a cement mixer can mix about 1m³ of concrete in an hour, so although readymix is probably only cheaper when you need more than a couple of cubic metres, it's nearly always worth the extra expense. It also provides a more consistent, higher quality mix. Mixers are more suitable for mixing bricklaying mortar. However, if you're building a very small extension or porch, or if lorry access is restricted, the mixing

may need to be done by hand. You really need two people – one to mix and one to pour, as continuously as possible.

Ready-mix is ordered by the cubic metre and a full truckload comprises about 6m³. To calculate the volume needed, multiply the depth x length x width of the trench or slab. As a rough guide, a strip foundation in a trench

10m long x 600mm wide (assuming the concrete strip will be 300mm deep in a 1m deep trench) would need about 2m³ of concrete. The same trench-fill foundation with 850mm deep concrete would need 5.2m³. When calculating the amount needed always allow a little extra – better too much than not enough. Any spare can be driven away or spread thinly on a plastic sheet and broken up for use as hardcore.

A typical foundation mix would be 1: 3: 6 Portland cement/sand/gravel (sand premixed with gravel is known as ballast). But when ordering it's often best to just explain what it's for and let the supplier work out the optimum mix. Also mention the trench dimensions, and whether it is to be poured direct or barrowed. Standard foundation mixes are known as 'GEN 1', whereas a stronger 1: 2: 4 floor slab mix is 'GEN 3'. Other specialised mixes are available for reinforced concrete and driveways etc. The lower the GEN number the less it should cost, but the price also depends on the delivery distance and how much of the truck's capacity is utilised.

Speed is of the essence when pouring concrete. Concrete cures (sets) fairly rapidly, so avoid pouring one load then waiting an hour for the next one. If there's a long delay between batches the first lot will start to harden and the new load won't bleed in with it, leaving a join that'll become a weak-point in the foundation. A full truckload can take about 20 minutes to pump.

The ideal situation is to excavate the trenches and pour the concrete the same day. Before pouring, ensure the trench bases are clean, level, dry, and free of any loose material.

If possible the concrete should be poured directly into the trenches down a chute from the lorry, saving the need for laborious wheelbarrowing of fresh concrete around the site. But you don't want a monster 20-tonne cement wagon parked too close to those fragile trench sides, so it may sometimes be necessary to rig up a temporary 'slide' out of spare timber lined with plastic sheeting to help guide the mix into the trenches. Normally the mix should be of a 'thick lumpy custard' consistency, not too wet, requiring just a little encouragement from a shovel or rake to move it along the trench. Special 'self-placing' foundation concrete mixes are a recent innovation that flow easily around the trenches. Or you can use a concrete pump to achieve an even spread. Note that readymix should not be watered on site, as this will interfere with the mix, and watered concrete is a major cause of foundation failure.

If site access is restricted the concrete may have to be barrowed to the trench in batches, which will obviously take longer. Under these circumstances, tell the supplier in advance to add some retarder to the mix, which will delay the drying out time to a couple of hours.

NOTIFY BUILDING CONTROL 3
Concreting of foundations – one day's notice

Working with cement – wise precautions

■ Wear protective gloves and boots – concrete burns the skin.

■ Check the weather forecast before concreting – overnight frost can ruin concrete. Foundations poured in winter conditions should be covered over.

■ Be prepared. Note the location of your nearest plant-hire firm in case of urgent problems, such as the need for a water pump in the event of flooding.

'Footings' – the below-ground walls

The term 'footings' has a rather quaint, old-fashioned ring to it. Way back before the widespread use of concrete, the main walls of Georgian or Victorian houses might have only had five or six courses of brick below ground level. As they got deeper, the brickwork would gradually be 'stepped out' to spread the load, like a big pair of feet protruding either side, each course being about quarter of a brick wider than the one above. But brick or stone footings were superseded in the early twentieth century by modern concrete foundations which spread the load adequately without resorting to stepped brickwork. However, the word 'footings' persists as a description for underground masonry.

After allowing two or three days for the concrete foundations to cure, the below-ground walls can be laid in brick or blockwork up to DPC level. In the case of strip foundations the walls must be built up centrally, so that a typical 280–300mm wide cavity wall built on top of a 600mm wide concrete strip should have at least 150 mm of concrete strip projecting out on each side. If at this point the builders suddenly realise the trench location doesn't actually correspond to that shown on the drawings, they may be tempted to build off-centre, which can later result in structural instability, so monitor this stage carefully.

With trench-fill foundations the concrete is substantially thicker, so it's possible to build off-centre, even near the edge. This is why trench-fill is often used where space is limited, such as where main walls need to be built close to garden boundies, or where awkward neighbours won't permit even temporary access.

The architect should have specified bricks or blocks that are suitable for damp underground conditions, such as hard engineering bricks. Not only must bricks and blocks be approved for use below DPC level, but so should the mortar, normally employing sulphate resistant cement. If the wrong materials are used, such as lightweight blocks (unless they are special 'trenchblocks') they can erode very swiftly, with serious structural consequences.

For extra strength the below-ground cavity in this lowest part of the wall is traditionally filled up to ground level with a 'sandwich filling' of lean-mix concrete or mortar. This normally stops about 150mm below the level of the DPC on the inner leaf, after being compacted (but even where ground levels are much lower, don't fill it any less than 225mm below DPC level). The fill needs to slope slightly outwards so any trapped water can drain away through weepholes in the outer leaf. A useful short-cut is to simply use special modern full-width foundation blocks, which saves having to fill below-ground cavities.

Celcon full width solid foundation blocks.

Photos: David Snell / Buildstore.co.uk

Where drainage pipes pass through the foundations concrete lintels will normally be needed to bridge over them. A space of at least 50mm must be left around pipes, and a flexible pipe surround fitted, to discourage uninvited guests in the form of insects and subterranean creatures (see next chapter).

Airbricks

Check if your existing house has suspended timber ground floors, very common in period properties and pre WWII houses. If so, there should be a number of airbricks built into the lower walls to provide a crucial through-flow of ventilation under the old floors. This allows any damp to evaporate and helps prevent rot and beetle infestation to floor timbers. Great care must therefore be taken not to block them with the new extension.

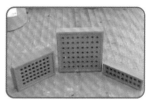

If you opt for a solid concrete ground floor in your extension, you'll need to run ventilation ducts through the floor so that the old house can still breathe. New plastic or terracotta airbricks can be built in to the extension's lower walls, ducted to the existing airbricks in the old external main walls. There should be a plastic sheet (cavity tray) placed above sleeves running across cavities.

If your chosen ground floor design isn't of solid concrete it'll be of either modern beam and block suspended concrete (see below) or traditional suspended timber. In both cases you'll need to install airbricks below DPC level, spaced roughly 2m apart, sleeved through both the outer and inner leaves and the cavity of your new walls.

Above: Laying the DPC.
Right: The DPC must overlap later with floor DPM sheet.

DPC – the damp-proof course

The purpose of the DPC is to prevent damp from the ground rising up the walls and making life a misery with rot, mould, blown plaster and unpleasant smells.

Once the foundations have been concreted and the walls have been built up to DPC level, the DPC itself can be laid. It should be positioned at least 150mm above the finished external ground level. Normally a long strip of black plastic will be bedded along both the outer and inner leaves onto a full and even bed of fresh mortar. Laying the DPC is a key stage that requires Building Control to pay a visit and inspect it before it's covered.

NOTIFY BUILDING CONTROL 4
DPC level – one day's notice

A bed of mortar is then laid over the DPC followed by courses of bricks or blocks. The DPC should cover the full width of the masonry and project out about 5mm beyond any external face (but not into the cavity). Joints between strips should overlap by at least 100mm. Sufficient 'spare' should be left projecting on the inside to later overlap with the DPM flooring membrane by a minimum of 50mm, forming a continuous barrier. Avoid having earth or flower beds banked up against the outer walls, otherwise additional protection with vertical plastic sheets or tanking can be required to stop damp penetrating.

Now work on the ground floor can begin. The area within these new 'dwarf' main walls is known as the 'oversite'. If it hasn't been done already, all topsoil here should be cleared, together with anything that could grow or rot affecting ground stability, such as roots, bits of wood etc. The actual depth removed will vary, but in rural locations may be as much as 300mm.

Ground floors

In Victorian houses the ground floors largely comprised timber floorboards suspended above the ground by timber joists resting on supporting walls. But problems with damp and rot led to timber floors being gradually superseded by floors made from of solid concrete.

Today, you basically have three choices for the construction of your extension ground floor. If you're a diehard traditionalist there's nothing to stop you building suspended timber joists and boarding, but this is the least efficient and probably the most expensive option. The type of ground floor almost universally used today for newbuild housing is 'suspended concrete', made from concrete beams and blocks. The third option, and the conventional choice for home extensions, is the solid concrete floor slab.

All three types have their pros and cons, but whichever method is chosen, measures must be taken to keep damp out of the building and to keep the house warm by minimising heat-loss. And as noted earlier, suspended floors of either type will require airbricks inserted in the walls below DPC level.

One consolation if you've already had to go to all the expense and trouble of building special raft foundations is that your floor structure will already be in place. The raft will double as your new floor, just awaiting a layer of insulation and floor screed to finish it off.

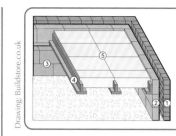

Drawing: Buildstore.co.uk

Beam and block floor
1 Outside wall
2 Concrete block inner wall
3 Sleeper wall
4 Concrete beam
5 Concrete block

Beam and block 'suspended concrete' floors

Imagine a Victorian suspended timber floor made instead from tough reinforced concrete and you'll have some idea of how a modern 'suspended concrete' floor works. Special concrete beams are laid like traditional timber floor joists spanning above the ground from wall to wall. But instead of nailing floorboards to them, the spaces in between are filled with concrete blocks.

Beam and block flooring became popular during the 1990s for use on sites with ground problems caused by subsidence, clay heave, sloping land, or contamination, since building above the ground is a simple way to overcome such difficulties. Today, most new houses use beam and block construction for their ground floors, regardless of ground conditions. But for home extensions, traditional solid concrete floors are still widely used, because they are cheaper for small floor areas and because builders are familiar with them – 'that's the way it's always been done'.

But beam and block isn't at pole position with budget-conscious mainstream housing developers for nothing. It offers serious benefits over other types of floor structure, and significant savings elsewhere in the build. It can be laid very quickly, even in adverse weather, and can span greater distances than timber joists without support, plus the void is a handy place to run the service pipes. Compared to solid concrete floors, 'B&B' is not only easier to install but is less prone to defects.

To ensure the correct beams are used for the required span the manufacturers can custom design and deliver the beams to fit your extension if you supply them with a set of approved plans. Your drawings should

show the location of any internal walls that need to be supported by the floor, and the details of any service pipes coming up through the floor, such as soil pipes for loos. But you may need to order up to 8 weeks in advance.

Another important benefit is that ground preparation is minimal, with significant savings in labour. Provided the ground isn't prone to being waterlogged, the soil under the floor requires no oversite concrete. All you need do to prevent the risk of any future plant growth is clear the topsoil and vegetation and lay some thick polythene sheeting over the ground, weighed down with sand (Building Control may also require a quick spray with weedkiller in any areas harbouring aggressively pervasive species like Japanese knotweed).

As with all suspended floors, the weight is taken largely by the wall foundations, rather than direct to the ground as with a concrete slab. The main limitation is the span of the beams, but they can normally manage up to about 6m ('Rackhams 225' beams can span up to 8m). If the dimensions of your extension are greater than this (which is unlikely) you may need to construct an additional load-bearing internal 'sleeper wall' for the beams to rest on (with proper foundations).

The void beneath the floor should be a minimum of about 100mm, although 150mm is often specified, and should be ventilated with air ducts. This is particularly important if mains supply pipes are run within the underfloor space or in areas at risk from radon or methane. These air ducts are of an odd looking 'periscope' shape (known as 'cranked ventilators') that zigzag from the outside wall down into the void. This allows a free passage of air under the floor without letting light in, creating a microclimate as inhospitable as the surface of the moon, thus prohibiting plant growth.

The special pre-cast concrete floor joist beams have a profile rather like an inverted 'T' and are manufactured reinforced with steel. Size-wise they're typically 150mm deep, but are also commonly available in 175mm and 225mm sizes which, being thicker, can manage longer spans without support. They can take the same standard 100mm deep building blocks used in walls.

Constructing B&B floors on site could hardly be simpler. Although concrete beams are fairly heavy, for smaller spans it should be possible for two people to lift the beams into place without needing a small crane to offload and position them. First, the beams are laid in

Busy grouting – Milbank floors.

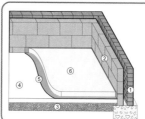

A solid concrete oversite
1 Outside wall
2 Concrete block inner wall
3 Hardcore infill
4 Sand blinding
5 Damp proof membrane
6 Min 100mm concrete oversite

Drawing: Buildstore.co.uk

rows with their ends resting on the inner leaf of the main walls, over the DPC (the DPC on the outer leaf may be a little higher). It's important to leave the correct intervals between the rows, so the blocks can simply be placed in the gaps between the beams. Then Hey Presto! – you have your floor structure. The blockwork infill between the beams can be done quickly and cheaply with standard 100mm thick concrete blocks (215 x 440mm) laid in either length or width direction. For very large spans the floor can be made stronger by simply laying more beams closer together with the blocks laid sideways.

At the floor perimeters, blocks can be cut to fit, or smaller sized 'slip' bricks may be used. Holes for services should be made at this stage to avoid subsequent cutting.

To prevent movement once all the blocks have been fitted, the floor surface should be grouted with a 1:4 cement/sand mix brushed into the joints between the blocks.

But why use ordinary concrete blocks when it's easy to beef up your insulation by fitting large purpose-made floor blocks? These contain integral thermal insulation, which can reduce heat loss through the floor by as much as 40 per cent compared to solid floor slabs. Laying larger blocks (560 x 440mm) of the same thickness can be done twice as fast as for normal-size blocks. Or you could fit high performance 'jet floors' that use expanded polystyrene (EPS) infill blocks between the beams. They are about 10% more expensive than standard, but you don't need to provide an added layer of insulation, just a screed (which must be placed immediately to protect the 'soft' infill blocks from damage.

There are two common methods of adding insulation and floor finishes above a standard beam and block floor, normally done at a later stage:

■ Insulation boards made from rigid polyurethane or polystyrene foam are placed over the surface. These are then covered with either a conventional cement/sand screed, approx 65mm thick, taking care to leave an expansion gap at the perimeter. The joints between the boards should first be taped to prevent wet screed running down between them. At the edges of the screed, the insulation boards should be extended up to form a 'warm' barrier with the cold wall surface. (See Chapter 14.)
■ Dispensing with the need for a later wet screed, special

highly insulated composite 'floating floor' panels can be used. These are made of a special insulating material bonded to a base of either plywood or chipboard. Before laying the floor panels, a 500 gauge polythene sheet is laid as a vapour control to protect subsequent floor finishes from any damp in the structure below. The floor panels are then laid, with their tongues and grooves glued with a PVA adhesive. Alternatively conventional floorboards can be set on battens over insulation boards, instead of a screed.

Note that pre-stressed beams are not perfectly level, having a slight upward camber (around 13mm on a 4m long beam) which is not a problem if you plan to later insulate and screed the floor, giving a nice level finish. But if you want a screed-free dry finish or floating floor, the use of a levelling compound may be required prior to laying the floor finish.

Concrete slab floors

Ground floors built exclusively of solid concrete were the standard form of construction in most new housing from the 1950s until superseded in recent years by suspended concrete. They are a tried and tested method, still popular with many small firms of builders and although very labour intensive, they are quite cheap on materials. But unless built with considerable care, solid floors can suffer from serious defects. If the preparation isn't right, floor slabs easily settle and crack up. Indeed, floor slab settlement is one of the most common problems with new construction. This may arise due to poor 'compaction', where the hardcore base hasn't been property compressed and instead starts sinking years later, leaving a cracked, hollow floor surface. Or problems may be down to poor preparation of the oversite ground, which later sinks, taking the floor with it. But sinking isn't the only problem. Solid floors can also suffer from 'sulphate attack' where they arch and bulge up, causing cracking. This is due to chemical reactions in damp hardcore expanding the concrete. 'Slab doming', as it's known, can be so severe that it even pushes out the bricks in adjacent walls.

So that the finished floor surface in the extension turns out level with your existing floor, considerable care needs to be taken to ensure all the various layers in the floor 'sandwich' are positioned at just the right levels. To achieve this it's best to work backwards from the finished floor level and calculate the required depths for each layer.

Solid concrete floors are built straight off the cleared oversite ground in layers comprising hardcore 'rubble', sand 'blinding', damp-proof membrane, insulation boards, concrete slab, and sand/cement screed topping – not necessarily in that exact order. Depending on ground conditions, the slab may need reinforcing with steel mesh prior to adding the concrete.

Above: Just the job for compacting hardcore (and loosening your fillings!)
Below: … Life's a beach – sand blinding.

NOTIFY BUILDING CONTROL 5
Oversite concrete – one day's notice

Laying a concrete slab floor

First, a base of clean hardcore at least 100–150mm thick (max. 600mm) is laid over the prepared oversite ground. This should be spread out evenly across the site. Clean broken bricks, roof tiles, concrete or crushed stone (washed) can be recycled for this purpose, as long as there's nothing measuring more than about 100mm (roughly half a brick).

The hardcore base needs to have good drainage qualities and be well compacted so that it doesn't start sinking or expanding years later. It should also not be affected by water or be prone to chemical reaction. Unless it's 'clean' (ie has had the rubbish sifted out) demolition rubble isn't suitable, since old plaster and bits of wood can hold moisture and rot. Avoid materials such as soft insulating concrete blocks, shale, loose chalk etc.

For this reason, 'ready-made' loose granular material such as 'type 1' hardcore is a popular choice, since it's fairly fine and compacts well. It can be ordered from builders' merchants and delivered direct to site.

The hardcore base must be compacted so as not to leave pockets of air. Whereas some materials, like 'type 1' and gravel, tend to self-compact, only requiring a quick going-over with a roller, others, like broken bricks, need to be specially compacted. For this you can hire a vibrating roller or a plate compactor 'whacker plate'. The hardcore should be compacted in layers no thicker than 225mm at a time.

The hardcore is then levelled with a layer of sand (known as 'blinding'). This should be raked to an even depth of about 20mm and either rolled or trodden down to compact it. Take care to remove any protruding sharp bits.

To prevent dampness from the ground getting through, a hefty 1200 gauge (0.3mm thick) plastic sheet damp-proof

Left: Type 1 hardcore.
Right: Compacting the hardcore.
Below: Sand blinding over hardcore with snazzy blue DPM, but no DPC or insulation yet.
Below Right: Damp proof membrane in place, awaiting insulation & screed.

membrane (DPM) is laid. If one sheet isn't large enough, the joints in the DPM must be overlapped by at least 150mm and taped. This can either be placed above the sand blinding (which prevents the sheet being punctured) or else placed higher up on top of the next layer, the concrete slab. The lower option is preferable where the ground is damp or where there's a risk that chemicals in the ground could rise up and damage the layers of insulation. Leave a generous amount of spare DPM sheeting around the edges, sufficient to be joined up with the DPC in the walls, so as to form a continuous barrier against rising damp.

Next comes the solid concrete slab or 'oversite concrete'. As with the foundations, the concrete can be delivered ready-mixed down the chute of a cement truck, or for a small project you could instead produce it on site with a cement mixer. The concrete for the slab is normally a stronger 1:2:4 'GEN 3' mix. As the concrete is poured it should be raked level to a depth of at least 100mm (taking care not to puncture the DPM). It then needs to be 'tamped' down using a long horizontal strip of wood called a tamping board. By applying a sawing motion over the surface this will remove air bubbles and release excess water as well as levelling the surface by skimming off any high points. The surface is normally left rough if a screed is to be added later, but some builders dispense with the screed, opting instead for a smooth finish on the concrete slab itself (assuming the insulation layer has already been placed under the slab). Once it's started to cure, the surface can be smoothed using a steel trowel. Or if you like gadgets, the slab can be levelled by 'power floating' – but don't get too carried away; take care not to slice through the projecting plastic DPM sheet. The DPM should extend up around the sides of the floor slab as described above, and needs to be 'dressed-up' around service pipe entry points. It will also be necessary to run a strip of insulation material around the edges before pouring the concrete, to protect against 'cold bridging'.

If your designer has specified that the slab needs to be reinforced (normally where ground conditions are a bit dodgy), special sheets of steel mesh can be sandwiched within the slab at the midpoint. You need to ensure that the upper layer of concrete is poured swiftly so that it bleeds into the lower layer and the reinforcement when still wet. Where slabs are thicker than 150mm, even where ground conditions are good, the addition of reinforcement will add strength, helping to avoid settlement cracks. The most common steel reinforcement used is 'A142' anti-crack mesh. It is usual to lay it within garage floor slabs and should be located towards the bottom of the concrete layer. In very large slabs, movement joints are needed to allow for expansion.

Waiting for the concrete to cure typically takes two to three days, during which time it will be very vulnerable to

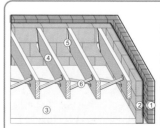

EPS insulation boards.

lapped up around the edges of the slab and screed to a width of about 25mm so that they're fully encased.

■ More commonly, the insulation is placed at a higher level, on top of the slab before the screed is poured, but with this method it's preferable for the DPM to also be placed above the slab, rather than below it. Once again, don't forget to lap the insulation around the edges of the screed. The insulation inside the cavity walls is supposed to start a little lower than the bottom of the slab, so as to form a continuous insulation barrier.

Insulation Materials

Assuming you decide to place the insulation on top of your concrete slab or B&B 'subfloor', before the final layer of screed or chipboard is laid, probably the cheapest material to use is flooring grade expanded polystyrene (EPS) which comes in 100mm thick rigid boards. 'Jablite' is a commonly specified brand. EPS is dense and strong, as well as having good water resistant properties. However, thinner 50 or 60mm high performance rigid insulation boards made from polyurethane (or polyisocyanurate) are now widely used as they reduce the total thickness of the floor construction. Kingspan and Celotex are well-known manufacturers.

Care must be taken to insulate service entry ducts and drainage stacks that pass through the slab. The insulation around incoming water pipes and soil stacks must extend below the ground under the slab to a depth of at least 750mm, to protect against frost. With all methods of flooring, air must be prevented from entering the building by injecting expanding foam around pipes passing through insulation boards, as well as where ducts pass through foundation walls.

Laying a screed

To finish a concrete floor and form a suitable surface for the usual floor coverings like carpets, laminate, floor-tiles etc, a fine 65mm deep sand/cement screed is normally applied over the concrete slab. This is normally put in place by the plasterers once the building is dry and weathertight. (See Chapter 14.)

Suspended timber floors

Timber floors are traditionally constructed from timber joists clad with floorboards or chipboard panels. At ground-floor level, extra protection is needed from damp, and the void below the floor timbers must be well ventilated. Unlike

damage from frost or heat (more than foundation concrete, which is not so exposed). Where it has been laid on a plastic DPM it can take longer to cure. It's best to plan the job so that concrete is not laid when temperatures are likely to drop to zero. Otherwise in very cold weather the exposed surface must be protected with suitable sacking, straw, or loose polythene sheeting material while it cures. Conversely, in hot weather concrete can dry too quickly causing it to weaken, crack and shrink, and you must keep it shaded and moist (but not soaking), giving it a periodic light sprinkling of water during the curing period and covering it with damp hessian sacks or old carpet.

An insulation layer now needs to be formed. One traditional problem with solid floors was substantial heat-loss through the cold floors, which could also lead to condensation and damp problems. There are two main methods of insulating slabs:

■ Rigid foam boarding can be placed on top of the DPM before the concrete slab is laid. The foam must obviously not be 'squashable' (ie it needs high compressive strength, which is why wall insulation is not suitable) and also needs good moisture resistance. It should be

Suspended timber floor

1 Outside wall
2 Concrete block inner wall
3 Concrete oversite
4 Wooden joist
5 Metal joist hanger
6 Herringbone strut

Drawing: Buildstore.co.uk

Left: Oversite concrete being poured over DPM.
Above: Floor joists positioned prior to DPC being fed under joist ends.
Below left: Joist hangers fixed to old wall.

their Victorian forebears, modern timber ground floors must be thermally insulated to reduce heat-loss.

Today, this is the least popular method of floor construction due to the expense and work involved in first having to clear the oversite vegetation and earth, and then effectively having to construct a concrete slab as ground cover. Plus there's the drawback that timber joists may only be able to manage relatively short spans, requiring additional 'sleeper walls' for support. If the main reason for wanting a suspended timber floor is the lure of traditional 'stripped pine' floorboards you'd probably be better off laying pine boards over battens fixed to a concrete floor.

Briefly, these are the key requirements for new suspended timber ground floors:

- The oversite ground must be cleared and covered with a concrete slab, minimum 50mm thick, laid over a 1200 gauge polythene DPM and a hardcore base.
- A space of at least 150mm is required between the surface of the concrete and the underside of the joists.
- A good cross-flow of air is required to the void beneath the joists, from airbricks built into the walls below DPC level.

- To prevent the risk of ground water entering and 'ponding' under the floor, drainage points may be required, such as surface water gullies in the garden.
- Floor insulation is especially important to reduce heat-loss, given the need for a flow of (cold) air below the boards. There are various methods, such as laying 150mm deep mineral quilt 'loft insulation' or 50mm thick polystyrene blocks between joists (with support from battens or plastic netting to hold them in place), or fitting special composite fibre insulation boards over the floor surface.

It's essential for your design to specify the correct size and grade of timber floor joists for their span (normally spaced 400mm apart). This must be calculated by your architect or engineer in accordance with Building Regulations.

Main trades needed on site
- **Groundworkers:** Excavation of trenches and drain runs.
- **Bricklayers:** Building the walls up to DPC level.
- **Labourers:** Mixing and pouring concrete for foundations and floor slab.

Materials
- *Floor slabs*: Use Ordinary Portland cement (OPC), not masonry cement. Sand must be sharp sand (coarse concreting sand) mixed with 20mm gravel aggregate. Specify sulphate-resisting cement where sulphates in hardcore such as brick rubble, or in subsoil, could attack the concrete.
- *Beam and blocks*: To BS 8110, with minimum half-hour fire resistance.

www.home-extension.co.uk

8 DRAINAGE

Don't plan on hanging up your shovel and mini-digger just yet. The groundwork isn't finished until the below-ground drainage system is all done and dusted. Of course, you don't have to do it right now, you may well opt to leave the drains to the end of the project. In fact, the only option you can't choose is to install the drainage halfway through your build, because scaffolding and materials will be in the way. But it makes sense to get all the excavation done at the same time while the equipment and labour is already on site, and before things get too busy.

Photo: Hepworth

Drainage falls into two categories, foul water and rainwater. Foul water from toilets, bathrooms and kitchens is sometimes subdivided into 'black water' (from toilets) and 'grey water' (everything else) – but you'll also need to provide a suitable dispersal system for surface water, the relatively clean rainwater that collects on hard surfaces like roofs and paving.

Even if your extension isn't going to need a new bathroom, kitchen or WC, you may still need to carry out some work on the underground foul drainage system, for example if any existing pipework to the main house needs to be diverted from where you want to build. Your approved plans should show how this is to be achieved.

NOTIFY BUILDING CONTROL 6
Draining commencement – one day's notice

Building Control will take a close interest in your drainage.

Top right: New rainwater pipework.
Below: Inspection unit awaiting burial.
Right: How to lay foul drains. photo Hepstore.com

Ever mindful of the typhoid and cholera epidemics in the nineteenth century caused by raw sewage from dodgy drains seeping into people's drinking water, any proposed alterations to your property's existing drainage system will require Building Regulation approval before work can start. And the Building Control officer will want to come out, inspect and probably test any new work.

Drainage works

Foul water is normally dispersed to sewage treatment plants via Local Authority maintained public sewers. Although some districts may have a combined system that can take both foul waste and rainwater through the same pipes, many have totally separate systems. Others may have no provision for surface water disposal at all. So unless you have approval to connect to a combined system, you must not mix these systems up by, say, inadvertently connecting rainwater downpipes to a kitchen gulley. If the system isn't a combined one, in severe storm conditions a sudden tsunami of rainwater cascading through the sewer system could overpower it, causing a deluge of liquid excrement downtown.

In some rural areas where there are no public sewers, the job of dealing with people's foul waste may instead be down to private cesspits or septic tanks, which require periodic emptying by specialist contractors. Most home-extenders will not need to worry about such matters, so the wonders of private sewage works are explained on the website.

If there's no surface water sewer, rainwater will often discharge via soakaways buried in the garden. So if one fine day your lawn starts furiously frothing and bubbling, it

may be because your systems have got inadvertently mixed up, with a washing machine waste pipe connected to a rainwater downpipe.

Common failings

There tends to be something of an 'out of site, out of mind' attitude to drains, and dodgy workmanship has often been covered up quickly and buried without a trace.

The most common cause of failure is bad joints between pipes. Joint failure may not sound too serious, but it can set off a chain of potentially catastrophic events. Small leaks only get worse over time, and where drains crack, they are an invitation to thirsty tree roots nearby to seek out water and start growing into the pipes. The result: blocked drains and leakage of foul effluent into the ground. Persistently waterlogged ground can risk localised foundation failure, with the potential to cause structural damage to the main walls of the house.

Conversely, if you live in an area with a high water table, groundwater from the surrounding land may seep into a drainage system that's not fully watertight, and the pipes will act in reverse like a land drain, dispersing water from your garden instead of from your bathroom.

Common causes of cracking to shallow drains include crushing from heavy vehicles parked above, and seasonal ground movement, particularly in clay soil that swells in wet weather and then shrinks in dry weather. Old inspection chambers may have been 'jerry built', perhaps of only thin (115mm) brickwork, or with porous bricks, and clumps of old rendering or mortar may have come loose causing blockages. Also, hidden soakaways may silt up and overflow, and if built too close to the house may increase the risk of rising damp.

Be especially vigilant for builders lazily chucking building rubble and paint down newly laid drains.

It's important when installing drains to 'go the extra mile' to ensure that new pipes are 100 per cent watertight before backfilling and leaving them in peace, hopefully forever.

Excavation

In some ways, adding an extension to your home can be more difficult than building a fabulous 'grand design' in which everything is 100 per cent new. For example, your new extension drains are basically a small addition to the existing system, which may itself not be too brilliant. Many drain runs on older properties are not particularly deep, which makes it harder to achieve a reasonable depth and gradient for your new drainage pipes.

To help calculate the required levels of new drain runs, architect's drawings normally show the levels of manhole covers along with 'invert levels' (*ie* the depth of the channel at the bottom of a chamber) at key points. The trenches should be as narrow as possible, allowing about 150mm space either side of the new pipes, which normally means a trench about 450mm wide (a digger's narrow bucket). There are no set depths for pipework in the Building Regs but going much deeper than a metre means trenches can start to become tricky to work in. However, they need to be dug about 100mm deeper than the required pipe level to allow for the granular bedding that the pipes will rest on.

Your approved drawings should clearly show the proposed new drain runs for your extension, and will also specify the type of materials to be used.

Photos: Hepstore.com

Pipe materials

Underground drainage pipes are either flexible (plastic) or rigid (clay or concrete). Rigid pipes have an inherent strength but can be damaged by movement, whereas flexible pipes can resist movement but may deform if overloaded so require good support when laid.

But damage can occur even before they're put in place. Storage and handling of pipes on site is important. If proper protection is overlooked and pipes are stacked without support, plastic pipes can become bent and distorted, and clay pipes may easily fracture.

Pipes made from vitrified clay date back to Victorian times but are still used today. However, most modern drainage pipework is of the heavy-duty plastic type, manufactured in an orangey terracotta colour to resemble traditional clay. Plastic is much easier to work with than clay, being both lightweight and simple to cut with a saw, plus they're very resistant to the kind of chemical attack that can be fatal to pipes made from other materials. Plastic pipes are commonly of 110mm diameter or sometimes 160mm. They are available in generous lengths of 3m, 6m and even 9m, minimising the need for joints.

Modern pipes have flexible joints which allow for a small amount of movement whilst still remaining watertight. These push-in joints are sealed with rubber gaskets ('snap joints') and are less likely to leak than their predecessors, since polymer jointing materials are both more flexible and more durable. Plastic pipes with flexible yet watertight 'O' ring joints came into common use in the 1970s.

But when the day comes to join up your gleaming new underground pipework to the old existing system, be prepared for some possible surprises. You may come across some strange and exotic materials. Victorian cast iron pipes may still exist, along with some made from innovative materials popular in the post-war years, such as asbestos cement, concrete, cement fibre and pitch fibre. This may cause a degree of head-scratching. See 'Joining it up' on page 105.

Pipe laying

Normally new pipes are laid starting at the highest point, *ie* the point nearest the new extension.

One the trench is dug, the first task is to ascertain the height difference between the point where the waste water will leave the property (typically at the base of a soil stack) and the point where the pipe will join the existing system or (if you plan to bypass the existing drains) the public sewer in the road.

Above and right: New extension drain runs may need to be fairly shallow.

The objective is to achieve the correct fall (gradient) so that the waste will be sent speedily on its way. But if the pipes are laid too shallow, the waste will hang around and the pipes will be prone to blockage. On the other hand, if pipes are laid too steep the water can be evacuated so swiftly that the 'solids' get left behind, again risking blockage. A gradient of about 1:40 (equivalent to a drop of 25mm on a 1 metre pipe run) is normally desirable, as consistent as possible along the full length of the pipes. Plastic pipes benefit from very smooth internal surfaces, so although gentler falls may technically be acceptable they're best avoided, as you need to allow for settlement occurring at a later date. In reality pipes are generally laid to an actual fall on site of between 25mm and 90mm per metre run. To find the recommended figure for your system, check with the pipe manufacturer.

Once the trenches have been prepared, but before laying the pipes, the gradients (shown on your plans) can be checked on site against a string line run between pegs set at each end of the trench, adjusted to the correct angle. Then a bed of fine gravel or pea shingle can be laid to this gradient, to a minimum 100mm depth, compacted along the bottom of the trench. The pipes should be carefully laid on top. Sharp inclines should be avoided, although a few gentle radius bends may be permitted provided they don't prevent rodding.

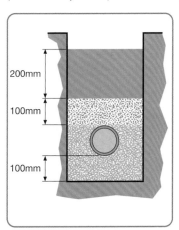

Next double-check the gradient, using a spirit level adjustable to pre-set levels (or alternatively you can take a standard 1m spirit level and attach a 25mm block of wood under one end).

Note that it's essential to keep gravel out of the collar joints, since if one of the rubber seals becomes displaced the joint will not be watertight. The connections should be a tight fit, and before fitting a joint the end of the pipe should be smeared with special collar lubricant, to help prevent damage to the rubber seals.

Deep pipes/shallow pipes
Where your new drainage trenches are deeper than the foundations of your main walls and the pipes pass within 1m of the foundations (or those of the neighbours), there can obviously be some risk of structural damage. So the Building Regs sensibly require that such pipes must be encased in concrete, at least up to the level of the base of the nearby foundations. Should the pipes collapse in future, this precaution means there won't be an ensuing seismic shift in the ground, robbing the foundations of support.

It's not just deep pipe runs near foundations that need extra protection in the form of concrete. Very shallow drain runs may need similar treatment to protect them. This is especially important for pipes run close to the surface, ie within about 600mm. Here a hard surface covering such as paving slabs would be required. Where they are run beneath driveways, or subject to unusual loadings – like cars parked over drain runs to the side of semi-detached houses – any depth less than 900mm will need a concrete capping over the drain.

Where only a very shallow fall is possible to your extension, perhaps because the existing system is so close to the surface, using larger diameter pipes will allow water to flow more easily at gentle gradients.

Pipes through foundations
Probably the most critical point of the whole exercise is where pipes cross under the foundations of a building. Pipes passing through walls or under buildings must be specially protected. This is normally achieved by installing a lintel above the opening, leaving a gap of at least 50mm around the pipe to allow for settlement. The pipes are surrounded by granular bedding (pea shingle etc), but the gap around the pipe can be an invitation to burrowing

creatures, and a flexible sheet material should therefore be fitted around the opening to stop them getting through. Such openings also need to be sealed against any localised risk of potentially lethal gases (radon or methane) seeping through and accumulating in confined spaces. The choice of material will depend on local conditions, so ask Building Control what they recommend.

Plastic pipes running through foundations may need to be supported on a bed of concrete, or even fully encased in concrete. But here a gap of about 12mm must be formed in the concrete at each pipe joint, or the flexibility will be lost.

At the precise point where pipes enter a building (or join an inspection chamber), there may in some cases be a serious risk of a large amount of movement between the pipe and the structure that it's passing into. To prevent the pipe fracturing, one solution is for the piece of pipe running up to the building to be kept short, say about 600mm, with a joint at each end. In effect this makes the pipe 'double jointed'. Because both the joints are flexible, they act like a pair of hinges allowing the pipe and the building freedom to move independently of each other.

Joining it up

Joining up the new and existing systems inside your garden boundary can be done in a number of ways – by simply joining one pipe directly to another, or by connecting at an existing manhole, or by building a new inspection chamber.

Although the amount of new pipework required for an extension should be very limited, as noted earlier you may encounter old pipes made from unusual materials that they need to be joined to. This can be a specialist task, particularly when confronted by decrepit asbestos cement pipes. These must never be cut or altered, since breathing in asbestos fibres is dangerous and professional advice should be sought. But it's not just the materials used for old pipes that can pose problems: modern metric pipes commonly need to be connected to old imperial sizes, normally of 4in or 6in diameter. This can present various difficulties, such as how to connect modern rubber collar couplings to old 'spigot-and-socket' pipe joints. Fortunately the manufacturers of modern drainage systems take account of such eventualities, and a wide variety of adapter couplings are available so that metric can be successfully joined to imperial, and modern plastic to old glazed stoneware etc. Only where old pipes are misshapen or damaged are you likely to encounter difficulties, when the only solution may be to excavate and replace the old pipes. And bang goes the contingency budget (again).

With luck, your addition to the existing drainage system may only consist of a single new pipe, requiring a simple 'saddle' connection to an existing one. First you need to identify the point at which the new pipe will hook up with the old one. This should then be carefully excavated. If the existing pipework is plastic it should be relatively straightforward to cut and connect with a 45° 'Y' connector. But it can be difficult to connect to old pitch-fibre pipes if they've become deformed after years of being squashed in the ground.

Where it's not possible to connect pipes directly to

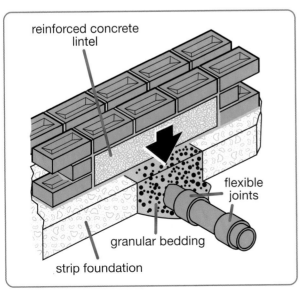

reinforced concrete lintel

flexible joints

granular bedding

strip foundation

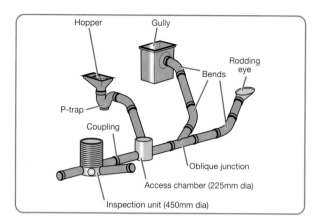

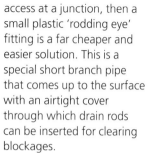

Rodding eye.

each other, a new underground junction will normally need to be constructed.

Manholes, inspection chambers, and rodding eyes

A manhole is a large underground drainage chamber big enough for a person (of either sexual persuasion) to enter. They aren't usually found in gardens, where instead you usually come across inspection chambers. These are much smaller, providing limited access for unblocking underground pipes by giving them a good 'rodding' (ie sticking special drainage rods into them). It was the Working In Confined Spaces legislation that sounded the death knell for manholes, but confusion between the two may arise since the words 'manhole' and 'inspection chamber' tend to be used interchangeably. And just to add to the confusion, there are two smaller modern alternatives – rodding eyes and inspection units.

Inspection chambers serve two main purposes: first, as a junction where several underground pipes can join up into one main outgoing drainage pipe; and second, to provide access for clearing blocked pipes by rodding (for which see 'step by step' guidance in Haynes house manuals).

All parts of the drainage system should be accessible for rodding, and should ideally have chambers at the highest and lowest points. But if the only reason for needing a chamber is for rodding

access at a junction, then a small plastic 'rodding eye' fitting is a far cheaper and easier solution. This is a special short branch pipe that comes up to the surface with an airtight cover through which drain rods can be inserted for clearing blockages.

At one time it was not permitted to fit rodding eyes as the sole means of access to an underground drainage system, and they had to be used in conjunction with inspection chambers, so that silt and debris could easily be removed. But they have since proved perfectly satisfactory when installed correctly and this rule no longer applies.

Chambers traditionally needed to also be installed at major bends in the drain run, since this is where problems are most likely to occur, but a simple modern alternative to building a new inspection chamber is to install a smaller plastic inspection unit. These are ready-made round mini-chambers that provide a 'junction' allowing new pipes to discharge into them whilst connecting out to the old system. Inspection units are a compromise between installing an expensive traditional full-size inspection chamber and a small rodding eye.

Underground drainage systems should be accessible without the need to enter buildings. So indoor chambers should be avoided. Indeed, Building Control may have already asked you to redesign your extension or re-route the existing drainage purely to avoid such an unsatisfactory arrangement. But if there is simply no other option, and Building Control permit it, special care needs to be taken with internal covers, so that they remain accessible and aren't hidden beneath washing machines or cookers. The covers must be double-sealed and screwed closed to prevent noxious stenches and 'solids' from seeping out and enlivening your dinner parties. Special deep recessed covers can be fitted which can be screeded along with the floor surface and tiled to match (or paved to blend in with patios etc).

Inspection unit connected up.

If you can't get away with simply installing rodding eyes or a small inspection unit, you have a choice of materials with which to construct a 'proper' inspection chamber. Traditional brick-built ones have been largely superseded by ready-made moulded plastic or concrete units. Plastic units are suitable for drains less than 1m deep and are lightweight and easy to install onto a concrete base. At greater depths you could opt to build in brickwork, or use pre-formed concrete sections. Because inspection chambers can be heavy and prone to settlement, flexible joints should be fitted to pipes where they enter or leave the chamber. When connecting pipes to new or existing chambers, it's important to note the direction of flow. Your new incoming branch pipe should merge via a side channel and should follow the existing flow direction, with the 'streamlined' angle of entry ideally not exceeding 45°.

And now for a quick moan about lids. In the good old days, inspection chamber covers were made of durable, virtually bullet-proof cast iron. Well OK, they may have cracked now and again when driven over by the occasional artic, but on the whole they did their job well. Today, however, many driveways are afflicted by flimsy light steel chamber lids, which are notorious for becoming dented and bending underfoot, with self-destructing handles to boot. If by some miracle they survive, rust will soon eat through and corrode them. So be sure to select covers that are tough enough for their purpose, especially if there'll be any vehicles in the vicinity.

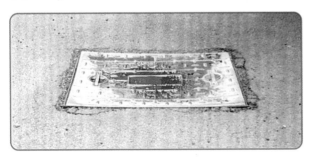

SVPs – soil stacks

An important element in the overall design of a drainage system is the above-ground soil stack, usually referred to as the 'soil and vent pipe' (SVP). If your house is 1960s or older, the chances are that this is a big vertical pipe running up an outside wall. More modern houses usually have them run internally and boxed in.

Older SVPs are usually of cast iron, whereas modern ones are of 110mm diameter plastic. Their main purpose is to connect to upstairs WCs for dispersal of foul waste (euphemistically referred to as 'soil' or 'solids'), but they're also a handy way of collecting 'grey' waste water from pipes serving baths, basins and sinks, which connect to the SVP with special collars. Branch pipes

connecting to the side of the SVP should normally be no longer than 3m with provision for rodding access to clear blockages, and must be properly supported with clips every 750mm. External waste pipes are usually run in grey plastic which is UV-resistant (ie it shouldn't become brittle as a result of ultra-violet sunlight).

This is the only part of your drainage system that is vented, being open at the top, at roof level. This helps prevent the dreaded problem of 'siphonage', which can occur when large deluges of waste water surge down the pipes pulling along all the air in their slipstream. Without ventilation, this can literally suck the water out of traps and gullies behind, thereby allowing the sweet aroma of drains to waft up into your bathroom. So if you detect a malodorous stench in the air, don't automatically blame the kids – it may be down to siphonage. Talking of essence of ordure, the top of your SVP should project at least 900mm higher than any nearby window, otherwise you risk foul odours seeping indoors. This means they normally need to terminate well above eaves level. At the

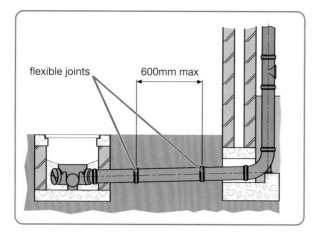

flexible joints | 600mm max

very top, fitting a 'bird balloon' may save you the job of having to pluck old birds' nests and dead pigeons from your drains at a later date. Venting internally via special roof tiles can be a simpler alternative.

Meanwhile, down underground, the SVP is connected to the main drainage system. Here there must be a gentle bend at the underground base, to prevent foaming from detergents and the accumulation of solid waste.

SVPs in modern houses and extensions are normally run internally, so the pipe will need to pass under and out through the main wall or foundations. To allow for different rates of settlement between the house and the drainage system, the two should be independent of each other. One way of achieving this is to fit a large diameter circular plastic duct in the foundation structure. The pipe can be run through this duct with a minimum clearance of 50mm all round. Alternatively, a small opening for the pipe can be left with lintels supporting both leaves of the walls above, as for a window or door opening. In each case rigid sheet material must be placed around the pipe to exclude undesirable visitors.

When fixing new SVPs in place, they should be secured to the wall by pipe clips spaced no more than 1.8m apart.

A simpler alternative to is to fit an 'air admittance valve' terminating within the bathroom or loft. These have a special one-way valve that prevents siphonage but keeps smells in. However, they must be located above the flood level of the highest sanitary fitting in the house, and are normally only fitted to serve a secondary bathroom, where the house already has one main SVP. In other words, they're ideal for extensions. See Chapter 13.

Rat attack

Readers of a nervous disposition look away now. If there's one thing that can spoil the thrill of a lovely new extension,

it's sewer rats putting in an unwelcome appearance. Vermin such as these may have been disturbed as a result of all the unsettling demolition work, and upwardly mobile sewer rats love nothing better than to take up residence in nice fresh drainage pipes. So to deter the possible ingress of rats into your new system, all pipes and sewers should therefore be kept closed as much as possible. Pipe ends should be temporarily stopped up, and manhole covers left in place. Disused drains, abandoned sewers and deceased cesspools should be excavated and completely removed, and old dead-end pipes packed with concrete.

Testing times

Building Control will need to inspect new drainage work before it's covered up, in order to ensure that all joints and seals are secure with no leakage. It's very much in your interest for the new waste system to be thoroughly tested, having first been checked by the builders who installed it. For the new above ground parts of the system, an air test is generally used. Below ground drainage will be either air tested or filled with water (for systems down to a maximum depth of 2m).

> **NOTIFY BUILDING CONTROL 7**
> **Drainage completion and ready for testing – one day's notice**

Now listen up. Here's a fun way to spend a few minutes. Hire some 'expanding rubber bungs' from a plumbers' merchant. Open the inspection chamber furthest away from your house and firmly place a bung into the pipe leading from the house. Next, pour water into the chamber nearest the house (making sure no one unwittingly flushes the loo in the meantime!). Keep a close eye on this, and if the water level doesn't drop for ten minutes, congratulations! – no drop in pressure means the system should be leak-free.

Alternatively, an air test involves pumping air into sealed-off sections of pipework via a nozzle in one of the bungs, and checking that the pressure remains constant without dropping (by attaching a pressure gauge, or a U-tube filled with water). Smoke tests can be a useful alternative method of demonstrating leaks in exposed pipe runs visually.

There's another reason for doing this now. Building Control may wait until completion before choosing to conduct a similar test. But leaving trenches exposed for weeks on end is to invite accidents and damage. So ideally, if you can grab your Building Control Officer next time they're on site, and demonstrate your pressure test, it should lay this one to rest.

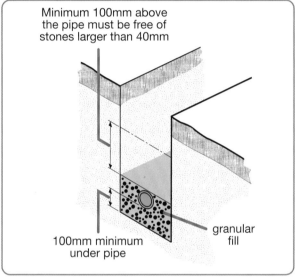

Minimum 100mm above the pipe must be free of stones larger than 40mm

granular fill

100mm minimum under pipe

Backfilling

Once Building Control have approved the new drainage work, the trenches can be backfilled. To protect flexible pipes, they must be fully surrounded by about 100mm depth of pea shingle/gravel. To get pipes well and truly 'tucked in' and protected from harm, no gravel stones larger than 40mm should be used, especially in the area immediately above them. This is followed by 300mm of soft soil which must be free of rubble such as rocks and bricks. The earth excavated from the trench is generally used for backfilling. The remaining topsoil is less critical but it will take many months for the ground to regain its stability. Heavy compaction should not take place until there's at least 600mm depth of soil over the pipe.

In areas where there could be damage from loadings above, such as parked cars or fence spikes, the pipes should be protected by concrete. Backfilling on top should not commence until at least 24 hours after concreting and traffic loads should be avoided for a minimum of 72 hours.

B.I.G.s

Ready-made plastic gullies are fitted at ground level outside the house where waste pipes from basins, baths, showers and sinks discharge directly into the drainage system (rather

than, say, being connected to a handy nearby soil and vent pipe that primarily serves upstairs WCs).

Gullies are similar to traps under basins and baths. Their U-shaped bend retains water at the bottom of the 'U', forming a very effective barrier that stops foul odours coming back up from the drainage system. Traditionally the problem with gullies was clearing blockages since unlike bath traps you couldn't just unscrew them and rinse them out. Enter modern 'back inlet gullies' (B.I.G.s) with built-in rodding access. These are covered with a grid, and

Traditional 'S' trap loo (in gleaming stainless steel!).

photo: stainlessdesign.net

when located level with the ground can provide additional drainage from the surrounding surface water, such as from patios (where permissible).

When extending to the rear or side of an existing kitchen, there will often be old gullies and pipes to deal with. Ideally, completely new drainage connections should be formed and the old pipes can then be blocked off and filled with concrete – taking care to first stop up the far end of redundant pipes, so that the entire drainage system doesn't get concreted!

But in some cases it may be necessary to leave an existing gulley in place so it can continue in use. This then becomes an internal gulley, which like internal inspection chambers is not an ideal arrangement and should normally be avoided. Otherwise it will need to be fitted with a screw-down sealed cover at floor level, for access purposes. First check any such proposed arrangement with Building Control.

Fitting a new WC

One of the many attractions of extending your home is the relief that an extra loo or bathroom can bring to a busy household. The Building Regs take a keen interest in such matters, particularly the need for good ventilation. The regulations on positioning of cloakrooms have relaxed in recent years. If you really wish, there's no reason why you shouldn't amaze your guests with a toilet that opens directly to your reception rooms or kitchen, as long as there's a wash basin installed along with the WC. Windows aren't essential to a cloakroom, so there are many ingenious locations where they can be installed, such as within former under-stairs cupboards. But even where you do have window ventilation, extractor fans are still required to achieve the necessary three air changes per hour with a 15 minute over-run timer.

Perhaps the terminology is slightly unfortunate, but modern WC pans are normally of a 'P' trap design, *ie* the pan waste outlet projects rearwards horizontally (rather than old 'S' traps that pointed down through the floor) ready to be mated into 'multikwik' or 'supersleeve' connectors.

Trees

In an ideal world there wouldn't be any massive trees growing near your proposed drain run. This is because trees are the enemy of drains. The roots of some species, such as willows and poplars, can be ruthlessly efficient at seeking out moisture, literally breaking through the tiniest of hairline fractures in drainage pipes in search of a drink. And when you start excavating near trees, or cutting through their roots, it can destabilise them. It's a hard problem to solve since, as noted earlier, cutting them down and removing them completely can cause ground 'heave', which is also potentially damaging.

In reality, there may be no option but to run the new pipes within fairly close proximity of trees (for example if the trees happen to belong to the neighbours). If so, there are some useful precautions that can help preserve your new drains:

- Where pipes are most at risk, they can be encased within concrete, with flexible jointing material applied around pipe joints within the concrete casing.
- Excavate drainage trenches by hand rather than using a mini-digger, to avoid cutting through roots larger than 50mm diameter.
- If possible, plan your drains so that the pipes run above or below any large tree roots.
- A 'root barrier' can be constructed as a shield in the ground to protect pipes, in the form of a deep, narrow trench filled with concrete, located between the pipe run and the trees.

'Grey water' reuse

There's no reason you can't save on water bills and do your bit for the planet by simply reusing all that 'clean' rainwater that otherwise disappears off into the ground. Such 'grey water' can be used for flushing loos and watering the garden. This is obviously more relevant if you're building an entire new house rather than extending, but it may be worth enquiring about diverting rainwater to water butts and then having it pumped to a separate water tank that serves your bathroom. You can even buy small purpose-made on-site treatment and filtration systems.

Rainwater drainage – soakaways

In many areas the water authorities discourage surface water from being combined with foul drainage. But rainwater needs to be taken well away from walls and foundations otherwise it may eventually cause structural problems. If connecting to the main system is prohibited, the best solution is to divert rainwater from the house into a handy ditch or nearby stream. If there are none, then a simple alternative is to construct a soakaway, assuming ground conditions allow.

Soakaways are the traditional 'hole in the ground' method of dispersing rainwater, and in recent years they've become more widely used in urban areas (when space allows) to help prevent overloading public sewers with water that doesn't require treatment. They're either made as conventional pits filled with rubble or as ready-made concrete chambers with holes in the walls, and must be designed to store the water run-off from roofs and hard surfaces, and to then disperse this stored water into the surrounding soil.

Trench-type soakaways should have at least two access points, including one at each end of the trench. To be most effective, soakaways work best in non-clay, low water table areas (otherwise ground water can fill the soakaway instead of the other way around). First, you need to arrange for Building Control to check the soil and advise on the required depth and distance from the house. This may involve digging a trial pit and filling it with water three times in succession to monitor the rate of seepage. The chosen site should also avoid any risk of waterlogging to downhill areas. In most cases where the soil drains well, and the roof area is less than 100m², you should be able to construct a traditional type of soakaway. (See website for details.)

But if a soakaway isn't built correctly there can be problems with overflowing or silting up. Maintenance can also be a problem – the main one being how to find it! Some form of inspection access should be provided (but often isn't) so that suction emptying and jetting equipment may need to be used to clear them.

Main trades needed on site
- **Labourers:** Excavate trenches, backfill.
- **Plumbers:** Lay and connect pipes.
- **Bricklayers:** Build inspection chamber.

Workmanship
- Requirements for workmanship to drains are covered in the code of practice BS 8000-14.

www.home-extension.co.uk

9 THE MAIN WALLS

Now's a good time to stand back and take stock. The walls are built up to DPC level and the ground floor structure is in place. In most cases, the drainage works will also be largely complete. So far so good.

Photo: David Davies

The opportunity should now be taken to get the site tidied up and to backfill the remaining trenches around the walls up to ground level with earth and rubble. This will set the stage for the next major phase – construction of the main walls.

It is at this point, whilst admiring your handiwork, that you may notice something rather curious, even slightly perplexing. The floor space appears incredibly small. Thankfully, however, this uneasy feeling results from an optical illusion that should pass once the internal walls are all nicely plastered and decorated.

The external finish

Nothing will affect the appearance of your extension as much as the choice of materials for the walls, although by now this will have already been largely determined. The Planners probably stipulated months ago that the new walls should match the 'visual character' of the existing, and Building Control will want see highly-insulated modern construction, not some quaint medieval throwback. The type of external finish will have been specified on your drawings and priced accordingly by the builder.

But even without the benefit of such official guidance, it's generally a good idea to build your extension so that it's similar to the main house. Experimenting with radically

different materials may only increase the risk of cracking later occurring at the joint between house and extension due to dissimilar materials performing differently.

The chances are that your extension walls will be of traditional cavity masonry construction, the type used almost exclusively in British homes since the 1930s. Today this commonly comprises a decorative outer wall of brick and a separate inner wall of concrete blocks, with an air cavity between. These two 'leaves' (or 'skins') are tied together with small metal wall ties across the cavity, the inner leaf normally taking most of the load. Finished walls traditionally measure approximately 280–300mm in thickness.

But there are several possible variations on this basic theme and local historic architecture can be a great source of inspiration. The outer walls could be of concrete blockwork finished in cement render. Or perhaps traditional lightweight 'shiplap' timber cladding, or decorative tiling. The premium material for walls is of course natural stone, but this is expensive and necessitates building

the outer wall a little thicker, at least 150mm, (traditional local building styles may dictate this). Modern 'reconstituted stone' blocks made from stone dust and cement, cost half as much as real stone. Exotic two-tone designs, such as brickwork with infill panels of flint or render can look great. Flint is either laid as whole stones or 'knapped' with the cut insides facing, although ready made flint blocks are an easier option. But it's worth noting that mixing materials normally means increased complexity at junctions, which will inevitably bump up the cost.

If you're adding to a period house, the brickwork on your extension might be designed to echo some original decorative features, such as string courses of dark

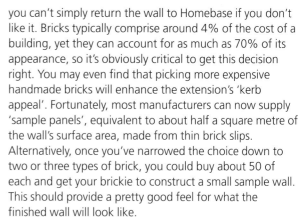

engineering bricks or contrasting bands in red brick. At roof level your brickie may relish the challenge of trying to match the original pattern of projecting moulded bricks.

Victorian solid brick walls were normally laid in either Flemish bond or English bond. English bond consisted of layers of bricks laid lengthways (stretchers) alternating with courses of bricks laid crossways to show their heads (headers), but by far the most common style was Flemish bond, in which stretchers were alternately punctuated by headers. Modern cavity walls make exclusive use of 'stretcher bond' with all the bricks laid lengthways. This can make blending a new extension to an old building quite difficult, so the planners may have stipulated that your modern cavity walls should be built to imitate Flemish bond, with the outer leaf using alternate bricks cut in half, known as 'snapped headers'.

Brick selector

Choosing bricks sounds like fun, but the problem is that if you get it wrong you're stuck with them. Unlike emulsion,

you can't simply return the wall to Homebase if you don't like it. Bricks typically comprise around 4% of the cost of a building, yet they can account for as much as 70% of its appearance, so it's obviously critical to get this decision right. You may even find that picking more expensive handmade bricks will enhance the extension's 'kerb appeal'. Fortunately, most manufacturers can now supply 'sample panels', equivalent to about half a square metre of the wall's surface area, made from thin brick slips. Alternatively, once you've narrowed the choice down to two or three types of brick, you could buy about 50 of each and get your brickie to construct a small sample wall. This should provide a pretty good feel for what the finished wall will look like.

However, getting a precise match with the walls of your existing property may not be too easy, because you need to take into account how things might look after a few years' exposure to the weather.

Luckily, the choice of bricks currently available is extensive, with hundreds of imported and home-grown varieties. Choose from colourful buffs, yellows, tawneys, or red Durham multis. Or how about bucking up your neighbourhood with some drag-faced or sand-faced styles? To blend in with an older house, there are historic-looking pre-war commons, stock bricks, wirecut, and handmade bricks, not forgetting single bullnose, double cants and squints for specialist detailing.

In terms of size, the standard UK metric brick is 215mm long x 102.5mm wide x 65mm deep, and you need 60 of them to build one square metre of wall. Most bricks are also available in greater depths of 73mm, and some as large as 80mm. To avoid the inherent problems associated with the use of fragile porous reclaimed bricks, you can buy modern frost-resistant ones that look very realistic. Manufactured with a traditional appearance, these ancient-looking bricks – such as small 50mm 'two-inchers'– are perfect for extensions to some 'Olde Worlde' period houses.

Common clay bricks can normally be used in footings and for internal load-bearing walls. Toughest of all are dense engineering bricks. Traditionally of a distinctive semi

White powdery 'efflorescence' – harmless salts in new brickwork should brush off

gloss blue/black or blood red colour, these are so hard and water resistant that they were employed in the construction of Victorian railway bridges and even for DPCs. Today they are often found in below-ground work or supporting steel beams.

Brick-supply specialists have libraries you can visit to obtain a match – but be aware that photos may not always faithfully reproduce the subtle hues of 'real-life' bricks. Ideally, take a sample with you of the ones you are hoping to match. If the bricks you want are no longer made, there are companies that will make replicas – at a price. If you're extending an historic building, local salvage yards can turn up hidden treasures, although old reclaimed handmade bricks can be surprisingly irregular in shape, driving bricklayers to distraction. Even bog-standard bricks have changed shape over the last 25 years, from old imperial sizes to metric, and this can make it virtually impossible to neatly line up extension brickwork with the existing courses.

But appearances aren't everything. Bricks are technically rated for both frost resistance and salt content. Frost can attack damp bricks, expanding the moisture by 10% causing the faces to crumble. Salts within bricks can chemically react with cement mortar and expand, causing cracking and spalling. In most parts of the country 'M rated' bricks should be sufficiently frost resistant, but if building in severe frost areas or mountainous regions go for the harder F (or FR) variety. Salt ratings are either N (normal) or L (low) and in very exposed, or wet locations, such as some coastal districts, the vile weather may require the use of L rated bricks along with sulphate-resisting cement.

Masonry needs to be protected as much as possible from the onslaught of the elements. Good design should ensure that the wall surfaces are spared the persistent passage of rainwater, by the construction of overhanging roofs, such as big umbrella-like eaves and projecting bargeboards, large sills on windows and doors, and generous coping stones on parapet walls.

Achieving the right 'character' isn't just about selecting the right materials. Good brickwork is taken for granted, so poor quality workmanship will ruin the whole appearance of a building. In case anyone tries to persuade you

otherwise, brickwork should be uniform, with the mortar joints of equal thickness in each course, and of equal width at the vertical side joints (the 'perpends'), plus the mortar texture and colour should be consistent throughout the wall. Different batches of facing bricks can vary slightly in colour, so wise brickies pick from mixed batches. This avoids 'shading', where it's obvious half the wall comprises an old batch of a different shade that the supplier has had kicking around for a year or two. To prevent staining, always keep stored bricks covered and dry on site.

Blocks

Concrete blocks are used to construct the inner leaves of cavity walls and sometimes for some interior dividing walls. If your walls are going to be rendered or clad externally, then the outer leaf will be made from blocks. The standard size is 440mm long x 215mm wide x 100mm deep, the equivalent of 6 bricks. You need 10 blocks to build one square metre of wall. Their strength is expressed in Newtons per sq mm ('N') and most qualify for the basic 3.5N strength.

You may think a block is a block, but actually the type chosen is very important. Dense aggregate blocks have a very high 7N strength but are poor insulators. They're used for foundations, external leaves of some rendered walls, and for internal load-bearing partitions. Lightweight aerated blocks which, as the name suggests, look a bit like an Aero chocolate bar inside, aren't so strong but have excellent insulating properties, and are widely used for inner leaves and partition walls (Celcon, Thermalite and Hemelite are well-known brands). Some have a rippled or 'striated' face, ready for rendering. Others have a warm buff stone-like colour. But with ever-increasing thermal insulation standards to meet, aerated blocks can be very prone to shrinkage cracking when drying out after being plastered. Although not usually of any structural significance, this can appear quite dramatic and tends to greatly alarm homeowners. So unless the finished interior walls are to be lined with plasterboard, builders may be tempted to revert to using more robust but 'colder' dense blocks when the architect's not looking.

Mortar

Where would we be without mortar, that trusty mix of sand and cement that magically glues buildings together? Simply take a shovel-full of cement, add four shovels of soft sand, mix it all up with a little water, and Bob's your Uncle. Sounds easy, doesn't it? But if the mix is too weak, with excessive sand, your mortar joints will eventually erode and crumble. On the other hand, if the mortar is too strong with too much cement, the joints will crack and the wall could fracture; too wet and it'll dribble away before the bricks can be placed; too dry and it may fail to bond properly.

This is where experienced brickies are a godsend. They'll know how to vary the mix so that it's just right for the strength of the bricks and the type of sand being used, as well as how to compensate for the effects of weather on drying-out times.

The colour of sand can vary considerably depending on the region from which it comes, and where consistency of appearance is important this should be taken into account. The type of sand used for brickwork is 'builder's sand', as opposed to 'sharp sand', which is coarser and more suitable for making concrete.

Mortar can be mixed on site, or you may prefer to buy dry pre-mixed bags where all you have to do is add water. If you plan to mix your own, remember not to mix too much at a time, as the shelf-life of cement mortar is normally only about two hours. Also, it should not be re-wetted after mixing.

A typical mortar mix for new brickwork would be 1:4 Portland cement/sand (a stronger 1:3 mix would be used in masonry that gets very wet, such as underground work).

This produces a strong mix with good frost resistance when set. However, it can also be fairly brittle. Adding a small amount of lime produces a less rigid mortar that is very slightly 'plastic', allowing any small settlement joints to 'heal'. Such walls should be less likely to develop cracks. The lime also gives mortar a traditional quality, lightening its appearance and improving workability. So a mix of 1:1:6 Portland cement/hydrated lime/sand is a good general purpose blend (non-hydraulic or semi-hydraulic lime can also be used), especially when laying reclaimed bricks or trying to blend in with the masonry of older buildings.

The performance of mortar can also be enhanced by additives. In place of traditional lime many bricklayers mix in liquid plasticiser, which adds tiny air bubbles to the mix, making it 'creamy' and easier to work. It also provides a degree of frost-resistance during the setting period, which is helpful when building in winter. A suitable mix which includes plasticiser would be 1:5 or 1:6 Portland cement/sand. Although such 'anti-freezing' agents can be added to the mortar, bricklaying should really only be carried out when temperatures are above 2°C, and fresh work must be protected against frost, especially overnight.

Special sulphate-resistant cement can be used for below-ground walls, or those with particularly high exposure to aggressive weather. Colouring agents, especially black, can be useful for blending in extensions to old houses, such as those with historic 'black ash mortar'.

If you want decent brickwork, a good start is to ensure that the materials are protected when stored on site so they're clean and dry. Cement should be stored safely off the ground, and loose piles of sand should be covered over when not being used. Taking truck deliveries of sand in one-tonne bags may be more manageable.

Striking and pointing

Although the word 'pointing' is widely used to describe the finish of mortar joints, strictly speaking the word 'striking' is more appropriate for most new work.

'Striking' describes the process of finishing the mortar joints between newly laid bricks. Bricklaying should be stopped at convenient stages so that the striking can be done. First, any small surface voids in the mortar are filled using a small pointing trowel. Then the mortar is 'struck' in the style required, doing the vertical 'cross joints' first, then the horizontal 'bed joints'. Finally, any crumbs of mortar from the wall are brushed away. If there are large pieces of mortar on the face of the brickwork, wait for about 12 hours until it has gone off before rubbing it away.

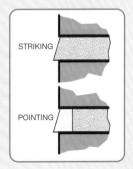

STRIKING

POINTING

Styles of finishing

Flush
Flush finishing is achieved by drawing a strip of wood about 12mm wide, 6mm thick and 100mm long along the joints.

Bucket handle
Formed by pulling a suitable shaped piece of metal (or a bucket handle!) along the joints. Also known as the 'hollow key' style.

Weathered
A weathered finish is good for throwing off rainwater from a wall, and is considered to be fairly durable. It is sometimes used on stacks to improve weather resistance. The vertical joints can be struck to the left or the right but must be kept consistent, otherwise the wall will look peculiar!

Struck
Struck jointing is not ideal for most exterior facings as it leaves the upper edge of the lower brick exposed to the weather.

Recessed key
Recessed key jointing suffers from the same drawback as 'struck'. Here the mortar is raked out and is then pressed back evenly using a special 'chariot' jointing tool.

Finishing mortar joints

Mortar makes up around 20% of the area of a brick wall, so getting the finished joints looking right is vital to the appearance of the entire building. At regular intervals the rough mortar joints on fresh brickwork should be carefully finished before the mortar gets a chance to harden. But this isn't just about getting your walls to look good. Most of the seepage of rainwater through outer walls actually occurs through the joints rather than the bricks. Good workmanship will help prevent this.

In locations exposed to howling gales and filthy weather, joints are sometimes strengthened by being pointed. Once the new brickwork has been completed, the joints between the bricks are raked out to a depth of about 12mm and then wetted before a 'line' of harder mortar is pressed in, to increase weather protection. The joints are then finished as normal using a special pointing tool or a smooth rounded piece of wood.

But what style of finish to choose? Don't be seduced by snazzy 'inverted arrow head' and 'recessed key' indented pointing. These are usually best avoided, since rainwater can collect and pond on the exposed ledge of each brick, which can lead to damp penetration and frost damage.

Depending on the style of the main house brickwork, it's often best to go for a simple, traditional style, such as a plain 'flush' finish. If you're using reclaimed or handmade bricks which are uneven in appearance, traditional 'bucket handle' joints (which are recessed in a curved shape) should suit the weathered character of the bricks.

The true masters of pointing and bricklaying were the Georgians and Victorians, who equated thin joints with top-quality construction. Incredibly fine joints (called 'tuck pointing') are especially evident on brick arches above many Georgian doors and windows. Today, trying to match such fine quality work may prove difficult. Modern finished mortar joints are typically about 10mm thick.

Brickies

It may sound obvious, but the secret to getting good quality brickwork it is to employ a good, experienced local bricklayer. Sir Winston Churchill famously stated that *"every man should build a wall"*. But good bricklaying is an

art that can take years to perfect. It is also one of the world's oldest professions, along with stonemasonry and prostitution.

It's important to have a clear understanding at the outset about what is, and what is not included in the price, especially if you're employing trades directly for a fixed price. There are a number of related tasks that also need to be done. Avoid prima donna brickies who consider it's someone else's job to do anything other than placing one brick on top of another.

Related jobs that are also done by the bricklayer

Included
- Setting out the walls on the new foundations.
- Fitting air bricks.
- Laying the DPC.
- Building in templates or frame ties to door and window openings.
- Installing cavity insulation.
- Fitting lintels.
- Building in restraint straps.
- Bedding on the wallplate at roof level.

Not included*
- Erecting scaffolding or towers.
- Supplying materials.
- Constructing timber templates for windows and doors.
- Plant hire.
- Cutting indents into existing walls and opening existing cavities for vertical DPCs.
- Fixing profiles.

*Unless agreed as an 'all-in-rates' package.

Communication at this stage is paramount. Remember, your prized extension is just another job to your brickie, so make sure your requirements are clearly understood and that he's equipped with a copy of the final approved plans, especially if there have been changes. Knowing in advance exactly where each opening is supposed to go is obviously crucial.

It's also essential that all the materials – including window templates – are available on site at the right time. If future visits have to be made after the main walls are built to complete any unfinished work there may be an extra charge.

Cavity walls can be built very quickly. Some highly motivated brickies, if well supplied with the raw materials, can steam ahead at a staggering rate. A team of 2 brickies plus a labourer should normally be able to lay up to 1,000 bricks a day or 30 to 40 sq m of blocks, or more likely a mix of the two.

Once work starts, the two leaves of each wall are, strictly speaking, supposed to be built up more or less together at the same rate. But in real life, in the race to the top, brickies often like to crack on with one leaf first, before catching up later with the other. Some prefer to build a few courses of the inner leaf blocks ahead of the brickwork, others favour a brickwork first approach. Either way, blobs of excess mortar should be scraped off the inner cavity walls as work progresses, as such obstructions can later risk rainwater bridging across the cavity onto the inner wall. To keep cavities clear of mortar droppings (known as 'snots') it's good practice for a protective batten to be placed over the cavity as work progresses above.

Insulation should be added as the wall is built. In walls

that are to be fully-filled with insulation it's common practice to lead with the outer leaf. Where they're only to be partially-filled, the inner leaf tends to lead (so the insulation boards can be secured to the blockwork with wall tie retaining clips before the outer brickwork is built up). Where the two leaves aren't built up together, a maximum height difference of 18 courses of bricks (about 1.3m) is acceptable. Finally, at the end of each day's work the bricks should be cleaned so that they're free of mortar splashes.

Render

As well as excelling in the field of mortar pointing, the Georgians also knew a thing or two about using render to disguise cheap brickwork so that it looked like expensive dressed stonework. 'Stucco', a hard external lime plaster that predated modern cement render, was applied to amazing effect. Render is a bit of a fashion thing, coming back into vogue now and again, such as on Regency and Victorian seaside terraces and many 1930s semis. It also has technical benefits, providing good weather protection and improved insulation, whilst at the same time allowing the use of cheaper materials for the main walls, which today means using concrete blocks instead of bricks.

For your new extension, you may rather fancy a smooth, clean, white-painted cement render finish. Or to match your existing house you may opt for pebbledash or roughcast render. Modern, sophisticated hard-wearing renders reinforced with alkali-resistant glass fibre are available in a wide variety of colours and finishes. You can even order render to be supplied premixed so that all you need do is add water – ideal for the self-builder. (See Chapter 16.)

Timber frame

Of course, you don't have to follow the herd and build your extension in boring old brick and block. If, instead, you plump for one of timber frame construction you may

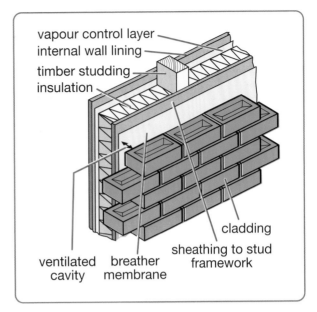

vapour control layer
internal wall lining
timber studding
insulation
cladding
sheathing to stud framework
ventilated cavity
breather membrane

well end up with a warmer extension at a cheaper price. And your existing house needn't already be of timber frame construction to go this route.

There's one thing that's very striking about the way timber frame houses look. That is, they look the same as any other house. The outer leaf of the cavity wall is made from the same brick or rendered blockwork as traditional properties, so you can immediately banish images of draughty old wooden scout huts.

It may be down to their superior insulation or the lure of possible financial savings as a result of their swiftness of construction, but timber frame houses are widely built in Scotland and Scandinavia, despite comprising less than 10 per cent of housing in England and Wales. In cold, wet, miserable weather, anything that substantially reduces time spent on site is obviously very welcome.

The actual 'timber frame' refers to the inner wall leaf, which is the one that takes the structural loading. The timber is pressure pre-treated with preservative and has a very low moisture content. The standard framework conventionally comprises 50 x 100mm timber studs, lined with large sheets of plywood to form manufactured wall panels which are delivered to site ready to be erected. They also arrive already fully insulated, with big chunks of glass mineral wool squashed between the timber studs (or you can request a higher performance insulation like polyurethane foam board). Thicker 125mm or 150mm studs are increasingly used which can accommodate more insulation for even better energy-efficiency.

As a result, it's possible for your basic timber frame structure to be erected in a single day, with a fully weather-resistant building ready in a couple of weeks. Note however that greater foundation accuracy is required – with conventional masonry walls the odd 30mm here or there can easily be made up by the brickies, whereas manufactured made timber frame panels require accuracy within 5mm.

Photo: timberdevelopments.com

Photo: UK Timber Frame Association

Ready made timber frame components delivered on site.

With the foundations and ground floor structure already in place, construction of the inner leaf walls begins with erecting the big ready-made timber wall panels. Special timber baseplates ('soleplates') are first fixed in position over a mortar bed and a DPC using special anchors direct to the ground floor structure, rather than to a wall base as you might expect.

The wall panels are positioned with their plywood sheathing side facing outwards into the cavity. The plywood has sheets of 'breather paper' stapled to it as a protective covering against any moisture that may get through the brick outer wall and cavity.

Looking from inside the building, all you'll see is a thick plasterboard lining, just like conventional modern dry-lined walls. Both make the same hollow sound when tapped. Hidden directly behind this plasterboard layer, however, is a huge polythene-sheet 'vapour barrier' stapled to the frame which acts as a deterrent to the old enemy –

condensation. Note the emphasis on keeping moisture at bay, for obvious reasons. Timber frame also incorporates small barriers in the cavity to prevent fire spread. Once the framework is fully in place, the brick or block outer skin can be built up as normal.

Suppliers normally also include the complete prefabricated roof structure within their package – a one-stop shop. Factory-produced roof panels can be delivered, ready to assemble on site, so your roof can be constructed using these already thickly insulated structural panels instead of messing about with the usual roof trusses.

If you like the sound of such ready-made, labour-saving 'open panel' house components, there's another more advanced timber frame alternative that's even better. Scandinavians favour 'closed panel' systems, where the wall panels are delivered already 'fully furnished'. This doesn't mean having your telly and couch already nailed to the floor, but it's not far off – the windows, doors, services and insulation are pre-installed, thereby saving you time and money with labour and materials on site.

If all this sounds a bit 'new-agey', it's worth remembering that homes built from a wooden framework are one of the oldest types of construction, known to generations of Tudors and Elizabethans, not to mention a good number of present-day North Americans.

However, the type that Shakespeare would most readily recognise today is 'Green Oak framing', which is enjoying something of a renaissance. This comprises a massive traditional oak skeleton with the gaps infilled not with traditional wattle and daub, but with modern rigid foam insulation board 'sandwiches'. The outside walls can then be partially rendered leaving the timbers exposed, Elizabethan-style. Alternatively, the outside can be clad with structural insulated panels (SIPs), leaving the beauty of the oak frame exposed only on the interior face.

The oak is known as 'green' because it has to be worked within 2 years after felling, before it gets too hard. But oak frames are expensive and in other countries good quality softwoods such as Douglas fir are used. Because timber is especially prone to shrinkage, flexible foam gaskets are sometimes fitted at joints.

Keeping warm

Being energy-efficient isn't just about doing your bit to save the planet. By designing-in the latest energy-saving materials you can boost the 'miles per gallon' factor of your extension by achieving minimal heat loss, thereby saving wads of cash. As Swedish folk never tire of reminding us over-centrally-heated Brits, living in a highly insulated Nordic home means you hardly need the heating on at all, thereby dramatically shrinking those fuel bills. So if you want a home that's warm in winter and pleasantly cool in summer, read on.

You'll find that the Building Regs are now very hot on the subject of insulation. This is explained in terms of 'U' values, which tell you how much heat is allowed to escape. The bigger the number, the more heat is being lost. So if, for example, the walls have a stated 'U' value of 0.30 it means 0.30 watts is the maximum amount of heat permitted to pass through each square metre of wall (technically that's watts per square metre x degrees Kelvin). This is one reason why solid brick walls are no longer acceptable. Whereas cavity walls should be able to achieve a nice low 'U' figure of say 0.25 without too much trouble, a naked solid brick wall may be hard pushed to go much below 1.25.

Today's Building Regs are careful not to single out any particular component, such as the walls or windows, for strict compliance with a specific 'U' value. Instead, you need to meet one overall target for the whole building. This means you can 'trade off' heat loss in one element, like floors (U: 0.25), with another, like windows (U: 2.0) or roofs (U: 0.16). Or you may be able to use less insulation in exchange for fitting a more efficient boiler. So if your architect is determined to install snazzy glass wall panels the size of a runway, thereby making your living room a little nippy in the winter, it's OK as long as everywhere else is thermally super-efficient.

Just to ram home the importance of energy conservation, there's a new legal requirement for all buildings to have an energy performance certificate (just like washing machines and cookers) when they're built, sold, let or even refurbished. This means your home will be officially labelled as anything from an excellent Energy Rating 'A' down to an embarrassingly chilly 'G'. Together with a similar Environment Impact Rating (which reveals your CO_2 emissions) this is neatly summed up as a 'SAP rating' that classifies your home on a scale of 1–120. The higher the number, the snugger your house. If you want to qualify as an environmental yob, your house needs only achieve a disappointing rating of 50 or less (the average British home only scores 51). So when, one day in the future, you come to sell your beautifully extended home, the highly insulated new part may drag the old house into a higher performance bracket – something likely to please potential purchasers.

'E' is for energy conservation.

Cavity walls

Walls made of traditional solid brick, much favoured by the Victorians, are today extinct in new construction. Even if you're building an extension onto an old period house, no way would they be permitted. In fact, it was already realised way back in the nineteenth century that problems with dampness penetrating through walls could be massively reduced by constructing two separate thinner walls with an air cavity sandwiched between them, rather than one big thick wall. If driving rain penetrated the outer brick wall, at least it wouldn't be able to bridge the gap and reach the inner leaf. Except, of course, that it can. Since the 1990s it has been common practice to stuff cavities full of insulation, either during construction or later by injection-pumping it through small drill holes. What wasn't foreseen at the time was that, in some cases, this could allow moisture to cross the void, causing damp patches and mould in the rooms of the unlucky occupants.

Cavity insulation

Polyurethane board partial fill.

There are two principal ways of installing cavity insulation in new walls. 'Total fill' and 'Partial fill'. As noted above, where cavities are totally filled up there can be a risk of rain penetrating through the outer wall, sneaking across the cavity and soaking through inner walls. So a traditional 50mm wide cavity that's stuffed full of rigid glassfibre or rockwool batts may be vulnerable to damp, at least in houses exposed to severe weather. Because insulation works by trapping air within its body, to work well it needs to remain dry, so having your cavities crammed with a lot of limp and soggy insulation won't do a lot to reduce your U values.

This may all seem slightly odd, since mineral-fibre or glassfibre insulation itself is perfectly waterproof. Indeed, if you place a batt of the stuff on a pool of water it will quite happily float for hours without absorbing a drop. But inside

Rubbish workmanship! – giant lumps of mortar and loose wall ties block cavity.

Photo: Birmingham City Council

the lonely world of a cavity, in the wrong conditions, it can convey water from the outside wall through to the inner leaf, and over time it may becoming virtually waterlogged.

This problem can be aggravated if careless brickies allow mortar droppings to fall down the cavity. When mortar 'snots' land on wall ties, or start to accumulate at the bottom of the cavity, you have the classic conditions for damp to bridge the cavity.

So seriously is this problem taken that completely filled cavities are now only acceptable when building in more sheltered parts of the country. Indeed some newbuild warranty providers require 'total fill' to be avoided altogether. So with ever stricter Building Regulations insulation standards to meet, what are you supposed to do?

One solution is to fit slimmer 45–60mm rigid boards of expanded polystyrene (EPS) such as 'Jablite' instead of old-fashioned fat woolly batts. EPS is the cheapest partial cavity fill. The boards are attached to the inner wall with special clips fixed to the wall ties. Thinner still are space-efficient 38–48mm Celotex or Kingspan rigid foil-backed polyurethane sheets. Polyurethane is the most efficient insulator, being twice as good as EPS or wools (but about 3 times as expensive). To be effective the boards must be firmly attached and not left hanging limply where the sun don't shine. Increasingly, cavities are now being designed 90 or 100mm wide in order to more easily accommodate both insulation and a decent-sized air void, which means an overall wall thickness of around 300mm. Partial fill should leave you with a clear 50mm 'defensive space' between the insulation and the outer leaf – which is exactly what original un-insulated cavity walls used to have in the first place.

New granular fill in cavity.

An exception to this may be seen on some new housing estates, where generous cavities are filled with tiny lightweight water-repellent polystyrene granules blown in once the walls have been built. Despite fully filling the void, major housebuilders are confident these will not allow damp to pass, even in the most dire weather.

Traditionally, it's the bricklayer's job to install the insulation in the cavities as walls are built, continuing all the way up to the top (not forgetting the gable walls). The cavities in unfinished walls should be covered over at night to protect insulation from damp, and unused insulation material should always be kept dry and clean when it's stored on site.

There are some additional factors to consider when deciding which type of cavity wall insulation to use. Insulation made from traditional mineral wool will offer good

protection from fire and noise transmission, whereas modern foam-based materials will provide better thermal efficiency. If you prefer an organic home extension, natural cellulose fibre made from recycled newspaper and sheep's wool can be blown into the cavities once the walls are completed.

In recent years remarkable progress has been made towards achieving super-low heat-loss figures in modern houses. Apart from improved cavity wall insulation, this has primarily been down to the development of lightweight insulating blocks for use in the inner leaf of cavity walls. But as noted earlier, some lightweight blocks tend to suffer from dramatic shrinkage cracking once plastered. And drilling into them to fix screws and wallplugs for shelves or cupboards can reveal their soft crumbly nature. Basically, the warmest ones can be so full of air bubbles that their compressive strength is poor. Most modern houses and extensions now have their walls dry-lined internally with plasterboard, which not only boosts the insulation performance but means you can fix things to the plasterboard-lining rather than direct to soft blockwork.

But there are other traditional ways of making the walls of your new extension walls super-snug. Applying traditional weatherproof timber boarding, tile hanging or cement rendering to beef up the outer walls has been standard building practice for centuries, in coastal districts or places exposed to regular battering by Mother Nature. Not only can this provide an essential extra line of defence against driving rain and howling gales but it will help further reduce your 'U' values. See Chapter 16.

them, or where old ones have rusted and failed, walls have been known to collapse spectacularly.

To achieve structural stability, the ties must be placed at regular intervals and fully bedded a minimum of 50mm into mortar joints, sloping at a slight gradient downwards and outwards so that any moisture heads out and not into your bedroom. The first row is inserted at ground level. As a general guide, ties are fixed in the wall about 900mm apart horizontally and about 450mm vertically, staggered in a 'domino five' pattern. Around door and window openings the density is normally increased and the ties are spaced vertically about every 300mm, positioned no more than 225mm in from the edge. You need at least 3 wall ties per sq m (4 per sq m for timber frame).

Until fairly recently the cheapest and most widely used wall ties were the 'butterfly' type. Looking a little like tiny coat-hangers contorted into a figure of eight, they have over the years proved adequate for the job in normal conditions. But today, 'double triangle' wall ties are the most widely used type. These comprise a 225mm long strip of stainless steel wire about 2mm thick with a small fold at each end. The squiggly bits in the middle of ties are known as 'drips' (because any water travelling along it should drip off before it can do any damage). The drip should be positioned roughly in the centre of the cavity. Of course, being covered by big blobs of bricklaying mortar will mess things up, so it's important that ties are kept clean. However, wall ties are designed to suit particular cavity widths, so where cavities exceed 100mm, longer 250 or 275mm ties can be used, while for walls in exposed locations stronger flat 'vertical twist' types are recommended.

Wall ties

For cavity walls to be stable and strong, the two leaves must be joined together with wall ties that bridge across the void. In fact the walls won't last long without them, so it's essential for wall ties to be fitted properly. Where lazy or incompetent builders have omitted to include

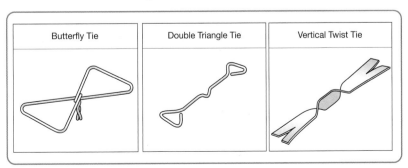

Thermal bridging

The more insulation you stuff into the fabric of your house, the greater the relative importance of any remaining cold areas where the walls can 'leak heat'. The weakest link when it comes to insulation is normally around windows and doors. It was common until quite recently for the sides of the cavities round wall openings to be 'closed off' with bricks or blocks, effectively creating a solid wall with the outer and inner leaves of the wall joined together. This created a 'thermal bridge' crossing from the cold outer wall to the inside walls of rooms, resulting in 'cold spots'. Cold spots in rooms can also occur where gaps are left in the cavity insulation, or where metal wall ties poke through into the plaster of the inner walls.

At this juncture, you might be thinking 'So what?' After all, just how life-threatening can a cold spot on a wall really be? The answer is, no one wants to live in an unhealthy house with damp, mouldy walls. Cold spots on the walls will irresistibly attract the warm, moist air circulating around a typical home. This will then promptly

condense back into water on the cold wall, causing damp patches which can eventually grow black mould.

Fortunately there's a simple solution. The problem of thermal bridging around openings for windows and doors can be prevented by installing special strips of polystyrene known as 'cavity closers'

which fit snugly into the ends of cavities, neatly sealing them off. Cavity closers can double as a DPC thereby tackling the problems of damp penetration and heat loss at the same time. When the frames are fitted, the cavity closer should overlap them by at least 25mm.

An alternative method of closing cavities around window and door reveals is the use of special 'warm' thermalite bricks. No longer is it sufficient to just stick a course of 'cold' bricks or dense concrete blocks across the wall leaves.

The other part of the solution in most newbuild construction is for the inner face of walls to be dry-lined with foil-backed plasterboard that stops the warm humid air in your house coming into touch with the wall, as well as providing an extra layer of internal insulation.

Nothing has escaped the attention of the energy-efficiency police, so the lintels you fit above openings now come ready-packed with insulation. Indeed, you can even compare different brands of lintel according to thermal efficiency by their respective 'R' values (a mirror image of U values – the higher, the more they resist heat leakage). Even so, the cold underside of metal lintels may still require an insulated lining to be applied.

Apart from door and window reveals, the other high risk areas for cold spots are where the walls meet the roof, which is why it's not unusual to see damp mould staining to some upper bedroom walls. The solution is for loft insulation to be carried over the wall plate to link up with

'Cold bridging' risk

A typical modern brick and block wall can be viewed as a sandwich, including cavity fill and internal dry-lining. The mortar is significant as a 'cold bridging' risk:

Layer	Material	'Cold' mortar content	Thickness
1	Outer leaf – brick	20 per cent mortar	105mm
2	Cavity – cellulose fibre insulation		100mm
3	Inner leaf – block, lightweight	6.5 per cent	100mm
4	Airspace/plaster dabs	20 per cent	15mm
5	Skimmed plasterboard dry-lining		13mm

Walls may be thicker if they have cladding or rendered blockwork externally.

the top of the cavity wall insulation (leaving space for air vents). A similar problem can arise at the bottom of the building, where the concrete floor screed meets the walls which is why the floor screed needs to be sealed from the cold wall by a strip of insulation around its edges.

Ventilation

If you reckon the rules on insulating your extension are a bit OTT, then you'll be delighted to know that Building Control pay similarly close attention to its breezy bedfellow, ventilation.

The problems began when sealing out draughts from our homes became a national obsession in the 1970s. Fireplaces got boarded up and rooms hermetically sealed with double glazing. At the same time, gas appliances would eat up valuable oxygen choking the over-warm centrally-heated indoor atmosphere. Steam from kettles, baths, washing and cooking with nowhere to escape then caused an epidemic of condensation, often manifesting itself as unsightly damp black mould.

The fact is that when the warm, moist air in your house hits a cold surface it will cool and condense back to water, causing damp. The source of all this water vapour is simply such ordinary human activities as breathing and sleeping. Add to this tumble driers, washing machines, showers, gas heaters and houseplants and you'll find an average home produces well over ten litres of water vapour a day – and it has to go somewhere.

The solution is to do exactly what you do in the car when it steams up: wind down the windows and turn up the blower. In other words, improve the ventilation.

The objective when designing a new house or extension is to provide controllable ventilation. This means that in addition to having openable windows and doors ('rapid ventilation') some element of permanent 'background ventilation' which can trickle through all the time is needed to reduce the risk of condensation. So small 'trickle vents' positioned in the heads of new window and door frames are now required. But because most water vapour comes from kitchens and bathrooms these rooms must be equipped with extractor fans that automatically expel steamy air before it can cause trouble. Finally, if you fully insulate your walls and reduce emissions of water vapour in the first place – like cutting down on boiled food – the problem should be solved.

Beams and lintels

Lintels are horizontal beams placed in the walls above openings for windows and doors etc. The purpose of lintels or beams is to safely transfer the loads from above down onto the walls either side of the opening.

You may be slightly surprised to hear that lintels were

omitted in many new housing developments from the 1940s through to the 1960s, often relying instead on metal window frames to take the loading. This wasn't a particularly brilliant idea, as many replacement window contractors have belatedly discovered amidst showers of falling bricks.

Traditionally made from timber, lintels are now normally of either lightweight steel or pre-cast reinforced concrete. They are installed as the leaves of the wall are built up by being bedded on mortar.

Steel is the preferred material for bridging openings in outer walls. Concrete lintels, apart from not looking too clever can suffer from cold bridging, whereas steel ones are pre-insulated and can be neatly hidden within the brickwork. The exception to the almost exclusive use of steel or concrete can be found on some contemporary designs, which have dipped into the past with manufactured 'stone' lintels and sills made from granite mixed with cement. Others have reverted to using large timber beams. These chunky 'railway sleeper' type hardwood timbers are extremely robust and are reminiscent architecturally of period cottages, a style briefly revived in the 1930s, though unlike those in Victorian houses these are not hidden away behind brick arches (where they are prone to rot). The whole point is to display them as a prominent architectural feature above windows and doors on the outer wall.

Your designer will have carefully calculated the imposed

loadings, and specified lintels that can safely take the weight. Or if you're designing your own extension, it's a good idea to make use of the free design and specifying service that some lintel companies provide.

Regardless of all the complex desk-calculations, some builders on site always know better and prefer to stick with the same familiar types of lintels they've used for years. Funnily enough, these usually happen to be the ones that are cheapest and most easily available. Worse, when a lintel doesn't fit, out comes the angle grinder. But cutting them to reduce the length can significantly weaken lintels, plus the exposed steel ends will be prone to rust. It's not entirely unknown for builders to put them in upside down – one possible clue to such an error is that you have to stand on your head to read the markings.

Suitability for purpose depends on the required loadings and spans. 'Catnic' and 'IG' steel lintels are available in lengths from 600mm to 4,800mm, with a range of sizes in between in jumps of 150mm. A popular standard-sized concrete lintel is 70mm deep x 100mm wide (available in common lengths from 600m to 1800mm), a perfect size to fit single leaf internal walls.

It's essential that each end of a lintel extends sufficiently onto the supporting walls either side (known as the 'end bearing'). The required length of any lintel is always going to be at least 300mm longer than the opening, needing a minimum 150mm bearing either end. Where the realities of working on site mean that a lintel is not perfectly level, a small amount of packing, such as with metal plates, may be permissible.

Things get trickier where your design dictates that the end of a large beam needs to rest on top of a lintel at a T-junction, for example where the end of a ceiling beam is supported on a main wall just where there happens to be a window below. Such 'point loads' must obviously be checked

early in the design stage by a structural engineer. In addition, Building Control will need to be satisfied that the type of lintel used matches those shown in the approved plans.

Many steel lintels for use in cavity walls not only come ready-insulated, but are also designed with a slight slope down to the front and their ends raised with special 'stop ends'. This helps direct any water in the cavity away and out through weep holes in the outer walls that the brickie will hopefully have remembered to incorporate (see 'Cavity trays' below).

Steels

As everyone knows, heavy, manufactured 'RSJ's are the Daddy of all beams. Rolled Steel Joists are used where extra large openings are needed, and come in a wide

range of lengths and cross-sections, but most commonly with an 'I' profile. They are highly adaptable for use in a wide variety of situations. Building Control will have requested structural calculations for any work requiring steels.

With wide openings, the load resting at each end of a beam can be so great that it can crush ordinary bricks or blocks, so the ends of steels normally need to sit on top of

'padstones', which usually comprise special dense concrete blocks, hard engineering bricks, or even steel plates. These will have been specified in order to spread the load on the wall at the end bearing points. Another way to help spread the load is by increasing the amount of the beam that projects onto the walls at each end beyond the minimum 150mm. The need for padstones will, of course depend on the precise load that's being carried (for a simple small opening like a typical door or window, ordinary masonry can normally take the weight of lintels unassisted).

Despite their tough image, RSJs are not indestructible. Steel reacts badly to fire, buckling, warping and bowing with potentially lethal consequences. Without some serious fire-protection measures you might not get a chance to escape before the walls start collapsing on top of you. So standard procedure requires them to be encased in a double layer of fire-resistant plasterboard with a plaster finish. Alternatively, special intumescent paint can be applied which expands to many times its normal volume when exposed to fire, protecting the surface of the steel.

If your extension design is fairly complex or has an exotic flavour, perhaps boasting galleried landings and mezzanine floors, there may be a need for an RSJ to be supported where there's no suitable wall to do the job. In such cases one solution is to construct new supporting columns, such as brick piers or steel stanchions, but these will need their own special concrete pad foundations. This is a fairly common solution when extending at first floor level over old garages with weak existing walls and inadequate foundations.

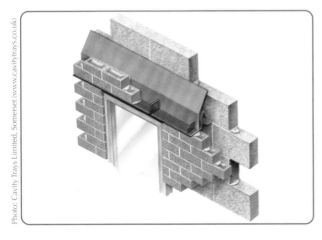

Photo: Cavity Trays Limited, Somerset (www.cavitytrays.co.uk)

Cavity trays

We've already established that it's not unusual for moisture to develop inside a cavity. It can penetrate from outside if severe rain soaks through mortar joints and brickwork, or from inside in the form of condensation. The problem is, once it finds its way in, how do you get rid of it?

Enter the cavity tray. Modern practice is to fit purpose-made plastic trays over window and door lintels, so any water that runs down the cavity will be caught and dispersed out of the wall through 'weep holes'. These are small vertical gaps left between a few bricks (at their vertical 'perpend' joints). They act as tiny drainage outlets, usually with small plastic weep-vents pushed into the holes. Weep holes should be installed no closer together than 900mm intervals, with at least two provided to drain each cavity tray above openings. They should also be placed near ground level so that any moisture that accumulates at the bottom of the cavity (on the concrete infill at the base) can escape.

Basically, trays should be provided over anything that interrupts the cavity – lintels, ducts, even recessed meter boxes – since these can all potentially direct rainwater onto the inside wall. Cavity trays are normally stepped at least 140mm from the outer leaf up into the inner leaf, and may have their 'tails' left projecting out slightly through the outer brickwork. Where the side of a roof slope joins a wall, a series of small stepped trays are usually provided.

To save time, some 'intelligent lintels' are now designed with built-in DPCs that function as their own cavity trays (but in walls exposed to extreme weather you still need to fit a 'proper' tray). Alternatively, plastic sheets (damp-proof membranes) laid over the lintel and turned up at the sides should, in effect, act as trays, collecting any moisture and directing it to the outside.

Remedial cavity trays

Building a single-storey extension against a cavity wall of the existing house can pose an interesting potential problem for the occupants. The original outside wall of the main house will now be enclosed downstairs by the new extension, in effect becoming an internal wall. But at first floor level it's still an external wall, exposed to all manner of foul weather and driving rain. The worry is that any rain that penetrates through the old brickwork upstairs could now seep down the cavity and cause nasty damp patches downstairs.

Thankfully there's a solution to prevent such a dispiriting and unwelcome intrusion. The builders will need to insert a new plastic cavity tray into the cavity of the old main wall, just above the point where the new roof joins it. This 'remedial tray' sits across the cavity and catches any water that penetrates, neatly diverting it out and away through new weep holes in the outer wall.

The work is done from outside. First a single course of brickwork needs to be temporarily removed in the old wall using an angle grinder (in some cases a second course may also need to be removed). About four to six bricks are removed at a time, enough to allow the tray to be fed through, piece by piece. Obviously, the tray needs to be at least as wide as the new extension below it. The bricks are then replaced, leaving a few small weep holes. Ideally this job should be done before breaking internally through from the extension to the main house.

Joining to the existing house

There are two main methods of building your extension walls onto those of the existing house, and the choice you make will be crucial for the stability of the finished structure.

Traditionally it was done by neatly 'toothing in' the new extension brickwork to the old, continuing an existing wall surface as seamlessly as possible. To make an invisible joint, a brick would be cut out and removed from every other course in the old wall, and the new ones stitched in. To look right your new bricks would need to perfectly match

the originals and be laid with the utmost care. But even if the finished job looked wonderfully neat, there could still be trouble in store.

The problem is the high risk of cracking occurring between the main house, resting on its old, shallow foundations, and the new extension with its deep bomb-proof boots. These two structures, although now joined together, are likely to be affected differently by seasonal ground movement. This typically results in a phenomenon known as 'differential settlement', where the old part of the house settles in

response to the ground beneath at a different rate to the extension. This in turn puts intense pressure on the junction between the new and the old. Result – vertical cracking.

Over the years different solutions have been attempted, but the obvious one – making the adjoining part of the old property's foundations deeper by underpinning them – doesn't solve the problem; it only moves the crack attack further back.

To avoid this, flexible wall-tie methods were developed. Thin vertical strips of steel known as profile plates (or 'crocodiles') are fixed to the existing wall with expansion bolts, one for each leaf of the new cavity wall.

The brick or block courses of the new walls are then built up against the profiles with a metal clip attachment bedded into each course and slotted onto the next 'rung' of the profile. This method can accommodate approximately 10mm of movement. When done, the visible vertical joint to the outer brickwork can be filled with a flexible silicone mastic to prevent cracking (brown is a popular colour). Visually the appearance of such a joint may be further improved by camouflaging it with a strategically placed downpipe, or by cladding the outer walls. A handy back door opening can sometimes be designed at this point so that the door frame disguises much of the joint.

If your new wall joins the old one at right angles (at a 'T' rather than just extending an existing wall run) the old wall can now effectively act as a bridge across the new cavity. Consequently there's a risk that rain could also bridge from outside across the cavity, so a vertical DPC must be installed where any part of an existing outside wall becomes a new internal wall. This is done by cutting a

vertical line in the old wall with an angle grinder, roughly centrally between the two new profiles, and feeding a new plastic strip (vertical DPC) into the slot. It is then lapped behind the new outer leaf in order to bar the path of any rain trying to bridge across at this point. Ideally the old cavity should be cut open wider so it extends round into the new cavity, but this could have structural implications and weaken the bolt fixings to the profiles. Ask Building Control for their opinion.

Templates for windows and doors

Fitting expensive new windows and doors into the walls as construction progresses can all too easily result in them becoming damaged. So it's normally better to make up simple 'dummy window' templates from timber which can be temporarily built into the walls. Later, when the walls are complete, the templates can be removed and the new frames fitted. In the meantime the templates can be boarded over for security. Even tough UPVC frames are now generally installed at a later date, with special 'cavity formers' being built in as work on the walls progresses.

Great care must be taken to ensure the template sizes are accurate to avoid the anguish and frustration of trying to later squeeze frames into openings that are too small. An alternative is to install the frames, without the glazing, as the wall progresses.

There are, of course, other openings that will be required in the walls, such as for pipes, flues, and various vents, but with the exception of those for meter boxes, they tend to be cut through the wall at a later date, rather than trying to build in fiddly small holes as you go. Pipes run through walls will require compressible packing around them to protect them from bending and cracking.

Lateral restraint straps

To be structurally strong, walls need a little extra support. This is provided by tying the new walls in to other parts of the structure. So, at each floor level horizontal L-shaped steel restraint straps are built in to the inner leaf blockwork. These are then fixed across floor and ceiling joists and roof rafters. Now, you may wonder how a few thin-looking steel straps, only 30mm wide and 5mm thick, could possibly make

Lateral restraint straps – the rules
- Straps should be spaced every 2m or closer, where joists run parallel to the wall.
- The long part of the strap should extend across no less than three rafters or joists (either above or below them) with timber noggins fixed under the strap in the spaces between joists or rafters.
- The wall end of the straps should be built into the blockwork of the wall, and the short 'L' turned down inside the cavity against the inner leaf, rather than being screwed in later.
- Where internal walls meet main walls, they should also be supported with straps to the ceiling joists at the top of each storey.

much difference, but they do. The Building Research Establishment (whose job it is to test houses to destruction in a massive airship hangar somewhere in Bedfordshire) have simulated extreme Hurricane Katrina type wind-load conditions, conclusively proving their importance. At particular risk in high winds are gable end walls, which particularly benefit from being tied to the roof structure.

Scaffolding

Once the construction of your main walls has progressed a few courses above ground-floor window sill level, the bricklayers may no longer be able to easily reach standing on the ground. Your scaffolding therefore needs to be ordered well in advance, so that it can be erected on site at this stage without delaying the bricklayers.

An alternative option where the required height is less than 2.5m, such as for single-storey extensions, may be to hire scaffold towers with decks made from planks. Your bricklayer may be willing to supply and erect them himself (for a reasonable charge).

The world of scaffolding has a terminology all its own. Ask what stage the construction of a new building has reached, and you may get a response like 'second lift'. This might seem a trifle odd given that stairs are normally the preferred method of ascending, but here the term 'lift' refers to the height that the build has reached, 'first lift' being the lowest scaffolding platform, just below head height. Later, when the wall has progressed to a towering height beyond the reach of human hands, it's up to 'second lift', and then higher still for roof work and stacks.

There are obvious health and safety dangers with erecting and dismantling temporary working platforms at height, and spectacular collapses have occurred from time to time. Scaffolding has to support a considerable weight, not just loads of burly builders but also lots of heavy bricks and roof tiles stacked up, making the possibility of overloading a real danger. Any platform over 2m high must have metal edge-guarding fixed to the sides, and if

people are likely to be passing underneath there should be protective netting to catch falling debris.

Erecting scaffolding is definitely not a DIY job, and must be carried out by a licensed specialist firm with plenty of insurance. To this end you must specify that it is erected in accordance with BS 5973, which will at least cover you in the event of an accident. Also, request a handover certificate once the scaffolding is all in place, which confirms it has been erected properly.

During the course of the works, check from time to time that it hasn't sunk into soft ground, and that ladders are securely tied and set at an angle of about 75°. The vertical tubular poles ('standards') must rest on substantial base plates. The horizontal poles ('putlogs') must not rest on the DPC in the walls.

Wall plates

When wall construction finally reaches roof level, a strip of 100 x 50mm softwood is normally bedded in mortar along the top of the walls. This is the wall plate, and its job is to provide a secure base for the roof timbers to rest on. In order to hold the wall plates in place, they're clamped vertically to the walls below using 30 x 5mm L-shaped galvanised steel restraint straps. The straps should be placed no more than 2m apart, and no further than 450mm in from the ends of the walls, extending at least 300mm down the wall. It's normally the brickie's job to fit wall plates and strap them in place, the carpenter having cut them to the correct size.

However, there's one part of the job that, with the best will in the world, the bricklayer cannot always finish until

later. This will only apply if your pitched roof has been designed with a gable end, rather than, say, a hip (see Chapter 11). Here, the gable brickwork may need to be completed only once the end roof rafters are in place. This is because the brickwork needs to be accurately cut to fit the profile of the roof (if it's to be left naked without bargeboards to disguise the joints under the verges). You may therefore need to programme an agreed date for the brickie's return visit to finish the job.

Internal walls

If your extension is going to have more than one room, you'll obviously need to build internal partition walls to divide the space. On the ground floor, blockwork dividing walls are generally preferred since they're relatively cheap to build and also provide good sound insulation between rooms. These are normally no thicker than 100mm, the width of a single concrete block, and not usually load-bearing. Lintels tend to be of the simple reinforced concrete type.

While you've got your brickies on site, it's a fairly simple job to build the partition walls along with the main walls, or soon after. Where they meet main walls, they should be well bonded in – something Victorian builders often shamelessly bodged. Any load-bearing 'structural' internal walls will need their own foundations and DPC, although the width of the trenches can normally be less than for main walls.

If you've opted instead to have your partition walls built of timber stud and plasterboard, these will need to wait until

later when the structure is fully dry and watertight (see Chapter 12). Upstairs, blockwork is not often used except for any 'structural' walls, which can be built straight up from the wall below. Otherwise it's generally considered better to build in timber studwork upstairs, since it is less than half the weight of a solid masonry wall.

Party walls and noise pollution

If your neighbour already has an extension that runs along the garden boundary right next to where you're now building, or if they're planning to build one, you might want to share this boundary wall between you. If this is to become your party wall, there are two key technical issues to consider – the risk of fire, and the possibility of noise pollution.

Achieving one-hour fire resistance shouldn't be a problem – a standard masonry wall should easily exceed this, especially if it's dry-lined with plasterboard. Sound insulation is a little more complex. Noise pollution is defined as 'unwanted sound', which comes in two varieties. Airborne sound such as loud music or shouting and screaming is one type. The other is 'impact sound', such as the thud of boots walking, although this tends to be more of a problem when designing floors, such as in flats with noisy neighbours upstairs.

Airborne sound is carried by vibrations in the air, like ripples in water. An effective barrier would be a thick, heavy wall, such as one made of dense concrete blocks. Stopping impact sound is a little harder, as you need some kind of separation in the form of a physical air-gap. A wall with a cavity can act as a barrier that sound can't track across. Dry-lining such a wall with plasterboard will improve it further, ideally incorporating an extra air void behind the plasterboard, partially filled with a layer of dense mineral wool. The edges will need acoustic sealant to block air paths. If all else fails, special composite acoustic sound-deadening panels can be fixed to floors and walls.

Main trades needed on site

- **Bricklayers:** Build the walls up to wall plate level.
- **Carpenters:** Build templates for window and door frames and cut timber wall plates.
- **Scaffolders:** Erect and later dismantle scaffolding.
- **Labourers:** Cut indents into existing walls, and fix profiles.

www.home-extension.co.uk

10 UPPER FLOORS, WINDOWS AND DOORS

As the main walls take shape, the upstairs floor joists are normally fixed in place. With a little help from some temporary boarding, these can provide a useful work-platform as your new extension grows ever taller.

However, expensive new windows and doors need not be fitted just yet, to avoid the risk of damage. Only once the roof is on, and breaking-through to the main house successfully completed, will the time be right for the eyes and soul of the new building to put in an appearance. Until that day, you may wish to keep them safely stored away, or simply delay their delivery.

First floors

The upper floors are traditionally constructed from timber floor joists spanning between the structural walls of the building, though the floorboards themselves will only be fixed at a later stage, once the building is dry and completely weathertight. In the meantime, a few sheets of thick plywood are sometimes casually flung over the joists to provide a temporary deck. This can pose a danger for unwary homeowners taking a leisurely after-hours stroll around the works, so take care not to come a cropper by stepping on overhanging edges.

The floor joists are one part of the structure where tradition still rules. Whereas mainstream housing developers now employ factory-made timber beams called 'I-joists', home extension builders have stuck doggedly to using traditional 200 x 50mm 'eight by two' softwood joists.

I-joists look rather like RSJs made of wood. Despite their thin appearance they're actually incredibly strong and light and are able to span larger distances (up to 6 metres) without support. One of main problems with ordinary joists is that they shrink, causing creaks and squeaks in floors – I-joists have greater rigidity and don't shrink. They take half the time to install, and services can be run through preformed 'knock-outs', rather than cutting or drilling notches. Apart from their expense, their main drawback is that they can't be cut, as this significantly diminishes their strength. Because home extensions aren't all built in standard dimensions like much new-estate housing, I-joists of the right size may not be readily available 'off the peg'.

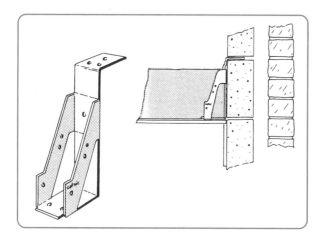

Spans and joist hangers

Joists are normally laid across the narrower span of the room. In most home extensions, the main walls will carry the floor load at either end. But once a room becomes wider than the maximum span for a conventional floor joist (about 4.5m – see span tables on website) extra support will be required, either from a structural beam (typically a steel) or a load bearing internal wall, which will add to the cost. Steel beams (typically 102 x 178mm) are not in themselves that expensive. They can either be hidden within the floor void, so the timber joists are hung off the steel, or placed below the ceiling, in which case they need boxing in with plasterboard.

On external walls, the Building Regs now require that floor joists must be slotted into galvanised steel joist hangers (small purpose-made cradles) that are fixed to the walls. This overcomes the problem in many older houses where joists bedded directly into walls would become damp and rotten, ultimately risking collapse. Of course, the new joists not only have to provide a level floor surface, but they're also responsible for creating a nice level ceiling in the rooms below, so it is essential that the hangers are carefully fixed in place, providing accurate levels at both ends.

Ideally, the joist hangers should be built into the blockwork inner walls whilst they're being constructed, in a similar way to the restraint straps. They also need to be secured by being screwed or nailed in place. It's not

considered good practice to use an angle grinder to gouge out slots in the walls or mortar joints for the joist hanger tongues to later be wedged into.

Although it's not normally recommended that joists rest directly on the blockwork inner skin of the main wall, if there's no other option and Building Control approve, they must be protected from the risk of damp by strips of plastic DPC. Also the joist ends must be pre-treated with preservative, and cut so as not to project into the cavity. Another problem with this method is that some often require packing underneath with small wedges of plywood or slate to get them perfectly level.

Where joist hangers have to be fixed to an existing wall, a horizontal timber wall plate should normally be bolted to the wall first, using M10 expansion bolts. Steel hangers can then be fixed to this. Alternatively, special 'face fix' hangers can be used which are designed to be expansion-bolted direct to the wall surface.

Of course, the floor structure does more than support your feet. As we saw in the last chapter, it also plays a crucial role in holding the main walls of the building together (called 'lateral restraint') with the help of horizontal steel straps, thereby preventing structural movement.

Fitting floor joists

Timber is rarely perfectly straight, and whereas a slight bow over the length of a joist isn't necessarily a problem,

Joist hangers are now required to main walls, rather than joists built into blockwork.

any badly twisted material should automatically be rejected, since it will only tend to get worse over time. Prior to fitting, all the joists should be compared and the straightest ones located near the edges of the room. Any that 'hump up' slightly should be positioned near the middle of the room (avoid placing them the other way so they sag over the ceiling). This is because any slight rise should gradually be compressed by the weight of furnishings in the room, and revert to a reasonably flat surface.

Floor joists typically comprise 200 x 50mm tanalised treated timbers set apart at either 400, 450 or 600mm centres ('centre' measurements are taken from the centre of one joist to the centre of the next). The precise dimensions will vary depending on spans, so check on your plans. (See website.) Structural timber like softwood for floor joists is supplied 'dry-graded'. Under the Building Regulations, the permitted moisture content is restricted to a maximum of 24 per cent (much higher than this and timber can become attractive to wood boring beetle and fungus). Low moisture content timber is defined as 'below 20 per cent', but the final moisture level in modern houses is only about 10–12 per cent, so shrinkage problems are still a real possibility.

New joists and floorboards are normally supplied 'kiln dried' and factory-treated with preservative to protect against rot and beetle attack and to prevent twisting or warping, the curse of much cheaper timber. The timber undergoes 'vacuum impregnation' treatment by being immersed in a vacuum pressure tank and is either 'tanalised', a water based treatment that lends the wood a faint green or brown shade, or is 'protimised', a spirit based process that leaves the wood uncoloured (or sometimes dyed red).

Treatment is especially important for timber ground floors since they're usually more at risk from damp.

Strutting and trimming

No matter how carefully the timber floor joists are installed, it's likely that some slight twisting will take place as shrinkage occurs. This can lead to distortion of the floorboards and may even damage ceilings below. To minimise this, some form of additional bracing is needed between the joists. The traditional solution is to fit small timber struts between the joists in an 'X' pattern known as herringbone strutting. For spans up to 3.5m, one line of strutting is adequate, but for every additional 1.5m further struts are needed. Modern construction makes use of purpose-made steel 'X struts'. Where floor joists rest on internal walls, additional strengthening is recommended to prevent 'rotation', usually by jamming small timber off-cuts called 'noggins' between the joists.

But where you need to make space in the floor structure for a staircase or a chimney breast to come through it, you'll need to construct a special framework of joists around the new opening. This is known as 'trimming'. Here, the joists that would otherwise be in the way of the stairs need to be cut short and 'teed off' (framed) with trimmer joists. These are special joists that are doubled up and bolted together, and then butted at right angles across all the ends of the shortened main

Above: State of the art 'I- joists'.

Left: Steel supports wall above.

joists. The main joists either side are also doubled up for strength. Special steel joist hangers can be used to join the timbers together. For floorboards, see Chapter 12.

Grading timber

Timber is an indispensable natural building material, but treat it badly and it will exact slow revenge, finding ingenious ways to retaliate by splitting, twisting, buckling and warping over the years. It can also be prone to swelling when it absorbs moisture, jamming doors and windows. So ideally timber should be well-seasoned before coming anywhere near a house. Victorian buildings and inter-war properties with their naturally slow-seasoned timber are often in better shape today than many 1970s houses, where wet rot has long ago devastated the windows and eaves.

Internally, a lot of modern houses have suffered from extreme shrinkage cracking, due to the speed of their construction. Timber that's still green and fresh from the tree may continue to season after the house is occupied, especially with the central heating on full blast, causing it to shrink and bow. Soon after occupation floor joists may shrink back from walls, and large gaps appear at staircase walls and at the edges of ceilings. So to minimise the risk of shrivelling and buckling, timber used for structural purposes such as floor joists and roof rafters must be kiln-dried. Even hardwood beams should be specified as 'well-seasoned'. It's advisable to allow new timber to adapt to the moisture content of the room before cutting and fixing it, by opening up packs and letting them become

conditioned so that any severe shrinkage will hopefully occur before it can do any harm.

Hardwood is the timber that comes from broadleaf trees such as oak, birch and beech. Softwood comes from conifers like spruce, Scots pine, firs and yew. Somewhat confusingly, despite the name, the classification has nothing to do with density or hardness, although most hardwoods (mahogany, oak, teak etc) are inherently more durable (as well as more expensive). However Douglas fir is a widely available resinous softwood that can perform as well as many hardwoods.

Most construction grade timber is spruce, known as carcassing, deal or whitewood. Joinery grade wood is usually of pine (known as redwood) which is more durable than spruce, and is used for windows, skirtings, floorboards etc, often sold with a planed finish.

As you pore through the left-over lengths of timber at your local DIY store, bear in mind that the pieces you select should ideally have straight grain with no knots or drying splits ('shakes') – which is precisely why all the old knotty and warped bits are left on the shelf. To save builders having to waste time judging every single piece of wood they use, timber comes ready strength-graded, the supplier having already assessed these features. For structural purposes new timber is supplied in strength classes that determine the allowable working stresses:

Photo: UK Timber Frame Association

Timber strength class

C14	C16	C18	C22	C24	C27
weaker --- *stronger*					

A few years ago timber classifications changed from the well-known popular SC3 and SC4 grades to the new equivalent classifications of C16 and C24. C24 costs slightly more than C16 as it is stronger and can be used over larger spans. The strength class depends on both the species and the grade of the actual piece of wood. In all there are 16 strength classes ranging from C14, the lowest softwood strength, through to D70, the strongest hardwood strength class. Softwoods are more difficult to assess than

Timber joists – points to check
- Stress grade as specified.
- Free from bow, twist, rot and woodworm.
- Depth and width as specified.
- Tops of joists level.
- Joists correctly spaced apart.
- Joists doubled up where supporting upstairs walls.
- Joist ends built tightly into brick/blockwork with no gaps (on inner walls).
- Joist ends securely fixed to joist hangers (outer walls) fixed tight to wall.

hardwoods, and there are two overall visual strength grades used as guidance for structural use: GS (general structural use) and the stronger SS (special structural use).

Basically all you've got to do is check that the material is stamped with its grading, and make sure you purchase the type that's specified in the approved plans.

Nails

The best types of nails to use in timber are modern 'improved nails'. These have tiny rings inscribed on their shanks, which give them a better grip. They bite hard into wood and are more difficult to pull out than conventional 'wire' nails or 'cut' nails. Improved nails are recommended for fixing structural items such as joist hangers.

Carpenters and joiners

The difference between a carpenter and a joiner is that traditionally carpenters do all the big structural timberwork (often called 'first fix'), mainly working outdoors, whereas joiners come along later to carefully perfect the finished appearance of the property using smoother, planed timber. Joiners tend to largely operate indoors, installing such things as architraves, panelling, fitted kitchen units, and staircase mouldings (often called 'second fix'). Joiners see themselves as craftsmen, regarding carpenters sawing and nailing lumps of wood together in rather the same way that portrait artists might perceive interior decorators. The

reality is that both are highly skilled trades. Many carpenter/joiners perform the full repertoire. But there's one important difference: whilst poor quality joinery is annoying, poor quality carpentry can threaten the very structure of a building.

It's said that the test of a good carpenter/joiner is how neatly they can hang a door. Although not exactly 'rocket-science' this does allow you to easily note the degree of care and attention to detail.

Floor insulation

The Building Regulations are especially rigorous about preventing heat-loss through floors, both solid and timber. Your approved plans must clearly show every detail of how the required levels of insulation are to be achieved. Upper floors, however, tend to only require insulation if their

underside is open to the exterior, such as where a passageway runs underneath, or over an unheated space like an integral garage. Insulating timber floors as they are built is simple and inexpensive. The insulation is slotted between the joists supported by timber battens nailed to the lower part of the joists.

Windows and doors

If there's one part of the build that's likely to spark a heated debate it's your choice of windows and doors.

Photo: eddystoneselfbuild.co.uk

Some folk harbour a slightly cynical view that any design that displays even the slightest artistic flair will inevitably be doomed, strangled at birth by the planning department. To be fair, the planners will be understandably keen to prevent problems such as windows that very evidently overlook the neighbours, whilst at the same time wanting to preserve the architectural character of the main house.

If your windows survive that process, Building Control will doubtless take a dim view of anything that allows undue heat-loss or poor ventilation. Conflict between the respective standards of these council departments is more likely to arise with listed buildings or projects in conservation areas, where simultaneously trying to preserve the old and enforce the new may prove incompatible.

Windows

The choice of available new windows is extensive. You can buy anything from quaint replica box sashes to conventional side or top hung casements or even zany tilt-

and-turn jobs. These are available in a variety of materials such as softwood, hardwood, UPVC, painted aluminium or galvanised steel, as well as in a range of colours and glazing styles. Taste is a personal matter, but as a general rule it's worth trying to emulate the original window architecture of the house you're extending, especially with pre-war or older properties. Sticking cheap plastic windows in an extension to a Jacobean cottage with traditional leaded lights, isn't going to do a lot for the property's resale value. Research shows that over a 30-year period, timber windows can actually turn out to be the cheapest option. Despite the magic words 'maintenance-free', UPVC may only last 30 to 40 years and is hard to repair. Decent timber should last longer if regularly painted or stained.

Most modern windows are 'casements' which simply means they open on hinges (rather than sliding like

sashes). Casements can be side or top hung, or pivoted in the middle. A window that doesn't open at all is known as a 'fixed light'. If you feel the need to add that elusive quality known as 'character', there are endless choices of 'cottage style' and 'Georgian' glazing bars as well as 'swept head' curved top inserts .

As a rule of thumb, your windows will cost twice as much per square metre as the walls they sit within. The cost of a basic timber window may double by the time you've glazed it and attended to all the detailing & decorating. And should you choose to buy custom-made windows in non-standard sizes, they could set you back up to 3 times the price of bog standard mass produced units. Most windows have to be ordered in advance, so plan for a 4–6 week delay. Perhaps the commonest size in new housing is the 1,200 x 1,200mm 'double casement' but there are a wide range of 'off the shelf' sizes.

The standard height options are:
450, 600, 750, 900, 1,050, 1,200, 1,350, and 1,500mm (sizes rising in 150mm jumps, equivalent to 2 brick courses).

The standard width options are somewhat less logical:
488, 630, 915, 1,200 and 1,770mm

Mass produced timber windows are commonly made from Scandinavian redwood, factory vacuum-treated with preservatives. Locks are now fitted as standard, and opening casements are ready-draught proofed. Windows and other joinery items are supplied with a base coat of wood stain which you can later choose to stain (or paint), or else a white primed finish for painting.

To compete with UPVC, factory pre-glazing of timber windows is becoming more common, so units should be delivered ready glazed as well as pre-finished.

From a technical viewpoint, new windows need to comply with Part L1 of the Building Regulations for thermal insulation (Part J if your extension is Scottish). Habitable rooms must have opening windows fitted with small trickle vents to provide background ventilation (fitted in the heads of window frames) which are now standard.

There are minimum size requirements for window openings. For all habitable rooms, the Building Regulations require the openable area of the window(s) to be equivalent to at least five per cent of the room's floor area. Perhaps due to their more northerly location, Scottish standards stipulate a minimum glazed area in each room equivalent to 15 per cent of its floor area.

But apart from looking good and keeping your home warm and bright, there are other factors that need to be considered:

■ Escape from fire, especially on upper floors.
■ Security, especially to ground floors and windows facing flat roofs.
■ Danger from broken glass.

If windows are located on a wall within 6m of a boundary with next door's house, there will be restrictions on their total size. This is to control the risk of fire spread between buildings. In the event of having to escape from a fire, the minimum opening that most people can realistically get through is 500mm wide x 850mm high, and the locks must be accessible since trying to smash your way out through sealed unit double glazing can be virtually impossible.

Reveals

The vertical sides of the walls around window and door frames are known as reveals. Even quite modern houses can suffer from damp and mould around the reveals because of those twin evils discussed earlier – cold spots and thermal bridging. But inserting special foam-filled plastic 'cavity closers' into the cavities not only breaks the cold bridge, but also doubles as a vertical DPC and provides a fixing point for the window frame itself.

Frame fitting

Photo: eddystoneselfbuild.co.uk

Something that will greatly affect the look of your house, and yet is sometimes overlooked, is the question of where exactly to align the new window and door frames within the wall openings. It's often left to the blokes on site to make this key decision on your behalf. The Victorians set their windows and doors well back into the brickwork, but this necessitated fitting huge masonry sub-sills underneath projecting well clear of the wall, adding to the cost. Recessed joinery not only looks better, but a softwood window that is sheltered from the weather by being set back in its opening can ultimately perform better than an exposed hardwood one. However, modern volume-produced joinery has integral sills and is designed to fit just 25mm back from the outside face of the brickwork, which on the plus side at least makes room for a nice big window ledge inside.

It's normally best to match the pattern of the existing windows, which means that for many older properties they need to be set fairly well back. Most importantly, this decision will also affect the outer sills, which must project out sufficiently from the wall in order to disperse rainwater.

The undersides of any exposed lintels may also need protecting.

Traditionally, new window frames were placed on a mortar bed, with a strip of protective DPC wrapped around timber windows, especially under the sills. Today, cavity closers provide a simple method of fixing frames, acting as a subframe to which the windows can simply be clipped at a later stage. The cavity closers are inserted as the walls are built, and fitting the windows can be left until later. Both UPVC and timber windows are available which clip into built-in cavity closers. But before fixing, the frames must be checked for correct positioning with a spirit level, to ensure they've been fitted square and plumb (upright and level).

There are various other methods used to anchor frames into the surrounding masonry. Traditionally, galvanised steel brackets known as 'frame cramps' were screwed to the sides of the frames and bedded into the mortar courses at the reveals as the walls are built up around the frames. Or metal brackets fixed to the sides of timber windows can simply be screwed into the masonry reveals. Alternatively, special frame-fixing 'hammer-in' screws with long plastic wallplugs can be installed by drilling holes in the frame and then keeping on drilling into the wall (using a masonry bit), finally hammering in the screw and tightening it. But whatever method is used, take it easy with the screwdriver as overtightening can cause distortion to the frames.

It sounds obvious, but always check that lintels have been correctly fitted above all openings. It is not unknown for builders to omit these, instead relying on the reinforcement in the frames themselves to hold up the brickwork above. However, even robust-looking UPVC frames aren't normally sufficient to take the place of a lintel. Above the lintels, cavity trays should be installed (or an equivalent sheet of plastic DPM angled up at the sides) to protect the lintel from condensation in the cavity.

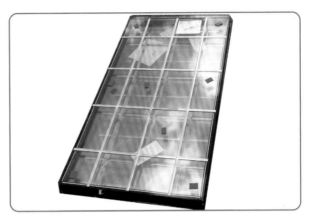

Finally, to banish draughts for ever, frames need to be completely sealed, by injecting a suitable silicone mastic between the outside frame and the reveal. Any gaps on the inside can be sealed with a few blasts of expanding polystyrene foam (wear gloves!).

Window fixing – points to check

- The sills have a thin 'drip groove' set back a few millimetres from their outer underside front edges.
- The sills project well clear of the wall (so rain can drip off freely).

- Timber frames are protected by DPCs or plastic cavity closers.
- Where the outer wall below the window is to be tiled or timber clad, a lead flashing 'apron' should be fixed under the sill (to be dressed down over the cladding).

Glazing

Double-glazing as a product has something of a chequered history. In terms of improvements that cut your fuel bills in an existing property, it actually comes way down the list, with an 'energy payback period' approaching 100 years. Worse, many units have been bedevilled by high failure rates within a few years of being fitted. The mysterious phenomenon of 'misting' commonly manifests itself as a result of moisture condensing inside the (supposedly) sealed units', due to wet edge seals breaking down and disintegrating. Fortunately, modern units are much improved, thanks to drained and vented bottom rails in the frames that allow moisture to drain away or evaporate, rather than accumulate. Timber windows with deeper glazing rebates have also helped, and being delivered already factory glazed has cut out the risk of 'Friday afternoon' fitting on site.

Of course double-glazing has other obvious benefits, such as improved security, sound proofing, and reduced condensation, and in order to meet the requirements of Part L1 of the Building Regulations it is now required for all new properties, home extensions and replacement windows. New double glazed windows must have a U value no higher than 2.0. So to reduce heat

loss to this low level, sealed units now come have thick 20mm or 24mm vacuum sealed air gaps, filled with inert argon or krypton gas. Built-in spacer bar 'thermal breaks' reduce condensation risks by separating the cold outer frame from the warm inner parts.

In Scandinavia, 'triple-glazing' is not uncommon, incorporating three layers of glass sandwiched with twin cavities thereby achieving even lower U values, way down at 1.3. But would it really be worth the extra expense? If you live next to a motorway or in Orkney this might be worth considering, but if you really want to intrigue the neighbours with some hi-tech glazing how

about fitting 'low-E' glass, which has an advanced micron thin coating to the inside of the inner pane that allows the sun's rays to pass through but reduces internal heat-loss (hence lower fuel bills). Or the amazing 'bioclean' self-cleaning glass?

Broken glass

To anyone with young children, danger from unprotected glass at low levels can be a real worry, so to cut the risk of accidents safety glass is now required in critical locations. That means any glazing within 800mm of floor level. And if you have windows next to your doors (ie within 300mm) then any glazing within 1,500mm of the floor must also be made from safety glass. Ditto for panes of glass anywhere that are wider than 250mm, and for internal doors with pane sizes greater then 250 x 250mm.

But what exactly is safety glass? There are two common forms of strengthened glass that comply with BS 7950. The type used in car windscreens is 'laminated safety glass', which is over 6mm thick and shatters into tiny pieces on impact rather than into big sharp shards. To achieve this, an invisible clear plastic sheet is sandwiched between 2 layers of ordinary glass, so that it all holds together on impact. When fitted in house windows, it gives glazing the added strength to resist intruders.

Safety glass also comes in the form of 'toughened glass' which is baked hard to five times the strength of ordinary float glass. Toughened glass is harder to break, but when it does break it shatters into relatively safe small nodules that hang together, but can be knocked through afterwards. Toughened glass costs about 50% more than standard glass. Of the two, it is reckoned that laminated glass is more secure, although it costs twice as much as standard glass. Small panes in doors etc may instead be made from tempered or annealed safety glass.

Children are, of course, naturally attracted to anything life threatening, so any part of your upstairs windows up to 800mm above floor level must not be openable.

However, this is a part of the building where you may find potential for conflict within the various regulations. Security rules demand windows that remain firmly closed, but fire escape regulations want them easily openable. New loft rooms with small skylight windows, for example, should be sufficient for easy escape in the event of fire (Building

Regs Part B), while at the same time they mustn't be easily openable by children intent on playing 'roof-exploration' games. A suitable compromise in such a situation might be reached by fitting special high-level child-proof handles.

Doors

Choosing the doors for your extension provides a great opportunity to add real character to your home. Fitting a cottage style ledge & brace door or some stylish French windows could be just the thing, as could glazed double doors in place of upstairs windows, enclosed externally by a small cast iron 'juliet balcony'. But before getting too carried away, note that doors are not exempt from thermal insulation standards.

It pays to take a little time when picking a new door as fitting a cheap one may leave you vulnerable to leaks as well as break-ins. Doors manufactured from UPVC are usually supplied as a complete unit with an integral frame. Their major advantage is that they're virtually maintenance-free, although they're not always as attractive as traditional wooden doors, which are still pretty much the most popular choice. Fibreglass (GRP) can do a fairly convincing impersonation of timber and may be worth considering. Steel doors are a serious modern alternative, popular in North America.

Door frames

It may sound obvious, but before attempting to fit a frame spare a thought for the direction you want the door to open. Entrance doors should open into the house, whilst

Door dimensions

The world of doors remains a stronghold of imperial measurements, the most common standard sizes being 78 x 33in (1,981 x 838mm) and 78 x 30in (1,981 x 762mm). For taller, wider folk 80 x 32in (2,032 x 813mm) doors are available. The standard thickness is 44mm. Including the frame, most UPVC exterior doors are available sized 82 x 36in (2,085 x 920mm), or 82 x 47in (2,085 x 1,190 mm) for French doors.

'French windows' or balcony doors normally swing outwards. On rare occasions, you might want a kitchen door, for example, to open outwards to save space internally. If so, extra precautions should be taken to prevent possible injury (*eg* kids running past just as someone flings open the door) and to protect the frame from the weather.

Timber door frames are usually of 100 x 75mm softwood and can be fitted in the same way as window frames (described above) and may require a protective strip of plastic DPC around them. Frames are normally pre-treated and primed. Once fitted, the joints between the frame edges and the walls are sealed with mastic.

Rainwater is prevented from entering under the door by means of the 'threshold', a hardwood sill positioned centrally to the underside of the door, incorporating a thin steel strip known as a 'water bar' or 'weather bar'. The threshold will need protecting against damp with a DPC strip underneath. It must also be installed at the right height in relation to the floor inside. Once fitted, timber thresholds should be

temporarily covered over until completion, to protect them from damage.

A small section of wood needs to be cut out from the bottom outer edge of your new door to form a stepped rebate so that when the door is closed it smoothly dovetails over the bar on the sill. This can be done with a circular saw.

But the metal weather bar in the sill can't keep the rain out just by itself. It needs to work in conjunction with an overhanging weatherboard projecting from the base of the front of the door. Some modern weatherboards are simply small, curved metal strips that just require screwing into place on the door.

Above: Door awaits weatherboard.

Fitting doors

New timber doors should be allowed a little time to acclimatise before fitting to minimise the risk of bowing, warping and sticking. The new door frames will have been specified to accept your precise choice of door, so theoretically it should all slip daintily into place. In actual practice, however, some planing may still be required to achieve a good fit.

As a rule, hinges should be positioned about 150mm from the top of the door and 200–225mm from the bottom. Heavier doors, particularly those containing glazing, require a third hinge, which should be placed mid-way between the two. Brass hinges are preferable since

they aren't susceptible to rust. The hinges should always be fitted to the door first, before the frame.

The new door is fitted by first being placed on some thin strips of wood to achieve a 6mm clearance between the bottom of the door and the sill, so the hinge points can be marked on the frame. This may seem rather a wide gap, but it allows for the fact that the door will tend to drop over time. A clearance gap of around 3mm at the top and sides is recommended. When any necessary trimming has been done and the hinge positions chiselled out, the door is temporarily wedged in the open position so the hinges can be screwed to the frame.

Finally, your door furniture and locks can be fitted. Mortises may need to be cut into the side of the door by drilling out and then chiselling. Timber doors should be painted or varnished soon after installation so that they don't get a chance to absorb moisture and swell.

Security

Police statistics tell us that the average British home suffers an attempted break in once every 12 years, of which more than half are successful. It's also a fact that around two-thirds of all break-ins take place through the rear of the house. But since this is the part of the property where most extensions are built, you may now have an excellent opportunity to beef up your home security. But what do burglars find at the rear of a typical house? Often it's the easiest doors to break in through – sliding patio doors and externally hinged French windows (aka 'French doors'). Patio doors are currently rather out of fashion and it's unlikely you'd be fitting new ones, but any existing ones should be fitted with special locks so they can't be lifted off their runners. If you plan to fit new French doors, specify additional bolts.

One obvious precaution with newly glazed windows and doors is to ensure that the beading that holds the glazing panels in place is fitted internally, so intruders can't simply prise it off and remove the glass from outside.

The NHBC newbuild standard is to fit 5 lever locks to all external doors (plus a cylinder rim/night latch to the main entrance door) and locks to all windows. Locks should be specified to comply with BS 3621. The easiest locks to use are mortise types with lever handles that automatically operate a latchbolt and deadbolt. To make escape easier in the event of fire, doors should be readily openable from inside without a key.

Conservatories

As noted in Chapter 3, provided they meet certain criteria, conservatories can qualify for exemption from most of the Building Regs. But regardless of how you link them up to the main house or arrange the heating, the glazing requirements of Part N will most definitely apply. For example, all critical and low-level glazing should be toughened safety glazing and, ideally, window sill heights should be minimum 800mm above floor level.

In modern homes, a large kitchen/diner is a highly desirable design feature and many new houses are built with an integral highly glazed 'conservatory' area creating a pleasant, bright, open room. So you may want to have your extension designed along these lines. Conventional conservatories can suffer from significant drawbacks (listed below), and it is always going to be a better option to build a 'proper' extension with big conservatory style windows and roof lights, than to stick a glorified prefabricated greenhouse onto the back of your house.

It is also a bit of a myth that conservatories are cheaper to build than normal extensions (unless of course they're cheap lean-tos). Furthermore they don't always add much to a property's value.

Most 'off the shelf' conservatories come ready-manufactured and are delivered from a truck, only requiring assembling on a firm, pre-prepared base. But this may not be as easy as it sounds. Apart from having to endure the hard-sell, and quite possibly paying over the odds, there are a number of important technical issues to consider:

- The cost of heating a conservatory through the winter can send your fuel bills rocketing, so building open-plan without dividing doors is not normally a good idea from a financial viewpoint. Flimsy polycarbonate plastic or sheet glass roofs will allow more than 15 times the amount of heat to escape than a normal tiled roof. From an energy efficiency perspective they provide so much 'solar gain' in summer that you may end up needing ecologically disasterous air conditioning. Roof blinds can't entirely solve the problem of unbearable levels of heat from the sun causing plastic roof panels to warp and occupants to swelter. And in winter conservatories can act as a heat sink sucking warmth out of the house.
- You'll need some kind of heating, such as an extra radiator, in which case the copper pipes should be surface run, not laid within concrete screed. Underfloor heating in polyethylene pipework is the ideal solution, but whatever the heating system it should be capable of being controlled separately from the rest of the house so that it can be set to a lower temperature or completely turned off.
- Most conservatories don't have much in the way of foundations, and may be built off nothing more than a

Photo: Potton Ltd

thin concrete floor slab, so ground movement can cause structural problems. Clay subsoil tends to shrink in dry summers and then heave up again when waterlogged in winter, making shallow conservatories something of a rollercoaster experience.
- Better-quality designs have dwarf cavity brick walls laid to normal foundation depths, upon which the superstructure is fixed. If a new conservatory is being built along with an extension it's best to build the foundations to the same depth.
- Because conservatories are relatively lightweight structures, they can suffer from a slightly scary phenomenon known as 'wind uplift'. Strong gusts of wind entering through doors or windows have been known to lift them clean off the ground. More commonly, wind pressure can build up within the structure, pushing the roof up from the inside causing the thin polycarbonate roof panels to fly away. To avoid such calamities, permanent roof ventilation should be fitted in the form of a ventilated roof ridge, to relieve the pressure.
- Finally, there's a quality-control test you can apply yourself to check the build quality of your finished conservatory. Invite your friends round and ask them each to lean heavily against different sections of the walls. If this causes any part of the conservatory to 'give', you can be fairly sure it hasn't been built strong enough!

Main trades needed on site
- **Carpenters:** Fit upper floor joists, doors, and windows.

www.home-extension.co.uk

UPPER FLOORS, WINDOWS AND DOORS

145

11 ROOFING

And now to the crowning glory of your extension. Not only will the new roof make a big design statement, but when the building finally has its 'hat' on you'll at last feel that the end of the project is in sight. You know you're on the home straight when a dark, damp shell is magically transformed into a dry, weathertight space – a home in the making. To mark the occasion in style, you may even find an excuse to enjoy a little celebration as the final roof tile is placed – the traditional 'topping out ceremony'.

First, there's the small matter of constructing one of the most complex parts of the build. Not only will it have to look good and perform well, it also has the added complexity of needing to marry up neatly with your existing building.

For most extensions there's a simple choice of roof styles: pitched or flat. Strictly speaking, a pitched roof is defined as one with a slope steeper than 10°, although in reality 17.5° is about the shallowest slope some roof coverings can manage. Flat roofs have something of a patchy reputation technically and are only likely to be permitted for single-storey extensions. There are, however, some intriguing possibilities that mix and match the two styles. You could opt for part-flat and part-pitched. Or perhaps an ultra-shallow lead-clad roof.

On the ground, the most obvious sign that your project is entering a major new phase will be the change of personnel on site, with the bricklayer handing over to the carpenter, shortly to be followed by the roofers.

The first thing the carpenter will need to check is that the building has so far been constructed square and that it's level on all sides at the wall plates, not forgetting to ensure that the scaffolding has been safely installed up to roof lift.

Even if you've succeeded in getting the roofing works scheduled for the (hopefully) dry summer months, it's

always wise to ensure that tarpaulins are at hand, to protect the building in the event of a sudden downpour.

If you're planning to employ your own roofing contractors, it's worth remembering that roofing is a trade that has a reputation for attracting rogue operators. Cowboy roofers tend to pop up after severe storms offering 'maintenance services'. They know that, safely out of sight, all manner of botched jobs can be carried out with impunity. So look for firms registered with the National Federation of Roofing Contractors (NFRC), who provide an independent warranty. Go and view some of their previous jobs and check out details like the neatness of pointing to verges and mortar bedding to ridge tiles. This is a good test, since messy pointing tends to be indicative of slap-dash workmanship. Always discuss the materials to be used with the roofer in advance, and try to inspect the work as it progresses, when it's safe and convenient to do so.

Safety and scaffolding

Roofs need to be treated with respect. Never try to carry out work in windy or poor weather conditions. On isolated sites, it's advisable not to do roof work alone.

A high proportion of building site accidents arise from poor erection of scaffolding or temporary work platforms. This should normally be the responsibility of the main contractor. Because of the real danger of serious injury and fatalities, scaffolding is the subject of much health and safety legislation. To help weed out cowboy scaffolding firms, it's worth quoting this little phrase when confirming instructions in writing:

'The scaffolding shall be erected and maintained in accordance with BS 5973 and 5974 "Access & working scaffolds and special scaffold structures in steel" and The Construction (Health, Safety & Welfare) Regulations 1996.'

Pitched roofs

As everyone knows, the basic structure of a roof takes the form of a simple triangle. The two main roof slopes meet on top at the ridge, whilst the base of the triangle is formed by the ceiling joists acting as collars.

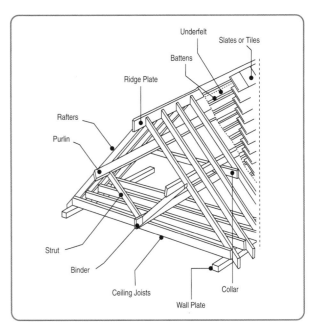

Roof slopes are constructed with timber rafters. Depending on the roof span (*ie* how wide it is) these are typically made from 100 x 50 mm timbers ('four by twos') which are typically spaced 400mm or 600mm apart. The tops of the rafters meet at a horizontal timber ridge plate that runs along the top of the roof. At their feet the rafters are fixed to the timber wall plates (the wooden beams running along the top of the walls). To stop the rafters spreading and pushing the walls outwards, they are tied together by the ceiling joists.

This describes a traditional custom built 'cut' roof structure. However, most roofs today are constructed using factory-manufactured 'trussed rafters'. The question is, are ready-made, standard-sized roof trusses likely to be at all suitable for your individually designed home extension?

Trussed rafters

The roofs of most new houses have been built from prefabricated trussed rafters since the 1970s. Because some can span over 7m without needing extra support from internal structural walls there are big potential savings elsewhere in the build. Although they're relatively expensive they're quick and easy to install, with additional savings on labour costs – except, of course, in non-standard designs, like most home extensions. Here your carpenter might have to spend a considerable amount of time customising them to fit, pushing *up* the labour costs, possibly making them uneconomic. In fact trusses should not be modified on site without authorisation, as cutting bits off can drastically weaken the structure.

When trusses are first delivered they need careful handling to prevent damage. They must be stacked well clear of the ground on bearers and sheltered from the weather. Building the roof is essentially an assembly operation, but because some larger trusses can weigh 30–40kg lifting them into position at a great height is no mean feat, requiring cranes to be hired. Once the trusses are lined up, they can all be connected together with binders and straps, and twice skew-nailed to the timber wall plate.

Another drawback of conventional trussed rafters is that the resulting loft space cannot easily be used for living

accommodation due to the intricate network of struts and bracing timbers. Trussed rafters in themselves are rather weedy looking things, held together with primitive metal connecting plates. So to beef them up extra bracing is now required as a result of some early un-braced examples collapsing spectacularly. This means a number of additional horizontal and diagonal 100 x 25mm timber strips and binders need to be nailed in place.

Straps and clips

We've already encountered 'restraint straps', used to anchor down the timber wall plates that run along the tops of the walls (see Chapter 9). The wall plate defines the point where the roof structure sits on the house. Without such measures to secure roofs, severe gales have caused roofs to fly off, a phenomenon known as 'wind uplift'.

But straps have other uses. 'Lateral restraint straps' are fixed horizontally, tying in the roof timbers to gable or party

Ends of lateral 'L' straps built into blockwork inner leaf.

walls, as well as being fitted lower down the structure, at ceiling and first floor levels. Each horizontal restraint strap should be secured across at least two rafters with plated screws (as well as being fixed to timber noggins or packing strips between the rafters) and downturned tight against the inner leaf blockwork. It's the bricklayer's job to build the lateral restraint straps into the cavity of the walls at rafter, ceiling and first floor levels, rather than regarding them as an optional extra – which makes this a good test of a competent tradesman. The straps are left ready for the chippie to screw to the rafters or joists.

As well as needing extra bracing, roofs built from trussed rafters also require small metal 'truss clips' to secure the trusses to the wall plates below. Then there are special 'vertical anchor straps' with distinctive twisted necks designed to tie the rafter feet of the trusses to the wall below.

Cut roofs

Because of the relatively small size of most home extensions, and the need to custom-build the new roof where it joins up to the existing house, traditional 'cut'

roofs are widely used. Here, the carpenter cuts all the various timber components to length on site. It's important this is done in accordance with your approved drawings and structural calculations, which will have taken into account all possible anticipated loadings, such as from heavy roof tiles, severe gusts of wind and drifting snow etc.

A traditional cut roof with two main roof slopes is known as a 'close coupled roof', essentially comprising two lean-to roofs leaning against each other.

Erecting the roof

One of the most perilous parts of your entire project is now about to begin. The skeleton of the extension roof first takes shape with a horizontal timber ridge board placed in position forming the highest part of the roof structure. This is attached at one end to the existing house, and at the other end to a highly trained volunteer holding it up in thin air! This provides the carpenters with a few short moments to carefully position the first rafters to take the load. The carpenters can now complete the roof structure, filling in all the missing rafters and ceiling joists. At this point you might want to quickly check that the

degree of pitch as built matches that shown on your plans.

The rafters are typically spaced 400mm apart and rest at their base on the timber wall plate. So that they're securely connected, a small V-shaped cut known as a 'birdsmouth' is made, joining neatly to the wall plate. At the top they're nailed to the ridge board.

But the job's not over yet. In larger roofs, additional support may be required about halfway up the rafters in the form of large horizontal 'purlins'. The problem with purlins is that traditionally they often needed to be propped up in turn with timber struts, and the load transferred to internal load-bearing walls. Not only was this expensive (requiring the building of 'structural' walls) but it took up valuable space. So today large RSJ steels are often used as purlins, which don't need any extra support.

A currently popular traditional-looking design might feature low roof slopes swooping down around bedroom dormer windows. Inside, the first floor rooms encroach into the roof space so that the ceilings slope around the edges of the rooms. Here you'll often find the rafters strengthened with steel purlins above the ceilings.

It's often been said that a good roof structure is a work of art, so it seems a shame to hide it behind great big sheets of plasterboard. Given that you're paying for a skilled carpenter to custom-build the roof at considerable expense, why obliterate all that craftsmanship behind ceilings? Your designer may have already recognised the potential for a bit of 'wow factor' here, leaving some of the structure on display for all to admire – in which case you'll need to take special measures with the insulation (see below). If your chippie is really good he might even be working on a traditional 'kingpost' roof structure, the perfect backdrop to that suit of armour and stag's-head trophy you've always promised yourself !

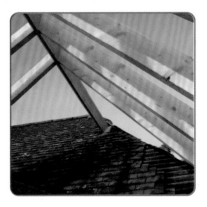

Lean-to roofs

The most common type of roof for a typical small ground-floor extension is the simple lean-to. This is just a single-slope 'mono pitch' roof where the tops of the rafters are propped up against the wall of the main house. Construction involves first bolting a horizontal strip of timber to the wall of the existing house, onto which the tops of the lean-to rafters are secured. At the bottom they connect to the timber wall plate on top of the main walls. As described earlier, the ceiling joists prevent them pushing out the walls. If your new extension has a gable end wall or, in the case of a lean-to roof, half a gable, then it may be only once the rafters are in place that the brickie will be able to finish building up the gable end wall. So don't be too hasty writing out that big cheque – you may still be due a return visit.

Hipped roofs

If you like pyramids this is the style for you. Instead of just having two roof slopes propped up against each other and a brick gable filling in the space at the end, hipped roofs have a third roof slope. Hips were especially popular on 1930s houses.

However, hips are more complicated to construct than a bog-standard 'close coupled' design. The difficulty is that the carpenter needs to make a lot of tricky angled cuts to all the different-sized 'jack rafters' near the angled hip corners where the three roof slopes meet. The corners themselves are made from special 'hip rafters', usually clad with round 'hip tiles' (similar to ridge tiles) or with perkily upturned 'bonnet tiles'. Due to their weight, hip tiles normally need a protruding metal strip called a 'hip iron' at their base, to discourage any loose ones from slipping off and maiming innocent passers-by. Neatest of all are 'close mitred hips' where the tiles either side are precision cut to meet over a hidden lead soaker, creating an 'invisible' join.

Felt and underlay

Roofs should have a secondary barrier beneath the tiles to keep out severe weather. This defence against wind driven rain getting under the tiles has traditionally comprised a layer of thick felt, used in most new housing since the 1950s. But the days of heavy, bitumen-soaked hessian underlay, drooping ponderously between damp rafters, are now long gone. Today, modern high performance lightweight roofing felts such as those made by 'Klober' and 'Tyvec' are normally specified. Rather like high-tech mountaineering clothing, these 'breathable membranes' cleverly prevent rainwater from getting in, yet allow water vapour to escape outwards from the loft by permeating

through the material. They are thinner yet tougher than the old felt, which was always prone to being ripped and torn on installation. Most important of all, modern underlay doesn't rot.

As soon as the basic roof structure is complete the felt can be installed (unless you want to insulate it first – see below). It is secured to the rafters with treated softwood roofing battens, starting near the bottom at the eaves and working upwards. An overlap of at least 100mm must be allowed where one sheet joins another. This has the advantage of swiftly providing a temporary waterproof cover so work can proceed in relative comfort down below.

In Scotland the rules are different. Rafters must first be covered with rigid 'sarking boards', a traditional form of timber cladding.

Battens

Tiles are hung from rough-sawn wooden battens running horizontally across the rafters. Battens help increase the lateral stability of the roof structure, which is especially important for trussed rafter roofs. To preserve their strength, the joints between lengths of battens should be staggered, and the smallest battens should span across at least three rafters.

Batten sizes are typically 32 x 19mm where the rafters are spaced no further than 450mm apart. Thicker 32 x 25mm battens are used where the rafters are spaced at up to 600mm centres.

The battens can't be finally nailed down until you've calculated the precise spacing between the rows, which will depend on the size and lap of the slates or tiles and the pitch of the roof. Tile manufacturers can normally assist if you provide them with the appropriate measurements.

Spacing your battens

- Starting at the top, first work out the position of the highest batten. This is normally fixed so that the ridge tile on top will overlap it by at least 75mm.
- Next establish the position of the lowest batten at the bottom of the roof slope. Here you want the lowest tiles, known as 'the eaves course', to project outwards above the centre of the guttering, so work back from this point to locate the necessary batten position.
- The trickiest part is calculating how many battens are needed in between the top and bottom ones. Measure the distance between the top and bottom battens, and transfer this to the ground and do a dry run, laying the tiles out as they would be on the roof.
- You need to calculate the 'gauge', which is the distance from the centre of one batten to the centre of the next. To do this, apply the magic formula: Maximum gauge = length of tile – its minimum lap (minimum lap is the manufacturer's recommended amount of overlap to cover the head of one tile by the tail of the one above). You're allowed to increase this gap slightly, bringing the battens closer together, but you must not reduce it, otherwise it will risk rain being driven underneath the tiles by strong winds. As a rough guide, the lap rarely exceeds a quarter of the length of a tile.
- It's not over yet. To calculate the actual number of spaces to leave between each row of battens, divide the overall distance between the top and bottom battens by the maximum gauge. If it's not an exact number, increase it to the next whole number. The number of battens needed (in addition to the top and bottom ones) will be the same as the number of spaces, less one.

Cold roof, warm roof

The conventional way to insulate a loft is to lay about 250mm depth of mineral wool or fibreglass quilt between (and over) the ceiling joists to achieve the required U value of 0.16. This means the roof space above is left cold, with a cross-flow of air from the eaves dispersing any rogue condensation and damp. This is known as a 'cold-roof'.

But increasingly, extension designers trying to make the best use of the limited available space need the bedrooms to encroach into the roof space. Normally, the tops of the walls should rise at least 1.5m above the bedroom floor level before meeting the sloped ceiling. But so that loft rooms don't become freezing damp garrets, the insulation needs to be moved higher up to rafter level. This is then known as a 'warm roof' and can be achieved by fitting polyurethane foam boards between (or on top of, or below) the rafters. A typical arrangement might be to fit 90mm Celotex boards between the rafters of the sloping ceilings around the bedrooms, plus another 25mm underneath. But you normally need to leave a clear air gap of at least 50mm above the insulation and below the tiles and underlay, which could be a little tricky if you've just stuffed your rafters with foam boards. The solution is 'counter-battening'. Here, the height of the rafters is raised by nailing an additional timber batten down the line of each rafter, once sheets of insulation board have first been laid across them (or between them). This not only holds the insulation in place on top of the rafters, but creates a ventilated air space above to prevent any build up of damaging dampness from condensation.

In recent years, a lot of roofers have rather uncharacteristically come over all 'hi-tech' in the insulation department. After all, why mess about with clunking great insulation boards and itchy mineral wool when it's easier to lay large sheets of thin 'Bacofoil and Kleenex' over the rafters. These shiny 'radiant heat barriers' are a fairly recent innovation, and despite being only 20 to 30mm thickness they can provide the equivalent of 210mm loft quilt insulation.

Once the insulation sheets have been laid over the rafters and secured by counter-battens, the breather-membrane underlay sheets are then spread over the top, held in place by conventional horizontal battens on to which the tiles or slates are hung.

If you're converting an existing loft, the insulated boarding can be fixed internally to the underside of the rafters, before being lined with plasterboard incorporating a vapour barrier. N.B. Some local authorities may not accept certain brands of 'radiant heat barrier' insulation – so check with Building Control at the design stage.

Ventilation

Once upon a time the subject of ventilation was not taken too seriously by the building trade. Today, however, the Building Regulations regard such matters very seriously. Damp from condensation can ultimately rot timbers, so having a decent amount of insulation as well as a good cross-flow of ventilation are key to preventing damage.

Your roof design must therefore incorporate an effective method of passing air through the roof space. This is conventionally done with vents in the soffits under the eaves (equivalent to a 10mm continuous gap along their full length) on opposite sides of the building. If you're building a 'room in the roof' design, this eaves air gap needs to be increased to 25mm, and ventilated ridge tiles provided at the top of the roof, in order to get a good draught flow running through the 50mm air space above the insulation. The good

news is that if you've specified an appropriate 'breathable' membrane instead of traditional roofing felt you may not have to worry about all that expensive ventilation work at the eaves and ridges, although counter battening is still normally needed to provide a continuous air gap.

However, if Building Control still insist on a conventionally ventilated roof, achieving the required 'through-flow' of air may not be so easy with lean-to extensions. Being propped up against the wall of the main house these obviously haven't got eaves on opposite sides of the roof. So instead, you could fit special roof tiles or slates with inbuilt vents rather than ugly 'mushroom vents' sprouting from the upper roof surface. These will allow air entering at the eaves to flow up through the roof and out again. Vented ridge tiles or roof tiles can also make useful outlets for soil stacks and extractor fans. Alternatively, if your design has gable ends, or small 'half-gables' either side of a lean-to roof, then extra ventilation can be provided via a vertical I-shaped slot, which can look quite fetching in a churchy kind of way, or perhaps a terracotta airbrick in each gable. But be sure to fit insect mesh over vents unless you relish the prospect of playing host to swarms of wasps, birds or bats.

Support to water tanks

It's unlikely that you're going to need to fit a new cold water tank in the extension loft, unless your old one is totally shot. But in case you do, the point to note is just how heavy water tanks can be. A typical main tank full of water weighs 250kg, equivalent to three fully-grown adults standing above your bedroom ceiling. Clearly the roof design must be able to handle this load. Thick timber bearers should be spread over at least three ceiling joists and any internal load-bearing walls used to support some of the load. The deck should be of exterior grade plywood rather than chipboard.

Joining it up – valleys and flashings

Where a new roof joins with the existing one at right angles, the roofers will first need to strip the tiles or slates from your existing roof to expose the structure around the area to be joined, so that new valleys can be formed. Valleys are found where one pitched roof joins another at an internal angle (so you shouldn't need to worry about them for most single-storey extensions or where simply building out from a side gable).

If your old roof isn't underfelted, which is perfectly normal in many older houses, you'll be left with precisely zero weather protection at this stage, so tarpaulins should be kept handy to prevent pouring rain and clouds of dust intruding into bedrooms and bathrooms below. If you can schedule the roofing process for the dryer summer months so much the better – just don't assume it won't rain!

Having stripped the tiles from the immediate part of the old roof, new timber 'valley boards' (or 'layerboards') are

Cutting & fixing a lead flashing.

Three different new extension roofs joining to the existing roofs.

accurately cut (mitred) to butt up against each other. Below the join runs a special lead-lined valley known as a 'soaker'. This achieves an almost invisible join that's not so prone to blockage with leaves etc. Your choice of valley will largely be determined by the design of your existing roof, and the type of tiles or slate coverings.

then nailed diagonally to the existing rafters, creating valleys where the two roofs meet. Your structural engineer will have considered whether the existing roof timbers are likely to need any additional support as a result of the extra load imposed on them.

Before tiling can start, a lead lining is laid over each valley board in strips no longer than 1.5m and a minimum of 100mm wide. The lead used should be 'code 4' or thicker 'code 5'. The strip higher up should be lapped over the one below by at least 150mm (225mm for shallow roofs of less than 30°). Modern fibreglass (GRP) valley linings and flashings are a cheaper alternative to traditional lead and easier to fix, although good old-fashioned lead is considered superior. Traditional 'open valleys' such as these

Coverings

The planners will have already taken a keen interest in your choice of roof coverings, possibly even requiring you to submit samples for approval before starting on site. But whatever materials you choose, there's a good chance that you'll want them to match your existing ones as closely as possible. However, new plain clay tiles can sometimes successfully complement an original slate roof, or vice versa. For some extension designs, modern artificial slates may look perfectly suitable adjoining a main house clad in old natural slate.

But good looks aren't everything. There are important technical factors to consider when choosing roof coverings. Some may not be suitable for use on modest,

have the adjoining tiles or slates cut around them, with any gaps along the sides of the valley pointed up with mortar.

Lead is notoriously prone to expansion, and needs to be carefully nailed so as not to restrict thermal movement which will cause it to crack. Special copper or stainless steel clout nails are used since they don't react with lead.

But there's more than one type of valley. A more desirable arrangement than using 'open valleys' is to fit purpose-made 'swept' valley tiles on plain tile roofs, very popular on 1930s houses. These are less prone to maintenance problems over time. Another traditional method, similar to an open valley, is the 'mitred valley'. Here the tiles at the facing edges of the valley are

PLAIN TILES

Plain tiles are rectangular and slightly curved to assist water discharge off the roof. They are available both in natural clay and manufactured concrete.

Sizes: A typical size would be 265 x 165mm. But being fairly small, the pitch of plain-tiled roofs cannot normally be much less than 35°.
Coverage: Only around 60 to the square metre.
Lap: Typically 65mm+.

The amount of nailing required to tiles depends on the pitch of the roof, and how heavy the tiles are. Normally only every fourth or fifth course might need to be nailed. But in exposed windy areas every tile may need nailing, as they do for some steeper pitched roof slopes above 45°.

PANTILES

Pantiles are traditional large tiles of Dutch origin with a wavy S-shaped profile, traditionally popular in the counties around East Anglia.

Sizes: Typically range between 342 x 252mm and 406 x 330mm.
Coverage: About 15 tiles per sq m.
Lap: Typically around 75mm.

Like plain tiles, pantiles are hung by their nibs but are lighter (per square metre) and can be laid to a shallower pitch – some as low as 22.5°. They are relatively quick and easy to lay. Pantiles overlap with each other at their sides, and so only need one short lap from the row above (single-lap).

INTERLOCKING CONCRETE TILES

One of the most cost-effective roofing materials, these low-profile tiles are similar to traditional Roman tiles and are quick and easy to lay. They are single-lap, with consequent savings on labour and battens.

Sizes: Typically 380 x 230mm or 420 x 334mm.
Coverage: 10 tiles per sq m.
Lap: Typically 75mm+.

Constructed from coloured concrete, some can be laid to a very shallow 17.5°, but they can look clumsy. The interlocking sides provide weather resistance without needing extensive overlapping like plain tiles, so the weight over an area is lower. However, they are considerably heavier than slates. Cheaper than plain tiles they work well at low pitch angles and in exposed locations. Worth considering where they match the original coverings to your property.

NATURAL SLATES

Natural slate is one of the most hardwearing of all roofing materials, being lightweight, frost resistant and durable, with a lifespan well in excess of a hundred years.

Photo: David Snell

Sizes: A 'Countess' is the traditional 512 x 255mm standard size, along with the 560 x 305mm 'Small Duchess'.
Coverage: Typically 18 per sq m.
Lap: Typically 65mm.

Some can be laid to a shallow 20° degrees or less. Unlike tiles, which are normally hooked over the battens, slates need to be nailed through two holes, either in their centres or their heads (tops). Nails are usually of copper or aluminium. They're typically treble-lapped, and laid in different grades of thickness, starting with the thinnest on top. Natural Welsh slate is the ideal covering, but is relatively expensive. Reclaimed slate is a good compromise as are new imported Canadian ones although the quality of some Chinese or Spanish slates can be patchy.

ARTIFICIAL SLATES

Modern artificial slates are a popular, cheaper alternative to natural slate and can look authentic. They are made from composite fibre and cement, or moulded with a mixture of 80 per cent slate dust and glass fibre resin.

Sizes: Typically 360 x 340 mm.
Coverage: Typically 12 per sq m.
Lap: Typically about 75mm.

They can be laid to a very shallow pitch, some as low as 15°, and most are lighter even than real slate. Some are manufactured with interlocking sides to create an easy-to-lay single-lapped roof. Now often the budget material of choice.

STONE SLATES

These are actually not slates at all, just heavy slabs of natural stone, in fairly irregular sizes. The most expensive of all roof coverings, stone slates are commonly seen in areas like the Cotswolds and the Pennines. For those working to a budget, it may be worth investigating modern artificial concrete moulded imitations.

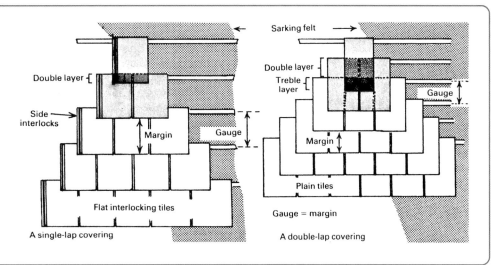

Single-lap tiles are made with interlocking side grooves. Double-lap slates and plain tiles do not have these grooves, and need to attain a treble thickness at their heads to keep out the rain. This necessitates many more battens.

Double layer

Side interlocks

Margin

Gauge

Flat interlocking tiles

A single-lap covering

Sarking felt

Double layer

Treble layer

Gauge

Margin

Plain tiles

Gauge = margin

A double-lap covering

shallow-pitched roofs. And when comparing the pros and cons of tiles or slates, their weight is another key factor to bear in mind. The loading they impose on the structure must be carefully considered at the design stage.

The lap factor

One crucial piece of information when selecting coverings is the amount of 'lap' required, ie how much the heads (tops) of one row of tiles or slates need to be covered by the tails (bottoms) of the row above in order to successfully keep the weather where it belongs, on the outside.

As far as the lap factor is concerned, there are basically two kinds of products – 'single-lap' and 'double-lap'. Deciding which type to use will dramatically affect not only the weight of your roof, but also the cost of labour to build it.

Traditional 'double-lap' coverings like plain tiles and natural slates can't be overlapped at their sides, so the only way to cover the joints between them is to overlap them from above. They are traditionally laid in rows (courses), starting at the bottom of the roof slope and working upwards. The vertical joints being staggered, like the bonding of brickwork. To keep out the rain at the joints between tiles in the same row, each gap must be covered by the tile above it and protected underneath by the tile below. This means that at certain points there'll actually be three layers, a triple thickness, which in turn necessitates using a lot of battens.

If this sounds like hard work, you're right. It's a lot easier to fix modern 'single-lap' tiles or artificial slates, specially designed with grooves at the sides so they can 'interlock', overlapping each other sideways. This means only a short single lap over the head of each tile is needed to make

them instantly watertight, resulting in a much quicker job requiring fewer battens.

But whatever type of tiles or slates you choose, the amount of lap is generally less on a steep roof (of more than about 45°) because the rain will run off more quickly. On shallow roofs, the rainwater runs slower and tends to 'fan out', getting under the edges, so a greater lap is needed. Lower down near the eaves, the pitch is sometimes made shallower in order to slow the rainwater for a safe landing into the gutter.

Another problem with modest slopes is that the flatter the roof pitch, the more risk there is of 'wind uplift' allowing wind-driven rain to penetrate under tiles – hence the need for a greater lap. It's important to ensure that the correct size and type of tile has been selected for the angle of pitch and laid to the correct lap, or else rainwater may well track-back underneath. Manufacturers can provide comprehensive information. To top it all off neatly, special purpose-made tiles are also available for ridges, hips and verges.

Blending in

Most of us don't want our new extensions to stick out like Blackfriars Heliport. But getting a new roof to blend in

naturally with an old one requires a fair bit of care and thought, especially when building to the front of the house. Nothing is guaranteed to make your extension look more glaringly obvious than vast expanses of shiny new roof tiles sitting self-consciously next to the mature, subtly shaded and weathered old roof. But how to instantly tone down those dazzling, bright new tiles?

There are those who claim that the natural weathering process can be speeded up by spraying your new roof tiles with liquid fertiliser. These are probably the same people who swear by other slightly dubious instant-ageing concepts, such as painting fresh stonework with organic yoghurt to help it 'acclimatise', or coating new brickwork with boiling linseed oil for a supposedly better match with existing brickwork. Fortunately, if you prefer not to become the laughing stock of the entire neighbourhood, there's a more reliable solution. Because achieving exact colour matches using new tiles can be an impossible task, one obvious remedy is to instead use matching old ones. You might well ask 'Where do I find those?' Easy – by simply stripping a suitable number of tiles or slates from your existing rear roof slope, the front can be clad to perfection, the rear roof slope then being reclad with the new coverings. You'll be amazed at the results.

If using reclaimed materials from your own house or from any other source, always be sure to remove any broken, cracked or frost damaged tiles or slates. Alternatively, if you find that your old roof is actually on the way out it may be cost-effective to carry out a complete re-roofing job, as much of the necessary labour and scaffolding will already be on site.

Slates or tiles?
Tiles, in all their many varieties and styles, comprise the majority of British roof coverings. A quick zoom back in time a couple of centuries would find many roofs clad with handmade plain clay tiles secured with small timber pegs (known as 'peg tiles'). Lightweight natural slate roofs became pretty much universal in Victorian times until manufactured plain clay tiles with projecting 'nibs' took centre stage during the Edwardian era persisting into the 1930s as the roof covering of choice. The advent of

cheaper manufactured concrete tiles and easy-to-lay interlocking tiles has ensured their continuing popularity in more recent years. Today, natural slate and clay tiles are relatively expensive, and similar looking cheaper alternatives such as artificial slate are widely used. The problem with some concrete tiles is that after about 10 years they can start to look rather washed out – one reason you never find them in salvage yards. Clay is at least 25 per cent more expensive than concrete, but it's often worth paying the extra for a quality product. The dearest coverings tend to be stone slates, natural Welsh slate, handmade clay tiles and thatch.

Ridge and hip tiles
The most exposed part of the roof is at the very top – at the ridge. This therefore needs to be well protected and waterproofed, which is traditionally done by being capped with special half-round or angled ridge tiles bedded in mortar. Hipped roofs have similar hip tiles laid along the 'corners' of the side roof slope. However, over the years the bedding mortar can become loose, allowing storms to dislodge them – and being hit by a flying ridge tile is no joke. Modern 'dry-ridge' tiles have overcome this problem by using special screws and fixing wires that tie them to the ridge timbers below. Some incorporate vents to enhance airflow within the loft space.

If you're of an artistic persuasion, this could be the perfect opportunity to embellish your design – by topping off the roof with an antique cast iron finial or a glorious terracotta crest. Salvage yards may stock some irresistible reclaimed items.

Verges
The verges are the side edges of a gabled roof or a lean-to. They typically project about 50mm over the wall, the end roof tiles being tilted up slightly in order to keep rainwater away from the edges. This is achieved by wedging an extra layer of tiles called an 'undercloak' underneath the batten ends (slates or cement fibre sheets are also used).

The verges are traditionally pointed up with mortar and often decorated with a wooden bargeboard fixed underneath or perhaps

some fancy 'dog's tooth' brickwork. However, the exposed mortar pointing often develop cracks or erodes over time. A modern 'dry-fix' alternative uses plastic cover strips secured with clips, or special one-piece tiles called 'cloaked verges' that wrap over the edges. The only snag is that modern maintenance-free materials may not be architecturally appropriate on extensions to older buildings.

To achieve a neat finish at the verges, the rows of tiles at the edges require specially wide 'tile-and-a-half' tiles on every other row. Similarly, to complete the roof at the bottom edge along the eaves, shorter 'eaves tiles' are used. These bottom rows of tiles are then raised or 'kicked up' with tapered wooden fillets fixed over the joist ends, in order to slow the speed of rainwater.

The roofline – eaves, fascias, soffits and bargeboards

The term 'roofline' refers to the detailing at the edges of roofs – *ie* at the feet of the rafters and at the verges.

There's no question that the external walls of a building are better protected from the weather if there's a certain amount of roof overhang, and this presents an interesting architectural opportunity to give the building some real character. So at the design stage, quite a bit of thought will have gone into choosing one of the various possible decorative facings around the roof's perimeter. The style that you finally plump for here will have a marked effect on the final appearance of your extension.

Fascia boards are horizontal boards of timber or UPVC that run along the eaves at the feet of the rafters, or they may sometimes be fixed directly to the brickwork. Normally the rafter feet project out beyond the main walls, so the roof overhangs the walls by between 50 and 200mm. The most widely adopted standard eaves style in housing since the

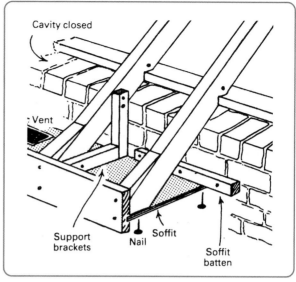

The overhang offered by a box eaves design helps to protect the brickwork below.

1930s has been 'box eaves'. Here, a traditional fascia board is fixed along the ends of the projecting rafters, in turn supporting the guttering. This leaves a gap underneath which is filled with a strip of plywood (or an asbestos cement) soffit, making a box shape, hence the name. The soffit closes off this entrance to the roof void, yet provides ventilation, for example with small vents fitted at intervals.

Today, however, some significant changes are afoot. There's currently a distinct preference for more traditional eaves methods. So you may instead opt for your projecting rafter feet to be left quite naked, and not to be boxed-in at all. Consequently, in order to prevent a mass influx of birds, wasps and creepy crawlies into your loft, the bricklayer will need to fill any gaps between the rafter feet on top of the wall, and any necessary loft ventilation must be provided with insect-proof wire mesh. A sheet of plywood is laid above the lower rafters, and gutter brackets can be fixed direct to the rafter feet.

There's another traditional eaves style that can also create a roof overhang without the need for any timber fascia boarding. If you're adding on to a Victorian house, you may want to match the decorative brickwork eaves. Here the upper wall brickwork is 'corbelled' in a projecting pattern, perhaps with protruding bricks alternately stepped outwards.

Bargeboards are similar to fascias, but instead run along the edges of gable roofs, under the verges. But once again you're confronted with various options. Most modern

houses simply leave the plain pointed up verges projecting over the wall, although the brickwork detailing below needs to be very carefully finished. Some designs may better suit fancy 'Victorian' brick corbelling under the verges, as described above. Otherwise simple bargeboards fixed to the brickwork can look just right. Or you might want to make a bold design statement and build your roof verges projecting assertively over the gable end wall with big overhanging 'Edwardian' bargeboards. If so, you'll first need to answer an important technical question, namely how do you prevent the overhang drooping and sagging under the weight of the tiles? Fortunately the Edwardians had a ready answer, which was to build a gable 'ladder'.

When the overhang reaches more than about 150mm the structure needs beefing up, so to extend the roof outwards rows of timber noggins are placed across the gable end wall like rungs in a ladder. On the inside, these are fixed to the end rafter, and on the outside to the new outermost external rafter. The decorative bargeboards can

then be fixed to this outer rafter.

Fascias and bargeboards are commonly made from 25mm thick timber. When extending an older property timber can be the best choice architecturally. But exposed or unprotected roof timbers need regular decorative weather protection to stop them rotting and to preserve their appearance. So builders will often fit 'maintenance-free' UPVC fascias, bargeboards and soffits secured with special stainless steel fixing nails, which can be disguised with small coloured plastic caps to match the colour of the board (usually white). Pre-moulded soffits should incorporate ventilation grilles. If you don't like decorating but want the look of real wood, then cedar is a more expensive compromise since it is naturally weather resistant and doesn't require painting or staining.

Dormer windows

Rooms built into roof spaces often have dormer windows projecting through the roof slopes. Dormers can be set back slightly, with the timber frame structure built up from the rafters or floor joists with a framework of upright timber studs. Alternatively, they can be built straight up from the wall below, Victorian style. The dormer sides are known as 'cheeks' and are traditionally clad in lead sheet, or else hung with tiles. At the junctions to the roof it's common to have 'soakers' hidden under the tiles. Like valleys, these 'secret gutters' are formed from strips of sheet lead.

Flat roofs

If you fancy the idea of stepping out of your bedroom on sunny mornings to enjoy a spot of breakfast on your private roof terrace, then why not put that flat roof to good use enhancing your lifestyle? Assuming the planners haven't already torpedoed such an idea, there are however some key differences between building a standard flat roof and one that's 'habitable'. To be fit for purpose, the designer will need to carefully consider matters like the type of surface treatment, the strength of the supporting structure, and how best to stop friends and family plummeting off the edges.

Timber 'firings' fixed above joists create the required roof fall.

Flat roofs are, of course, not actually flat. By definition, anything up to a 10° pitch counts as flat. In fact they need to be built with a decent 'fall' because the slow rate at which rainwater discharges from the surface poses a greater threat to this type of roof than to a pitched one. The steeper the slope, the greater the self-cleansing effect as rainwater passes over its surface. The Building Regulations encourage a minimum fall of 1:40, but that hasn't stopped some roofers actually building them totally flat. If built correctly however, rainwater should discharge efficiently into the gutters without stopping en route to cause damaging 'ponding' on the surface.

Hitting the deck

Flat roofs have had something of a bad press in recent years. Lifespans can be alarmingly short, perhaps only ten years or less. But if built with care, using the correct materials, they can perform perfectly well. Construction involves two main elements – the supporting structure, and a protective covering.

When building a new flat roof structure, the joists spanning from wall to wall are actually set perfectly level, so that the ceiling below will also be level. To create the required fall for the decking, tapered strips of timber the same width as the joists, called 'firings', are nailed along the tops of the joists (timber merchants can supply firings cut to the correct fall).

But before ordering your roof joists, you first need to consider the required size, grade and length (which should already be specified in your plans). Common joist sizes are 200 x 50mm, 175 x 50mm, and 150 x 50mm.

Where a new flat roofed extension (normally single storey) meets the existing house, a horizontal timber wall plate is first bolted to the wall of the house. Metal joist hangers can then be secured to this wall plate, and the ceiling joists slotted in to the hangers. The joists will span to the outer wall of the extension, normally spaced apart at either 400mm or 600mm centres. The precise dimensions of joists and their respective spacings will have been calculated according to the loads imposed on them.

As with pitched roofs, the support structure joists rest on timber wall plates on the tops of the main walls.

To complete the structure, a deck of 18mm or 25mm thick marine grade plywood is then laid over the joists and secured with galvanised nails. Ordinary chipboard is not recommended as it can disintegrate when damp. To keep rainwater from spilling over the edges, the sides of the roof surface are built up slightly with triangular pieces of timber called 'tilt fillets' nailed to the edges of the decking (except, of course, for the lowest edge where the guttering is). A protective covering, normally mineral felt, is laid on top once any necessary insulation has been placed on top of the decking. Try not to leave too long a time before the naked decking is covered, or it will need to be protected from rain with temporary sheets.

Coverings

When specifying flat roof coverings, the designer will need to consider key factors such as whether anyone is likely to be walking on the structure, as well as taking account of the direction the property faces, since south-facing roofs are more likely to fail early.

Historically, flat roofs, such as in the timber decks of sailing ships, were waterproofed using asphalt, a black, gooey, bitumen-based substance. It occurs naturally in liquid form (in asphalt lakes etc) or can be distilled from some types of limestone rocks and shale, or manufactured from petroleum distillation. Tar is a compound with similar properties produced by the distillation of coal or wood (or cigarettes).

The cheapest and most common covering material for domestic flat roofs is roofing felt, normally laid in triple layers bonded together, and to the deck, with hot bitumen tar. But working with asphalt, tar or bitumen has its dangers. There are potential skin cancer risks from persistent exposure on site unless protective clothing and gloves are worn. And as if that wasn't bad enough, care

must be taken to avoid the risk of nasty burns. So keep your distance when scolding bitumen or tar is being laid.

One major reason for felt roofs having a short lifespan results from the effect of the sun's heat on such dark surfaces. This can be intense, effectively cooking the felt in summer and freezing it in winter. The continual expansion and contraction this causes is very damaging, so felt roofs need protection. This is often achieved with a solar-reflective finishing layer of white mineral chippings. The snag is that invariably the wind blows these away unless securely bedded in hot bitumen, so you may end up with more chippings in the guttering than on the roof itself. Also, the chippings cannot be walked-on as they could puncture the surface. One alternative is for flat roofs to instead be painted with bright silver solar-reflective paint, which helps protect them from the effects of ultraviolet radiation.

Today, however, much of this work can be avoided by fitting two to four layers of high-performance glass-reinforced polyester, which doesn't need to be covered with chippings or solar-reflective paint.

If your extension design means that people are going to be stomping around on the roof, the surface layer will need to be formed from a hard-wearing material, such as asphalt or purpose-made paving slabs. These are placed above small raised supports to allow rainwater to disperse invisibly away under the paving, along the waterproof sub-surface.

Other materials traditionally used for covering flat roofs include metals such as lead, zinc and copper which can provide a more durable, if more expensive, solution. Of these, lead is the most realistic for home extensions, being less expensive than copper and more durable than zinc, lasting 100 years or more.

In today's metric world it's heartening to find that lead is still specified traditionally in pounds per square foot, varying from 3 to 8 psf (Code 3 to Code 8). The higher the

Lead sheet with plenty of 'rolls'.

code number, the thicker and more durable it should be. Code 4 lead is the one builders tend to use unless instructed otherwise. Flashings should typically be made of Code 4 or 5 lead (1.8mm or 2.24mm thick). Flat roofs and valley gutters need to be of heavier Code 6 lead (2.65mm thick) or higher.

However, lead is notoriously prone to expansion in hot weather, so any large areas without expansion joints will eventually cause splits and buckling. Sheets should therefore not exceed about 2.25m length. Expansion cracking can be prevented by building in expansion joints known as 'rolls' and 'drips'. Rolls are formed from a strip of lead wrapped around a wooden pole (rather like a broom handle). Drips are basically steps in the flat roof covered with overlapping sheets. Lead is also prone to 'creep' – extremely slow movement downhill – so the roof pitch or fall needs to be laid just right, between 25–60mm per 2.25m run. At joints with walls, the sheets should be turned up and lapped over by a separate lead flashing.

Insulation

To comply with the Building Regulations, flat roofs over habitable rooms must include thermal insulation. Traditionally there have been two methods of insulating the roof – a 'warm' or a 'cold' roof – depending on exactly where you place the insulation. Today, however, 'cold roofs' are banned in Scotland and are frowned upon in the rest of the Britain.

So the obvious choice is to build a warm roof, which is the simpler option anyway. Here, a plastic vapour barrier sheet is first laid on the deck, and special thick polyurethane foam insulation boards are placed on top. The surface layers of weatherproof felt are then laid over the insulation boards. This is far more efficient than the old 'cold roof' method, which involved placing loft insulation above the ceiling leaving a clear air space above, like in a conventional loft.

With warm roofs it's not the end of the world if a little moist air from the room below percolates up through the ceiling into the roof void. Because the insulation is directly below the roofing felt, there's no cold surface for warm air to hit and condense against (although some degree of ventilation is still considered desirable).

If you're feeling really lazy, for smaller extensions you can buy ready-made 'composite' decking that combines a triple sandwich of plywood, insulation and felt covering all bonded into one.

Joining it up

The biggest weak point on flat roofs is normally where the roof meets a wall, typically to the main house. Here the roofing felt should be dressed at least 150mm up the wall (known as the 'upstand') and fixed into a chased out mortar joint and bedded in mortar. The sharpness of the 'corner' where the felt is folded up the wall is reduced by fitting a small strip of timber 'angle fillet' under the felt. Finally, a lead flashing cut into the wall above is dressed down over the joint, finishing no closer than 75mm above the roof surface. Any pipes or ducts passing through the roof are another point to watch, so the joints to any soil pipes etc poking through the surface must be carefully waterproofed.

Combination roofs

If you like the simplicity and economy of flat roofs, but don't like the way they look, don't despair. One way to disguise a flat roof is to hide it behind a small 'pretend' pitched roof. With such 'false hip' roofs, the visible lower part is built as an apparently normal pitched roof, but the upper central part that you can't see from ground level is actually flat.

Designing a single storey rear extension can be tricky because a lean-to pitched roof may cover the existing bedroom windows. One solution is to go ahead with the

pitched roof, but cut away the parts outside the upstairs windows, instead building them flat. So you basically have a mini flat roof outside each window within the overall pitched design.

Another solution is to build a roof that defies description either as flat or pitched. Actually it's a lean-to roof of an extraordinarily shallow pitch of around 10°. But instead of being covered in cheap felt, it could be clad in fabulous, long-lasting leadwork. This is a good compromise, being shallow enough to allow freedom at window level, yet steep enough to look attractive and to efficiently disperse rainwater.

Rainwater fittings

When the roof is complete, and whilst the scaffolding is still in place, it makes sense for the gutters to be fitted and the downpipes connected to the waiting surface water

drain connections below. But first, the fascia boards or rafter feet that the gutter clips will be fixed to should be painted.

There's a wide variety of guttering on the market, and you'll probably have already considered the style that best suits the character of your extension. Most popular is good old black PVC, which is relatively cheap and adequate for most purposes. But you could equally opt for low-maintenance aluminium or traditional cast-iron. You'll need to decide between the various shapes, such as moulded or ogee, half-round or squareline, and colours – black, white, brown etc.

But remember, your new guttering will normally need to match the existing system, so think carefully about compatibility before selecting your preferred choice of bright orange extruded aluminium. Given safe access, installing a rainwater system should be a relatively simple task – see box.

The Building Regulations stipulate that rainwater systems (*ie* your gutters, downpipes and gullies) should be able to cope with at least 75mm of rainfall per hour – in other words, they have to be capable of putting away a full 3in per 60 minutes. This means making sure your gutters are carefully fitted so that they're fully supported by brackets and don't sag, and are set to the correct falls. They must also be served by sufficient downpipes so rainwater will glide smoothly away. It's worth noting that dormer windows, unless set well back, tend to cause complications with the rainwater system, often needing a separate gutter and pipes either side.

Installing a rainwater system – key stages

■ Guttering needs to be laid to a slight slope (fall) so rainwater will run along it and disperse easily. Aim for a fall of about 10mm for each 3m run of guttering.

■ If there's a fascia board, make sure the board is perfectly level so that you can use it as a guide for setting the gutter fall.

■ Start at the highest point of the run, marking the position of the clip, and do the same at the lowest point by the downpipe. Run a string between the two marks to get the right fall.

■ Gutter brackets can be screwed to the fascia. Where there's no fascia board, special brackets are available for fixing to rafter feet, or into the brickwork. Brackets should be fixed about 900mm apart, closer where there are junctions to bays etc.

■ At their lowest point, the gutters should be no more than about 50mm below the edge of the tiles. Also, the bottom edge of the roofing felt should lap down into the gutters – so don't trim it back.

■ Assemble the sections of guttering and fit them to the brackets.

■ Connect the gutters to downpipes. Because the eaves normally project out, overhanging the wall below, upper downpipes often need a 'swan neck' to bring them back near the main wall. This may also be needed again lower down the wall if the upper wall projects out with tiles or timber cladding.

■ Plastic downpipes should simply slot together, requiring support-brackets every 2m or closer.

■ At their base, the downpipes will either discharge over a gulley or connect directly into the underground drainage system.

One possible downside of having swish new guttering is that it could make the adjoining old fittings on the main house look less than impressive, not to say embarrassingly outmoded. In which case you may decide to go the whole hog and fit new replacements all around the house. Otherwise, it may prove a little tricky connecting up the new guttering with the decrepit old stuff, although universal adapters are available. If the extension is built right up to the neighbour's boundary, and your gutters overhang next door, you might also want to check your legal rights of access for routine maintenance and cleaning out.

Note that intricate details of rainwater fittings can be found in Haynes' *The Victorian House Manual* and *The 1930s House Manual*.

Chimneys

Most home extensions don't have chimneys. But if your existing home doesn't have the benefit of a fireplace, or you have your heart set on a fabulous showpiece living room, it might be worth considering.

Fireplaces

Although it's a lot of extra work and expense, a new fireplace can transform an ordinary extension into something quite extraordinary. Far be it for us to try and dictate taste, but if you don't want run of the mill pseudo-Victorian, you could cause a stir by fitting a cool art-deco fireplace, or perhaps a surreal 'flame and stone' contemporary feature.

Photo: eddystoneselfbuild.co.uk

Photo: capitalfireplaces.co.uk

Photo: capitalfireplaces.co.uk

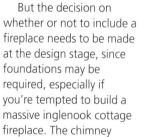

by a stainless steel flue which can be run independently up through the roof structure – subject, of course, to fitting the appropriate fire-resistant materials. This obviates the need for expensive chimney breasts and brick stacks, and is normally easier to incorporate in a single-storey extension, unless the steel flue is run externally. Alternatively, some modern living flame gas fires only require a balanced flue through the wall, like a wall-mounted boiler (although you may need to fit a protective cage-guard to the terminal externally). Note that if you plan to burn wood or coal on an open fire it may be legally prohibited, *ie* in smokeless zones.

Flues

Building a new fireplace will normally necessitate the

But the decision on whether or not to include a fireplace needs to be made at the design stage, since foundations may be required, especially if you're tempted to build a massive inglenook cottage fireplace. The chimney breast can be built at the same time as the walls.

A simpler solution might be to install an attractive log stove, served

Good chimney design

Stacks should be built so that rain driving against them in severe weather is dispersed, to prevent damp in the structure below. Some good design features are:

- The chimney should terminate at least 900mm above the main roof ridge to avoid turbulence, downdraughts and 'smoke blow back'.
- Lead flashings should protect the joint where the stack meets the roof, around the base. Flashings are fixed into a mortar joint in the chimney brickwork about 150mm above the level of the roof covering. They should be embedded at least 25mm into the masonry, fixed in place with metal wedges, and sealed with mortar.
- The top brick courses should project about 30mm so they overhang to throw rainwater clear of the main stack. The flaunching (the big lump of mortar at the base of the pots) should slope outwards.
- To prevent water soaking through the masonry and down into the roof structure there should be a damp-proof course (DPC) through the chimney approximately 150mm above the roof, and another one below the brickwork head.

insertion of extra air vents in the walls of the room. Air for combustion is drawn from the room, and an open fire needs at least six changes of air in the room per hour to burn well. In fact you need an astounding 110m³ of air supply per hour for rooms harbouring any kind of solid fuel appliance.

New stacks and chimney breasts can be built incorporating ready-made concrete flue liners inserted section by section. These liners are easy to construct, being simply pieced together and the joints sealed with special fire-cement. The resulting space between the liner units and the surrounding brickwork is then back-filled with a weak mortar mix.

At chimney pot level, there are a whole range of caps, cowls and hoods available to protect flues and stop rain from pouring down. Specialist advice is useful here, as the wrong choice of cap may affect the way the fire draws, causing it to smoke.

Detailed advice about stacks, flues and fireplaces can be found in Haynes' *The Victorian House Manual* and *The 1930s House Manual*.

And finally...

When the roofers have all finished, the rainwater fittings are in place, and the carpenters have completed all the eaves and bargeboard details, the scaffolding may no longer be required.

But don't be too hasty. The 'snagging' process (see page 221) may yet reveal defects at roof level, such as leaking skylights, loose flashings, or leaking gutter joints. Also, fitting upstairs windows and decorating the external joinery will be a lot easier whilst direct access is still possible. So hang on to the scaffolding while you can.

Main trades needed on site

- **Roof tilers:** *Included* – laying all felt, battens and tiles, forming valleys and bedding ridge tiles and verges. Most will also do small amounts of leadwork, like fixing valley linings and lead flashings, but work to flat roofs and large valleys is a specialist trade.
- **Felt roofers:** *Not included* – inserting cavity trays or fitting lead flashings.
- **Carpenters:** *Included* – building the roof structure, except for battens which are fixed by the roofers, cutting and fixing timbers to form valleys, stripping existing tiles from the old roof where the new roof will join it. Fitting fascias and soffits. Fitting the guttering is *not included*, unless specified.
- **Bricklayers:** Building up gable ends walls after the carpenter has fitted the rafters.

www.home-extension.co.uk

12 BREAKING THROUGH AND INTERNAL WORKS

Well that's all the big stuff done. But before officially pronouncing the building 'watertight', it might be wise to wait until the first rainy spell has passed without the need to erect umbrellas indoors. Roof leaks tend to manifest themselves fairly swiftly.

Next comes one of the messiest parts of the entire project – the moment of truth when the building work comes crashing into your private life.

What used to be your garden will now be looking like a war zone, but it no longer needs to. Surplus materials should now be removed, and drain runs covered up. This will help set the scene for the next phase. As the internal works start to take shape, you should finally begin to see the fruits of your labour.

But first it's worth taking a few moments to sit down with the contractor and assess whether the programme is realistically still on course for the agreed completion date. Your timetable may need to be amended if, for example, unusually vile weather has held up progress. The good news is that from now on bad weather can no longer be an excuse for delays, as the remaining work will be largely indoors. It's also a good time to take stock of your finances, particularly if there have been any 'extras'. So get your calculator out and update all those overly optimistic projected expenditure figures.

Looking back to the design stage, you may have included some approximate figures in the specification for things like kitchen units and bathroom fittings if the prices weren't known at the time. Although a useful way of buying yourself some time early on in the project, there inevitably comes a day of reckoning, and you'll now need to firm up any such estimated costs. Right now, it's especially important to check if any potentially crippling delivery delays are in the pipeline for big ticket items on order, like windows, glazing and kitchen appliances. High value items need to be delivered in good time so as not to delay things, yet not too early because of the risk of theft.

The masterplan

From now on there'll be a bewildering number of trades buzzing around the site, hopefully not getting under each other's feet. As a result it can be fairly easy to lose track of precisely who's supposed to be doing what, and when they're meant to be doing it. Some events are time-critical and must be done in the correct order, some less so. A rough guide to the order of internal works would be as follows:

- External doors, windows and glazing fitted & protected.
- Breaking through.
- Upper floors boarded.
- Internal partition walls.
- First fix – plumbing, heating, electrics.
- Plasterboard ceilings and walls.
- Plastering and ground floor screed.
- Second fix – plumbing and bathroom fittings, heating and electrics.
- Second fix internal joinery – doors, skirting, kitchen units, architraves.
- Loft insulation.
- Tiling, painting and decorating, external finishing.

One of the busiest trades at this stage will be the chippie, fresh from earlier triumphs building the roof structure and fitting floor joists. He'll shortly need to start installing the windows and door, followed by construction of internal stud walls, and fixing floorboards and door linings. Unlike most other trades, the chippie's work is spread over much of the build and isn't always rigidly programmed. There are also a couple of internal joinery jobs that may possibly be required, such as building the staircase carcass (where necessary), and preparing loft hatch openings and decks for any water tanks. The more intricate joinery works will be left until all the plastering and floor screeding is complete.

When all the windows and external doors are fully fitted, and the extension is secure, it's time for another milestone in your build. One of the messiest parts of the entire project is about to commence – breaking through the wall between the new building and your home.

Of course, it helps if your builder has bothered to run this past you in advance, rather than for example finding your viewing of *Coronation Street* rudely interrupted by a giant demolition ball. It's surprising how often otherwise good client-builder relationships are suddenly ruined at this stage. So it pays to plan this highly intrusive stage carefully, to avoid the risk of simmering grievances flaring up into outright warfare and spoiling an otherwise professional job.

External doors, windows and glazing

Until now, the builders may have managed to get in and out of the extension via an ingenious temporary door knocked up out of a bit of old plywood screwed to the door frame. However, before your home is opened up to the extension you'll want the reassurance of decent security, in the form of a robust new entrance door. On the other hand, you don't want your expensive new portal scarred by paint and plaster splashes and damaged by trades coming and going. So once hung, be sure to retain the protective plastic coverings until completion.

We covered the installation of windows and doors in Chapter 9, because some builders will want to install the frames as the main walls are built, rather than using templates, but for most projects it's a safer option to wait until all the major roof works are done, to minimise the risk of damage.

Most external timber doors are of the traditional 44mm thick solid timber panelled variety. Hardwood is still the most popular choice. Cheap flush doors with a plywood finish over a lightweight frame are best avoided. But whether you opt for timber or UPVC, you'll normally want to match the style of the other doors on the rest of the house. Having said that, you might want to add a bit of 'cottagey' character, perhaps with a split top-and-bottom opening stable door to the rear or side of the house. Fitting brand new doors and frames is always a lot simpler than messing about with peculiar-sized ancient items salvaged from reclamation yards.

Regular viewers of Channel 4's *Grand Designs* may have noticed that one of the most common reasons for

Photo: Potton Ltd

disasterous delays is the late delivery of the windows and glazing. This may have something to do with the fact that the architect specified a unique triple-glazed design, hand-crafted in Iceland from titanium alloy. But the point is that by placing your window order early you should hopefully avoid holding up the entire project further down the line.

The days of messing about with putty and metal 'sprigs' to fix a bit of ill-cut glass into its frame are now long gone. The Building Regulations require double-glazed 'sealed units', and these are normally supplied along with the windows or more likely factory pre-fitted. Obscured glass will be needed for bathrooms and cloakroom windows, and safety glass for any at low level. However, for custom-made windows the services of professional glaziers may still be required. See Chapter 9.

Breaking through

Knocking an opening through the wall of your house directly into your living space obviously won't do a lot for dust allergy sufferers in the family. So before work starts, it's essential to protect furnishings and floors with sheets and to close off the doors to the rest of the house.

The least messy way of breaking through is to use an angle grinder to cut most of the way through the wall from the extension side. Then, when you're sure everything of value is protected, finish the job off from inside the house with a bolster and chisel, which makes less dust than using power tools. But unless your builders are advised of this approach, they'll automatically use the quickest method and blast straight through in one go.

Building a two-storey extension can mean double trouble when it comes to knocking through. One of the all-time classic home extension mistakes may only become evident once the builders break through upstairs. The plan may have been to construct a door opening leading from the new side extension to your existing landing. But strange as it may sound, the somewhat inconvenient fact

Above: Now you see it...
Below: ...now you don't.

that the stairs are smack in the way can sometimes get overlooked! The Building Regulations don't allow new doorways to open straight out onto steps – for obvious reasons there must be a clear landing. This is the kind of problem you may encounter if the drawings and design stage are rushed, and if you don't get this right you can forget about Building Control issuing that all-important final certificate upon completion

The job of breaking through and creating a new doorway will be considerably easier if you only need to adapt an old window by converting it into a full-height door opening. Simply cutting out the section of masonry below the window means there's no need to mess about fitting new lintels. But where a new, or wider, opening is necessary, structural work will be needed. Building Control will want to inspect this to ensure the work matches that shown on the approved plans and calculations.

Below: 'How I broke my neck' – unacceptable opening onto staircase.

Making an opening

The wall above must be supported temporarily while a slot is cut for the new lintel. This is done by first cutting holes about every 600mm just above the position of the proposed new lintel.

Steel or timber 'needles' of about 150mm x 50mm are then placed through these holes in the wall, and are supported each side by adjustable steel 'acro' props, in turn resting on a scaffold plank to spread the load. (On weak timber floors, the joists must be checked first to improve support.) Be careful not to overtighten the props – they just need to support the wall, not jack it up!

The new lintel is inserted in the wall and must extend either side of the proposed new opening by at least 150mm. To spread the load, additional support will be needed under the ends of the lintel, such as a dense concrete block, a padstone or hard engineering bricks.

The lintel is bedded in mortar and the masonry above built up. The space between the top of the new lintel and the brickwork or blockwork above it must be packed with mortar. It's important that there's minimal shrinkage in this mortar as it dries out, otherwise the brickwork above will 'drop' onto the beam – a surprisingly common sight in the walls of houses where patio doors have been replaced. The solution is 'dry packing'. This is normally a 1:3 cement/sand mix which isn't actually dry, but is dampened with a small amount of water. The mix should be rammed hard into the space and allowed to dry for at least 24 hours before the props are removed.

The new opening below the lintel is marked out on the wall, then the plaster is chopped out vertically with a bolster and the masonry cut and removed. The side reveals (jambs) can later be made good with plaster. Alternatively a timber frame liner can be screwed to the reveal. Finally, the surrounding masonry and gaps to the floor are filled and levelled.

Internal walls

Before the electrician and plumber can start working their special magic, all the internal walls and floors should first be in place. As noted in Chapter 9, if your extension comprises two or more rooms then simple non-structural partition walls may be all that's needed to perform the basic task of divding up the space. If your internal walls are built of concrete blockwork, they'll probably have already been constructed by the bricklayer at the same time as the main walls. But internal walls built of timber studwork will now need to be erected – see below.

If you have an eye for interior design you might want to add a little glamour to your internal walls, perhaps in the

Photo: polarlight.co.uk

form of glass blocks. These are best encased in a surrounding timber framework within the wall. But you don't need to go mad and glaze every square metre. Just one or two strategically placed blocks can do wonders to brighten an otherwise plain bathroom or kitchen.

Blockwork walls

Non-structural walls built from lightweight concrete blocks can be built very rapidly and provide better sound

insulation than stud walls. However, because they impose greater loads than timber frame walls they're often confined to the ground floor – but not always. Normally 100mm blocks are used at ground floor level, whilst lighter, thinner 75mm blocks are preferred upstairs. Which is fine if they're built directly on top of the ground floor wall. Otherwise support must be provided with doubled-up joists bolted together, so the new wall can be built directly above it. Alternatively, if the wall runs at right angles to the joists below, then the blockwork can be built off a 75 x 75mm timber sole plate.

However, even if the joists have been doubled up to a satisfactory strength, some degree of movement in the timber can occur as a result of timber shrinkage or deflection of floors, and this can cause cracking. So upstairs it's probably better to build in timber studwork.

Structural walls

A different kettle of fish entirely is the load-bearing internal 'structural' wall. These are built of denser concrete blocks, or brickwork, and should be clearly shown on the drawings since they may be supporting loads from the

roof, as well as from ceiling and floor joists, and therefore need proper foundations. Internal door openings in such walls must employ lintels (normally the concrete variety). However, in all but the largest home extensions load-bearing walls won't normally be necessary, since the floor joists usually only need to span less than about 4 or 5m and shouldn't need extra support. So if the upstairs internal walls don't need to carry any weight, it should be possible to simply divide the rooms with inexpensive timber stud partition walls.

Stud partition walls

Many traditional builders are deeply suspicious of stud walls, regarding them as 'cheap and nasty'. Given the

choice, most homeowners also prefer solid walls. Nevertheless, partitions are cheaper and easier to build, and the perceived drawbacks, such as poor sound insulation, can be overcome.

Lightweight timber frame 'studwork' walls normally comprise 100 x 50mm softwood timber studs, clad on both sides with plasterboard sheets. Upstairs, stud walls can be securely fixed to the floor joists below and the ceiling joists above and needn't have a ground floor wall directly underneath supporting them. At ground floor level they can be built directly off a beam and block floor or off a concrete slab. Equally they can be built off the finished screeded floor surface (sometimes reinforced with steel mesh along the line of the wall).

But at what stage should partition walls be built? They definitely need to be in place before the electricians and plumbers run their pipes and cables, which in turn has to be done before plastering, so the partition walls are generally built soon after the structure is weathertight. Floor screeding is normally done later, along with the

Building a timber stud wall

■ To build a stud partition, you first need to mark out its top and bottom position with lines on the ceiling and floor. Horizontal timbers can be fixed along the lines, to make the header plate and base plate respectively (also known as the top plate and sole plate). For added strength, nail through the floorboards to joists where possible. Fixing to concrete floors is done with screws and plugs.

■ Where the wall is built on an existing timber floor, such as to upstairs rooms, fixing is straightforward if your new wall runs at right angles to the floor joists. If it runs the same way as the joists then unless it's directly above a joist you'll need to provide extra support for the new base plate in the form of strips of timber 'noggins' (minimum 50 x 38mm) between the joists. The same applies at ceiling level.

■ Next the vertical timber studs are fixed in place, normally at 400mm or 600mm centres. But the precise spacing should match the size of plasterboard used. Standard plasterboard sheets are 1,200mm wide, so the studs should be placed to allow the boards to join over a timber stud.

■ To provide strength, you need to fit at least one row of horizontal studs (noggins), between all the main vertical studs at about half height, which also provides an essential fixing point for the plasterboard sheets. When constructing the frame 'skew nailing', with nails hammered in at an angle, is the quickest method of joining the various pieces. It helps to drill a pilot hole first.

■ If you know you'll later need to hang stuff off this wall, such as kitchen wall units, or even sockets or pictures etc, now is the time to fit extra rows of noggins at the appropriate height so that you'll have something substantial to drill into.

plastering (being a 'wet trade'), so where the timber base plate has already been fixed to the concrete floor slab, it must be protected with plastic sheeting so that the wet screed doesn't cause damp and rot to the timber.

A quicker modern alternative widely used by mainstream housing developers is the metal frame partition system wall. These tend to be thinner at around 50–75mm but can also be clad with plasterboard. You can even buy 'off-the-shelf' ready-made plasterboard sandwich partitions with a cardboard cellular core, which just need cutting to size.

One drawback with stud walls is the perceived problem of sound travelling through them, which is of particular importance for bathroom walls. But it's a fairly simple task to fill the hollow cavities with thick sound-deadening mineral wool quilt, and double plasterboard them to improve sound insulation qualities. Nonetheless, solid masonry walls normally provide a better barrier to sound, so you might want to specify solid partitions where this is especially important. On upper floors where this may not be structurally possible because of the additional weight, specify special acoustic boarding in place of ordinary plasterboard.

Once the framework for the stud walls is complete the door linings can be fixed in place and the wall left awaiting any cabling and pipework runs before being plasterboarded. Instead of a plaster finish, the boards may be left unplastered with the joints taped and filled ready for decoration. This is the preferred, cheaper option for many mainstream housebuilders, although a plaster finish is normally preferable in kitchens and bathrooms because of their moist atmosphere.

Finally, like the old joke about painting yourself into a corner whilst decorating a floor and not being able to escape, when building a stud wall don't box yourself in forgetting to leave a way out via a door opening!

Door linings

Openings left in internal walls for doors will need door liners to be fitted. These are simple planks of wood (or MDF) rather than the purpose-made door frames used for external doors. The linings can be fixed in place now, or you could leave them until after the floors have been screeded or boarded. But they should normally be installed before the walls are plastered.

Linings have traditionally comprised some handy leftover floorboards, but today ready-assembled kits are available in differing sizes to fit walls of varying widths.

Internal door liners are deliberately wider than the walls in order to accommodate the depth of plaster, and are typically made from 130 x 30mm planed softwood for installation against 100mm thick internal walls, or where the walls are thinner – say 75mm, such as upstairs – 105 x 30mm liners may be used.

Timber liners are easier to fit to stud partition walls since they're screwed or nailed directly to the timber sub-frame.

Where the internal walls are built from blockwork, liners are sometimes fixed to them using cut nails driven directly into the masonry. However, it's better to use special frame ties, or screws driven into wallplugs. The screws should be fitted in pairs to prevent frames from twisting as doors are opened and closed.

Fitting doorstops is normally done later, towards completion, at the same time as the doors are being hung. Remember that the door linings have decorative surfaces that will be on view in the finished extension, so protection from damage will be needed, especially if they're later to be varnished or stained.

Timber flooring

Now that the building is dry inside, the timber flooring can be safely laid on the joists. The general idea is to get this level with the adjoining floors in the main house, but in many extensions even a blind person would have little trouble pinpointing the boundary of the new extension, thanks to the pronounced 'hump' in the floors where this was badly judged. To be fair, achieving an 'invisible' join to the existing floors isn't easy. The only way to get this right is by regular measuring and checking at the floor joist stage.

Of course, the aesthetic appeal of traditional timber flooring will be somewhat diminished by blobs of plaster, paint, mastic and heaven knows what raining down, so once fitted take care to keep them protected during the next few gruelling weeks.

Floorboards versus chipboard panels

You have two main choices when selecting your timber flooring: floorboards or chipboard panels. For a traditional floor that you can leave exposed with an attractive stain or

Photo: realoakfloors.co.uk

varnish finish, pine floorboards are ideal. But chipboard panels are cheaper and quicker to lay, although they need to be covered – perhaps with laminate or carpets – which obviously adds to the cost. Plywood panels are a possible third option, but although cheap they're rarely used today. Whichever type you choose, a 10mm expansion gap should be left to at the edges by the walls that can later be concealed under the skirting.

Softwood tongued-and-grooved (PTG) floorboards are commonly available in 18 x 121mm sizes sold in varying lengths. The floorboarding adds strength to the floor structure.

However, unless the timber has been slow-grown and well-seasoned, or has been carefully reclaimed, wood floors can suffer from shrinkage between the boards. Even expensive solid hardwood floors can develop unsightly cracks. So it's best to first let the new boards dry out before laying by storing them for as long as possible in a centrally heated environment. By the time they have acclimatised, the moisture content should ideally be down to less than 12 per cent.

Floorboards are traditionally fixed to the joists using special large flat nails called brads, typically 55mm in length, the heads being easily embedded in the boards without the need for punching-in afterwards. The ends of boards should be staggered at different joists. For added strength the tongues can be glued into the grooves. Softwood boards are best sanded and sealed.

Flooring grade chipboard is widely used by most mainstream housebuilders. It's manufactured with tongued-and-grooved edges and is sold in various sizes, such as 2,440 x 600mm panels. The 18mm thick panels can span 450mm between joists, and the thicker 22mm ones can manage 600mm. Although chipboard is unlikely to shrink, it has been known to disintegrate when wet, so it's best to select the moisture resistant 'green' type.

However, unless fitted with scrupulous care, over time chipboard is very prone to creaking as a result of panels springing away from the joists. It's also very difficult to lift and replace intact should access be required for future maintenance to pipes or cables.

When laying, the boards should be PVA glued at the joints, and then secured using purpose-made screws or special lost-head round 'ringshanked' nails at 75mm centres. Chipboard is notorious for blunting tools because it's so dense, so it's worth drilling pilot holes first. The tongued-and-grooved edges of the panels can become easily damaged, so never hammer directly onto it near the edges without first protecting them under an offcut. Also, beware sharp particles that can often fly out when sawing, so eye protection is essential.

If noise transmission is an issue, special sound-deadening acoustic floor panels can be fitted instead of conventional chipboard. Made from high density cement-impregnated chipboard, these look similar to standard 19mm tongued and grooved panels.

Timber floorboarding can also be fixed to concrete ground floors on battens. But laying a timber floorboard finish above the screed will raise the floor height and therefore needs to be planned early on in the build. Whilst on the subject of floor finishes, note that most laminates and parquet timber floor coverings are not sufficiently moisture-resistant for use in kitchens and bathrooms.

Stairs

How many home extensions need stairs? Very few. You might need an extra staircase for a granny annexe, or perhaps your design boasts spiral stairs leading to a cool galleried mezzanine landing, but the most likely requirement would be for a loft conversion.

Stairs are one of the most complex parts of the internal

Stairs and the Building Regulations

Briefly the requirements are:
- Landings should be at least the width of the stairs (both in length and width). No doors should open outwards onto a landing.
- The pitch of the staircase must be no steeper than 42°.
- Headroom: there must be minimum 2m clearance above each step.
- The tread of each step must be minimum 220mm deep (strictly speaking this refers to the 'going', which is the tread without its 'nosing', the bevelled front bit that sticks out).
- The height of each 'riser' must be a maximum of 220mm (the riser is the vertical part of each step).

joinery, but because of their lack of relevance to the vast majority of home extenders, readers are referred to the Haynes House Manuals for more detailed descriptions. If you are planning to fit a staircase, note that once the carcass is in place at this stage it is best to leave it devoid of banisters and balustrades for the time being so that they don't get damaged.

Stairs are potentially dangerous places, a prime location for accidents in the home, hence the eagerness with which the Building Regulations cover the subject. So it's a little surprising that they can be rather relaxed about stair widths. Although standard widths are normally a minimum of 800mm, you're allowed to reduce it in some circumstances. In restricted spaces, such as access to lofts, a 600mm width may be acceptable.

Space-saving loft stairs are even permitted with 'paddle shaped' treads that alternate from right to left on each tread, forcing you to descend back down them facing forwards as if on a ladder.

There's another surprising apparent loophole. Handrails need only be provided to one side, unless the stairs are unusually wide (over 1m), in which case both sides need one. Handrails and banisters are normally fixed at a convenient level, about 900mm above the treads. The banister spindles known as 'balusters' mustn't have a gap

between them bigger than 100mm, to prevent small children from plunging to their doom. And 'ranch style' horizontal balustrades should always be avoided, purely on the grounds of good taste.

Externally the rules are different. For added safety, parapets to external steps or balconies need to be placed a little higher, at a minimum of 1,100mm.

Spiral stairs

Spiral stairs are a great way to add some instant style to a development, but before you're temped to splash out on a wonderful cast-iron antique masterpiece remember that it may not comply with current standards for internal use. Check compliance with BS 5395: Part 2.

In fact the Building Regs are not at all kind to spiral stairs. Designers like them because they don't need support from an adjoining wall, being reliant instead on a giant central newel post. This clearly offers the design freedom to do something wacky, like appearing to be freestanding in the middle of the room. But if you do this it could upset the fire-regulations people. Unless new rooms upstairs have access to a conventional staircase as an escape-route, they may need to have special escape-sized windows fitted. The simplest option is to specify off-the-shelf spiral 'loft stairs', which come in kit form. One final thought from bitter experience – be sure to tell the builders whether you want your spiral stairs erected clockwise or anticlockwise. Or they may just bollix it in their own special way.

Integral garages

For those whose first love will always be the car or bike, moving it into the house with you isn't an unreasonable idea. But sadly, the truth is that vehicles don't always make very good housemates. For a start there's the exhaust fumes, then there's the potential for oil and fuel spillages, and of course the risk of explosions and fire.

As a result, the Building Regs take a close interest in the safety of integral garages. First, they demand that the garage floor surface must be a minimum of 100mm lower than the house, and second, that any door from the house into an integral garage has at least 30 minutes' fire resistance.

To get the floor down this low the garage floor slab

simply lick their way around the frame. So fitting purpose-made fire-resistant frames is the best option. Standard frames can be modified, with large 25 x 25mm doorstops glued and screwed in place. Alternatively, special intumescent strips can be indented around the frame, which are not dissimilar in appearance to draught excluders. These will resist fire since they react to extreme heat by instantly expanding and sealing the gap between the frame and the door, thus delaying the advance of lethal smoke and flames. There's some debate about how good an idea this really is, since they also have the effect of sealing the door firmly closed, which means that anyone trapped in the garage couldn't escape through the door. In reality, however, that person would have been overcome by smoke and fumes long before the door jammed.

It's a good idea to fit a combined intumescent strip and smoke seal that does two jobs for the price of one, acting as a barrier to poisonous exhaust fumes.

As far as the walls between the garage and the house are concerned, a standard brick or blockwork wall should have no trouble stopping the spread of fire, but timber stud partitions must be boarded on both sides using two layers of 12.5mm plasterboard, with their joints staggered, followed by a layer of skim plaster. The same double plasterboarding solution applies to garage ceilings. The floors above integral garages also need insulating to minimise the chill factor in the bedroom above, and this is normally achieved by laying loft insulation quilt between the joists.

Other areas that are vulnerable to fire include any exposed lintels, which will also require plasterboarding, and the joints between walls and ceilings may need extra 'fire-stopping' with insulation material to protect nearby joists or roof timbers.

One final thought. Adding gas supply pipes to this already heady mix may sound like a dubious idea, but because of all the fire protection garages are actually excellent places to site boilers, and are increasingly the location of choice on many new developments. Boilers should be of the conventional modern wall-hung, balanced flue type, safely positioned well away from potential car impact zone, at a reasonably high level.

Left: Firedoor with self closer.

should ideally have been built lower than the rest way back at foundation stage, although you should gain at least 50mm by not needing a screed finish. The floor levels in the new accommodation will be designed to line up with those in the existing house and will influence doors and kitchen units, so raising the screed level another 40 or 50mm above the garage floor may not now be possible. A simpler solution may be to fit a raised concrete threshold to the new garage/house doorway, which in effect raises the immediate floor height at the crucial point.

A fire door with 30 minutes' resistance ('FD 30') can be identified by a small plastic marker (a blue circle with a white centre) embedded in its side. It's worth paying careful attention to fire door requirements, as you may need quite a few of them if you're also doing a loft conversion.

Fire doors need to be self closing, so special door-closing devices need to be fitted which, despite driving everyone in the house potty, can save your life in a fire. But it's no good having a fire-resistant door if the flames can

Main trades needed on site

■ **Carpenters:** Building studwork walls, fitting door linings, loft hatch, and doors and windows.
■ **Bricklayers:** Making good around openings.
■ **Labourers:** Demolition.

www.home-extension.co.uk

13

FIRST FIX
The Services

The time is now right for 'first fix'. This means routing all the new pipework and electrical cables through the building whilst its skeleton is still exposed.

Photo: designer-radiators.com

Photo: eddystoneselfbuild.co.uk

Pipes supplying hot and cold water to bathrooms, kitchens, loos and utility rooms will now need to be tucked away behind wall surfaces and in ceiling voids. The central heating pipework and some of the waste pipes also need to be installed at this stage. But, as the name implies, there'll be a 'second fix' stage later, when these jobs are completed, so don't be too alarmed when you notice lots of disconnected pipes with their tails poking forlornly out of the walls. Similarly, the electrical cables are only run as far as new boxes fixed in the walls, with their ends left loose and drooping (but obviously not live). These unfinished services will then spend several weeks awaiting 'second fix', which will only take place once all the messy 'wet works' (such as plastering and screeding) have been completed and the new pipes and cables concealed behind sheets of plasterboard.

One piece of good news is that compared to building a whole new house, you'll save a huge amount of expense and aggravation because all the incoming mains supplies – electricity, water and gas (or oil or LPG) – will already be in place. Which means the utility companies can't sting you a king's ransom for the privilege of connecting a new supply.

Thankfully, you should only be faced with the relatively simple task of extending the existing systems from your main house into the new extension. But just when you thought the gods were at last smiling upon you there may be a shock in store. It's not unusual at this point to make the

unwelcome discovery that your existing electrics and central heating are, frankly, getting a bit past it. At best they would struggle to cope with the extra load imposed by having to serve the additional accommodation. This is always fertile ground for builders seeking profitable 'extras' in the shape of unanticipated upgrading of old systems, which is why

it's very useful if you can price extra work on the same basis as the competitively tendered prices for the main job.

Electrics

Unless you've already provided the contractor with a set of drawings showing the exact positions for all your new sockets, switches and light fittings, the electrician will most likely apply his own skill and judgement – *ie* do it the easiest way. Even if you're well prepared, there's a fairly good chance the information will not have got through to the person actually doing the work.

Electricity is the biggest killer in the house. At least a thousand fires and more than 50 deaths each year are due to electrical faults. Wiring usually lasts only about 35 years and should be tested at least every decade. Most houses have electrical systems that are unsatisfactory in some way, either due to poor-quality alterations or just through sheer age.

Electrical work is not really an area for the DIY enthusiast, unless you know exactly what you're doing. Anything with a risk of death attached isn't normally worth saving a few quid over. In any case, much DIY electrical work is now restricted under Part 'P' of the Building Regulations (see website). If in any doubt, always consult a qualified electrician.

That said, it's slightly worrying that just about anyone possessing a pair of hands and a functioning brain is entitled to call themselves an electrician. No licence or formal qualifications are required, which is a little surprising given the risks of being fried to death from a moment's absent-mindedness. However, if your extension is being managed under the terms of a building contract it will require that the individual employed must be at the very least a 'competent person' (which legally means 'someone capable of signing a BS 7671 installation certificate').

But what should you look for when picking a suitable electrician? It's essential that they're registered with an appropriate organisation, such as IET (Institute of Engineering and Technology), the ECA (Electrical Contractors Association) or, probably the best-known of

all, NICEIC (National Inspection Council for Electrical Installation Contracting). If employing subcontractors directly, as always get more than one quote, and make it clear that payment for the job will be subject to first receiving an IEE test certificate upon completion.

The electrician's first job, after checking your plans, will be to route all the cables around and fix the boxes in place. He'll return at a later stage to do the second fix work, installing covers to the switches, sockets and ceiling roses once the plastering of the walls and ceilings is out of the way. Now is the time to add any last minute extra positions for power point sockets or light fittings. Don't wait until everything is all beautifully plastered. You'll need to clearly communicate any special requirements, although there are limits to what you can request. Remember that the Building Regulations now require that power sockets must be positioned no lower than 450mm above the floor, and light switches no higher than 1200mm from the floor, and no sockets are allowed in bathrooms.

Adding style

This is a perfect opportunity to add a little creative lighting to your design. Features like discreet LEDs embedded in floors, recessed ceiling lights, wall-mounted fittings and outdoor uplighters can all make the new extension feel super-stylish. Why stick with boring old white plastic sockets and switches when there's a choice of brushed aluminium, brass, or chrome? If you prefer something less contemporary, there are distinctive antique designs making something of a comeback – repro versions of deco uplighters and rounded bakelite-style switches.

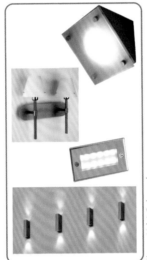

Photos: LightInStyle.co.uk

How many sockets?

One of the most common complaints amongst house buyers is the belated discovery upon moving in that there are insufficient power points for all the various Playstations, PCs, printers, scanners, foot spas, toasted sandwich machines and smoothie-makers that modern life requires. So be generous with the DSSOs (double-switched socket outlets) in your new rooms, since the cost of adding a couple of extra ones here or there at this stage is peanuts.

Depending on room size, a modern household requires about three or four DSSOs for each bedroom, five or six each for kitchens and living rooms, and a couple for halls and landings. But in the bathroom, only shaver sockets are allowed (run from the lighting circuit).

Running cables

Traditionally, cables running along masonry walls would be buried in channels known as 'chases' gouged out of the walls. Today, cables are normally run through protective trunking, such as special plastic conduit tubes, or behind flat steel shields or 'cable covers' which are pinned to the bare walls and then plastered over.

Cables should be laid either vertically or horizontally from the outlets they supply, so the following trades know where not to drill holes. Any outdoor cables must be run in special external grade protective conduits.

Having gone to so much trouble at the design stage carefully calculating that your extension would be structurally safe, you don't want the joists to now be seriously weakened by having huge chunks cut out of them for the various pipe and cable runs. Timber-frame houses are particularly vulnerable, so don't allow your electrician to hack away at load-bearing timber studs in order to neatly recess his socket boxes. Any holes or cuts made in the timber frame's vapour barrier must be sealed, using special adhesive tape.

Electricians normally need to run cables through floors, which means drilling holes in timber joists and feeding them through. The critical points structurally in joists are at their centres and ends, so there are strict rules about how to do this without weakening the joists:

- Holes should be drilled about halfway down the joist.
- Don't drill near the joist ends – not within the first quarter of the joist's span from the wall.
- The size of holes should be no bigger than quarter of the depth of the joist.
- Don't drill holes too close together (no closer than three times the hole's diameter).

Electric cables run within thermal insulation, such as loft quilt, can be at risk of becoming overheated, and any contact with polystyrene insulation can react with and soften the PVC sleeving. If there's no other option in a loft, run them immediately on top of the plasterboard ceiling rather than being totally encased within thick layers of quilt, and use a higher capacity cable than necessary in the immediate area.

The basics

The first question to ask when extending an electrical circuit is whether your existing consumer unit is capable of coping with the additional load. Now may be a good time to replace it, especially if it is an older type made of metal

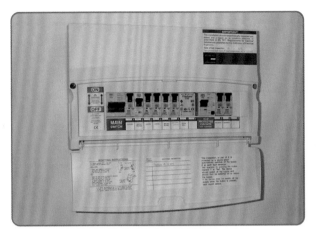

Photo: LightInStyle.co.uk

or bakelite (hard dark plastic) or if it has ancient rewireable fuses. Modern consumer units have MCB's (miniature circuit breakers) for each individual circuit. These are special fuses that automatically switch off when they sense a fault or overload, thereby potentially saving lives (rather than the traditional method of struggling in the dark to replace bits of blown fuse wire). Increased protection against electrocution in the event of contact with live wires is provided by RCDs (residual current devices) which are now mandatory. But they are very sensitive, often cutting out whenever a lightbulb blows.

The power circuits that supply the socket outlets in the walls are arranged as 'ring mains', usually with one circuit per floor. The 2.5mm^2 'twin and earth' cable connects from the 30amp MCB in the consumer unit, looping round all the 13amp socket outlets on one floor in series and then back to the MCB. One circuit can normally serve a floor area up to 100m^2 (an average semi having roughly 50–60m^2 floor area for each storey) but any number of power points can be provided within this. The kitchen, being a high demand area, has its own circuit. Also, electric cookers and immersion heaters have separate 45amp and 20amp MCB fuses respectively but use 'radial circuits', where a single cable is run from the MCB direct to the unit. Cables run to outdoors should have their own mini consumer unit and separate circuits.

Electricity will always head for earth, taking the easiest route (normally along its circuit). But in the event of a fault, leaking current could pass to earth through you, your shoes, the floor and the walls, and especially through anything wet or metallic. So to protect against electric shock, all exposed metal components should be connected with an earthed cable (green and yellow sleeved) to prevent them becoming 'live' and retaining any dangerous shock current. The requirement is to bond metal items such as incoming service pipes (water, gas, oil etc), central heating pipes, hot and cold water pipes, and all metal in bathrooms. New copper piping for heating and water may need to be earth bonded to the electrical system. However, pipework run exclusively in plastic shouldn't need to be bonded. Bathrooms and kitchens are high risk areas, so

nothing electric should be touchable from where a person could be in contact with water at the same time.

Only specially protected fittings are allowed in bathrooms and light switches should be of the pull-cord type or else located in the landing/hall outside the bathroom door.

Lighting circuits are also arranged in a ring or 'loop' with one circuit per floor, in the same way as power circuits. The thinner 1.5mm^2 'twin and earth' cable connects from the 5amp MCB fuse in the consumer unit, looping round all the ceiling rose lights in turn and then back to the MCB. Each room switch is wired directly to a rose via a single cable. New lighting circuits may also need to incorporate smoke alarms and shaver points.

Extractor fans

Today's Building Regs demand that kitchens, bathrooms and utilities are fitted with extractor fans and that all other rooms should be ventilated, either in the form of trickle vents fitted to windows or via airbricks in walls. This is in addition to the special ventilation requirements for roofs and suspended ground floors where structural timbers can be at risk from damp and condensation.

Building Control are very keen on the subject of ventilation and extractor fans, so they won't be fooled by a posh-looking, charcoal-filtered stainless steel cooker hood that is not actually vented to outdoors and just recycles stale air.

There's a good reason for all this official consternation. To get rid of all those litres of humid, moist air swirling around the atmosphere of modern homes, rapid ventilation is needed to prevent problems from condensation and toxic mould. And nowhere is it needed more than in kitchens and bathrooms where steamy air from laundry, showering and boiling food will do the most damage, condensing against cold surfaces, such as loo cisterns, and then dripping into puddles on the floor. The Building Regs Part F1 requires kitchen fans to be capable of shifting 60 litres of air per second, utility rooms 30 litres and bathrooms 15 litres.

In bathrooms, fans must not be located anywhere someone using the bath could touch them, and away from the risk of shower spray. If the bathroom is so small this isn't possible, consider fitting special low voltage bathroom units. Ideally fans should be sited on the opposite side of the room to the windows, to encourage a decent through-flow of air.

Most of us have experienced noisy

'first generation' fans that whine on for hours long after you've departed, like a particularly irritating swarm of bees. Not only are they annoying but they're largely ineffective unless you bathe exclusively after dark – no matter how steamy it is in the daytime, such fans don't work unless you put the light on. Thankfully, there are now 'intelligent' extractor fans known as 'humidistats'. These relatively quiet, automatic humidity-sensing fans only come on when needed, regardless of whether the light is on or not. But it's worth noting that they need to be set to operate at 70 per cent RH ('relative humidity') since once the humidity of the air in your house rises above this, black mould growth can form on your walls and ceilings.

Some first generation fans were also very effective at keeping the neighbours awake at night, since the slightest breeze could cause their small louvered shutters on the outside wall to rattle annoyingly. Thankfully, modern thermo-electric shutters have solved that one. Another recent improvement is the requirement for isolator switches in bathrooms, so that defective fans can be worked on without having to disconnect the entire lighting circuit. These are usually located high up on the outer wall as you enter the bathroom.

Fans may be built into walls, with the moist air directly expelled to the outside, or they may be fitted to ceilings and linked to outdoors via a length of round flexible 'concertina' ducting that runs up through the loft space to a roof vent. To prevent condensation dribbling back down, ducting can be insulated, or have 'condensation traps' fitted near the fan to divert moisture to an overflow pipe.

Another problem with ducting is that the longer duct, the weaker the fan's performance gets. Flat ducting such as the type used for kitchen chimney hoods running along the top of the wall units will reduce airflow even more than the rounded type, so a beefier fan unit may be needed.

But before you rush to install the biggest air-sucker you can get your hands on as a final solution to airborne dampness, first take a look around the room. There may be competition for valuable air, notably in the form of open-flued appliances. Whilst modern 'room-sealed' boilers aren't a problem, open fires need to take their combustion air

directly from inside the room. If this air supply is stolen by your new turbocharged extractor fan, the consequential air starvation can leave the occupants gasping.

This is why solid fuel appliances like Agas and wood burning stoves aren't necessarily compatible with extractor fans (if fitted, fans should have a reduced output rating). So in rooms harbouring such open-flued appliances, the Building Regulations will demand air vents inserted in the walls, in order to introduce sufficient fresh air changes per hour and prevent any risk of you and the family suffocating.

If you want to be truly eco-friendly, check out that latest thing, 'passive stack ventilation' (except that the Victorians had passive-ventilation systems too – known as 'fireplaces'!). Based on the principle that warm air rises, modern passive 'stack vents' are special vertical flues that extract stale moist warm air which naturally rises upwards with air pressure through the colder air in the roof space, and then away through a vented ridge tile. (An open fireplace and chimney will 'self ventilate' extracting about 20 litres of air per second.) The tekky bit is the heat exchanger in the roof space, which extracts the heat from the old exhaust air and uses it to warm the fresh air entering the house.

Smoke alarms

The biggest killer in most house fires is not incineration by flames, but being overcome by smoke. Deadly, silent smoke can engulf the average home in a few minutes, snuffing out lives in an instant. This may be your worst nightmare, yet the threat is not always taken seriously at the design stage. Smoke will always get you long before the flames, so a smoke alarm waking you up in time can literally be a lifesaver.

Yet in many homes the smoke alarms have been incapacitated by having their batteries violently torn out. Distraught homeowners deafened by the wretched things bursting to life in error have been driven to take desperate measures to silence the uncontrollable 110 decibel shrieking. This would seem to be another case of poor design – only some more expensive ones come equipped with a simple silence button to stop the ear-piercing racket in the event of a toast-burning false alarm.

Photo: eddystoneselfbuild.co.uk

On new buildings the alarms must now be wired to the mains (normally the lighting circuit) so they can't be shut-up so 'easily'. The recommended solution is of course to position them correctly in the first place, sited away from corners of rooms (which smoke tends to avoid) but not too close to light fittings (which can obstruct them). There should be smoke detectors fitted on each storey, no more than 3 m away from each bedroom. Locate them away from cooking areas, heaters and bathrooms, since steam and fumes can set them off, and don't fit them in boiler rooms, garages or kitchens. But because nearly half of all domestic fires start in kitchens, one should be sited nearby. If you still get false alarms, a modern consumer unit may allow you to temporarily turn the circuit off by simply flicking up the appropriate MCB switch.

Talking of gruesome deaths, what could be more ironic than cheating the Grim Reaper by taking all the correct fire precautions only to be overcome in your sleep by carbon monoxide poisoning? So if you find yourself nodding off in your armchair in front of a cosy fire in a draught-sealed room, it might later turn out to be a matter of some regret that a CO alarm wasn't fitted. Any appliances that take their combustion air direct from within the room, such as gas fires and solid fuel fireplaces, are a potential risk. So although there's currently no legal requirement to install a CO alarm, while you're at it why not fit a combined smoke/CO alarm for peace of mind?

Gas

Modern mains supplies are run in yellow polyethylene plastic underground pipes, which have long superseded metal. The incoming mains gas pipe should be buried at least 375mm below ground, terminating at a stop valve by the gas meter. To extend the existing supply, perhaps to a new boiler or gas fire in your new extension, copper gas pipes are normally run externally along the outer walls near ground level. As a safety precaution, gas pipework inside the house should be kept at least 25mm away from

electric cables, and no gas pipes may be run in unventilated voids to floors etc. Gas plumbing must always be done in copper pipe, not plastic.

Natural gas is not poisonous; the main risk is that of explosions. Hence work on gas appliances and pipework must by law only be carried out by qualified CORGI registered

engineers (Council of Registered Gas Installers). For oil-fired heating systems, incidentally, the equivalent body is the less cute sounding OFTEC (Oil Firing Technical Association).

Plumbing

If your home extension includes a new bathroom, WC, kitchen or utility room, the existing cold water supply will need to be extended. You're also likely to need some new pipes run to serve additional radiators. All pipework should be properly secured with clips so as to discourage leaks and banging noises developing later in life.

But before the first monkey wrench is taken out of the toolbag it's always a good idea to discuss the

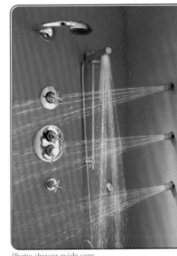

Photo: shower-guide.com

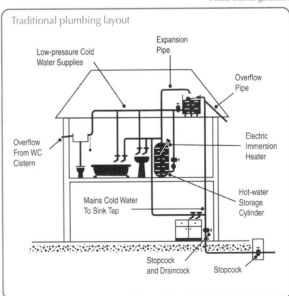

Traditional plumbing layout

Low-pressure Cold Water Supplies

Expansion Pipe

Overflow Pipe

Overflow From WC Cistern

Electric Immersion Heater

Mains Cold Water To Sink Tap

Hot-water Storage Cylinder

Stopcock and Draincock

Stopcock

desired layout of new pipes and appliances with your plumber. There will, of course, be physical limitations as to where pipework can be run, but with a little thought you can normally agree simple solutions, perhaps saving a lot of unnecessary expense.

Unlike doing work to electrics and gas appliances, the only restriction on DIY plumbing is competency. If you feel confident, there's no reason why you shouldn't carry out some of the work yourself. Even installing new bathroom fittings shouldn't be too difficult. The fact that all the pipes and fittings are brand new makes it a lot easier than trying to connect a stunning new suite to decrepit old imperial-sized pipes. But if you feel the urge to tackle some jobs yourself, it's essential to first tell the main contractor – you can't suddenly announce your new-found interest in plumbing when they've already scheduled a plumber to do the work.

Cold water supply
Cold water is supplied to your home below-ground from

the mains in the street, via a stopcock in the pavement or front garden. On older houses it may be a shared supply, perhaps even crossing through back gardens. Underground water pipes should be buried at least 750mm deep to protect them from frost. Where run any higher or above ground they must be lagged to protect them.

Pressurised cold water supplies were originally run in pipework of cast iron or lead. If you still have original supply pipes contact your water company, as replacement with modern heavy-duty blue plastic (alkathene) pipework is often advisable.

The incoming mains supply normally runs through the house direct to the kitchen sink (suitable for drinking water). There should be a stopcock inside the house, typically in the kitchen or cloakroom, that can be shut off in an emergency. The 'rising main' then usually continues up to a cold-water storage tank in the roof space, which supplies water for bathrooms and WCs. The hot water supply will be from the hot water cylinder (airing cupboard) or direct from a combination boiler.

The average 4 person home will typically use about 185cu m of water a year, the equivalent of over 2,000 baths, and in order to provide adequate flows of water to the taps, pipework must be correctly sized. Baths are generally supplied with 22mm pipes (hot and cold) and

washbasins and WCs with 15mm pipes. Shower mixers may require either 15 or 22mm supplies so check with the manufacturer, as some mixers only work well via a pump. Plumbing is slowly going plastic, although many plumbers remain loyal to copper. The Building Regs require all new water supply pipes to be fitted with simple non-return valves to prevent back siphonage, and these can also provide a handy on/off control to allow maintenance work.

Whilst you're in plumbing mode, you might want to take the opportunity to run a small branch pipe through the new wall for a handy garden tap, making sure, of course, that the pipes are insulated against frost and fitted with an internal stop valve.

Cutting joists

Water pipes may be concealed in suspended floors, or else buried in solid floors within ducts. Keep a record of the location of any hidden pipe runs in case access is required in future. Where pipework is surface-mounted along walls, some of the pipe-fitting work can be left until after the walls have been plastered (but before decorating).

The rules for cutting notches into joists without inviting disaster are similar to those for electric cables. As noted earlier, the critical points structurally in joists are the centre and the ends:

- Don't cut too near the joist ends – not within the first quarter of the joist's span out from the wall.
- Don't cut notches closer than 100mm to holes drilled for cables.
- Cut no deeper into a joist than an eighth of its total depth.
- Joists should always be notched from the top.

It's a good idea to fit small steel shields over the top of cut notches to protect pipes from subsequent puncturing should anyone carelessly hammer nails into floorboards.

Waste pipes

To some folk, what happens to the bathwater after they pull out the plug is a complete mystery. But just taking a quick look down below shows that the waste water discharges via one of the great inventions of modern civilisation – the U-shaped trap under the plughole. Traps cleverly prevent nasty sewer odours coming back up the pipes, since smells can't get past the water trapped in the bottom of the U, which forms a seal. The waste water then usually discharges into the main soil stack (SVP) and away through the underground drainage system to the sewers, as described in Chapter 8.

Waste pipes can tell you a few things about the person who fitted them. A couple of good signs to look for are sufficient rodding eyes provided on pipe bends, and sufficient support clips fitted to prevent pipes sagging (one at least every 500mm).

Whilst on the subject of picking a good plumber, it's worth taking the trouble to inspect some of their previous jobs before letting them loose on your designer bathroom. The airing cupboard is a good place to check the quality of their work, since if the pipework is neat and tidy in a place that's hidden from view it has to be an encouraging sign.

Modern plastic waste pipes should be relatively trouble-free if properly installed with sufficient support-clips and suitable falls – plumbers seem to sometimes forget that water runs downhill. Internal white plastic waste pipes and fittings are push-fit, usually either 32mm for basins, or 40mm for baths, showers and sinks. External pipes are usually run in UV-resistant grey plastic.

Your design must take account of the fact that waste pipes are only effective up to certain lengths before there's a risk of siphonage occurring. As noted in Chapter 8, this is a peculiar phenomenon which can allow foul odours to enter your house, accompanied by a cacophony of rude gurgling noises. It is caused when the protective seal of water in traps (to baths, basins, toilets etc) is literally sucked out by a deluge of outgoing waste water creating a build up of pressure in its slipstream. To avoid such horrors, there's a maximum permitted length to which pipes of each diameter can be run before siphonage becomes a risk. Hence there's a maximum distance that you can safely locate your new sink, loo and bath from the waste stack. This constraint can profoundly influence the layout of new bathrooms. These distances are typically 3m for baths or showers, and less than 2m for most basins. For WCs you normally have 6m to play with.

Cover openings to new waste pipes.

Maximum pipe lengths			
	Max length	Pipe diameter	Fall (per metre run)
Basins	1.7m	32mm	18–90mm
Baths and showers	3m	40mm	18–90mm
Toilets	6m	110mm	10–30mm

If this restriction cripples your otherwise excellent bathroom layout, it may be possible to work around the problem by fitting special 'anti-siphonage' traps or bigger bore pipes. Or you can cheat by using non-return valves that don't need a water sealed trap at all, such as 'HepVO' valves.

If you want to install a new bathroom or WC, fortunately you don't need to add another soil stack (SVP). Because your house will already have an SVP, you are allowed to use a short version known as a stub stack to serve extra bathrooms and loos, usually terminating with an 'air admittance valve' (AAV). Unlike SVPs these are not permanently open. Instead, they're capped with a rubber diaphragm which opens automatically to relieve pressure and admits air into the system before sealing closed again, relieving excess pressure without emitting odours.

Because no unpleasant stench is emitted, they don't need to terminate way up at roof level, and instead can be neatly boxed in. They're not usually suitable for outdoor use, but are often placed unobtrusively in loft spaces.

WCs

At the design stage, one of the first questions you need to ask is where the drain runs are. This tells you where it would be realistic to fit new WCs and bathrooms without running into major plumbing problems, such as trying to fit a loo in the east wing of the house when your drains are perfectly happy over in the west wing. Indeed, such toilet exclusion zones were a hard fact of life until an anonymous genius came up with the concept of the 'macerator' one day whilst idly gazing at the food blender in the kitchen.

The famed Victorian toilet pioneer Thomas Crapper tested the flushing power of his early WCs by simulating foul waste solids with apples bobbing about in the pan. Similarly, the macerator inventor realised that if you can liquidise fruit in a smoothie-maker, why not apply the same technology to toilets? Mashed up liquid waste could then be pumped out through conventional narrow-bore 40mm pipes rather than requiring the normal cumbersome 110mm WC pipes. Quite ingenious – except for one tiny problem: macerators rely on electric power to do the crucial pumping, so in the event of a power cut they're totally unserviceable. This means you're not allowed to rely exclusively on macerators. A home must have at least one conventional loo. But when building a new extension, the extra cost of excavating proper drains should in most cases be marginal, so macerators will not normally need to appear on your shopping list.

Showers

Unlike other sanitary fittings, showers need to be thermostatically controlled. The water temperature is adjusted automatically, preventing unwitting shower-users suddenly getting scalded with super-hot water because someone else has just run a nearby cold tap and upset the hot/cold mix.

Showers also need a consistently powerful water supply for which modern mains pressure hot water systems are ideally suited. Otherwise flow rates may need to be beefed up by fitting powerful pumps. It's also often necessary to install a separate cold supply direct to the shower from the cold water tank.

To surveyors, shower trays are rather like flat roofs – almost guaranteed to leak and cause problems at some point. If damp doesn't get down the seals at the edges of the tray it'll probably infiltrate the tiling. Which is why it's advisable to tile onto a marine plywood base rather than ordinary plasterboard.

The worst offending trays are thin acrylic ones, which can be prone to flexing and distortion, especially when timber floor joists shrink. Ceramic or stonecast trays are preferable. Or take no chances and fit a modern all-in-one moulded cubicle. But whichever type you choose, it's important to build in an access point so the trap can be cleared. Alternatively, you could dispense with the tray altogether and build a 'wet room' with a drain fitted inside the floor void (which must be able to cope with a flow of 30 litres per minute). The floor needs to be waterproof and should slope towards the drain at 1:40 for a 1 metre zone around it. This is easier to achieve on a solid floor where you can build a 25mm depression into the screed; timber floors may need to be built up instead. If you'd rather keep life simple as well as conserve the budget, a standard shower-mixer over the bath should do nicely.

Heating

Central heating

Your well-laid plans defining precisely where each piece of furniture is to be placed in your new rooms can be utterly ruined when you suddenly discover in horror that someone's stuck a radiator in the wrong place. So remember that

unless you provide the plumber with a clear set of drawings showing exactly where you want your radiators positioned and pipes routed, it'll get done the way that suits them – probably with the all the rads bunched back-to-back on internal walls, to save running much pipework.

Conventional CH systems pump hot water from the boiler to steel radiators in each room via pipework which comprises separate parallel 'flow and return' circuits, usually in 15mm or 8mm copper or equivalent plastic pipes. The 'flow' circuit feeds the hot water to each

radiator and the 'return' circuit takes the old cooler water back to the boiler.

For timber floors the pipework can be installed within the floor space. For concrete ground floors the pipework needs to be run in special ducts in the screed, or can be surface-run along walls and boxed in. Poorly supported pipes can be noisy and prone to damage, so 15mm pipework should be

supported with a clip at least every 1.4m and at each change of direction. Larger sized pipes can have supports a little further apart.

Before installing radiators you need to calculate their required sizes to heat individual rooms. Radiator output is measured in BTUs (British Thermal Units) and is calculated according to the size of each room and its level of insulation (see website BTU calculator).

Gone are the days when you could have any radiator you wanted, as long as it was oblong and white-panelled. Today, adding a new rad means an opportunity to splash out on some seriously cool design. For the style conscious, the sky's the limit with all kinds of fun shapes to choose from.

For optimum room warmth, the best position for radiators is under windows on outer walls since this is the point where the room is normally coldest. For bathrooms, a radiator towel rail is a useful addition.

Central heating systems need periodic maintenance including flushing-through to reduce limescale, and ideally should be checked annually under a service contract. Pressurised 'combi'-type systems require more frequent bleeding to release built-up air.

Electric heating is quite common in areas without a gas supply, typically comprising fixed storage heaters. These take down cheaper off-peak electricity at night, store it in special bricks and release the heat the next day. But electric heating is not only the most expensive system to run, but is also the most uncontrollable and the biggest CO_2 emitter. Popular alternative fuels in areas without a mains gas supply are oil, bottled LPG/Calor gas, and solid fuel (coal, coke, wood etc).

If you quite fancied the idea of having a living flame gas fire to add some glamour to your bedroom – tough. They're only permitted in

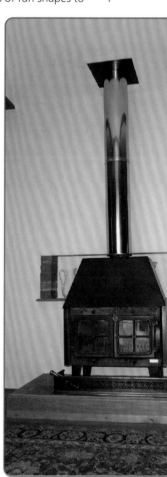

Photo: roycebathrooms.co.uk

necessarily as straightforward as it sounds. A typical home of 4 people typically needs around 230ltr of hot water a day, heated to about 60°C. But the required volume of hot water is only one factor. Your choice of system will also depend on the required pressure of delivery (the flow rate), and how much space is available for boilers, hot water cylinders and tanks.

The standard British system typically stores hot water in a copper cylinder in the airing cupboard, which also usually incorporates an electric immersion heater. Cold water from the large cold water tank in the loft refills the cylinder as hot water is drawn off at the taps. The water is heated by copper tubes inside the cylinder, which contain hot water from the boiler, transferring the heat to the water in the cylinder. The domestic hot water (DHW) doesn't pass through the boiler at all, so it's known as an 'indirect system'. An emergency expansion pipe from the cylinder leads up to the 'feed and expansion' header tank above.

reception rooms. Not only that, but all living flame gas fires, and most open-flued heating appliances (with a higher than 7kW input rating) require additional room ventilation usually in the form of a 230 x 230mm airbrick in the wall.

Hot water

Deciding on the hot water system that's best for you isn't

Modern pressurised unvented hw system.

But things are changing. Today over 50% of systems in new houses are built with pressurised hot water systems such as 'Megaflo' or 'Vantage' which do away with the need for tanks in the loft. Because there are no tanks for emergency expansion they are referred to as 'unvented' systems and any expansion is instead taken by a vessel connected to the hot water cylinder that's capable of storing hot water at mains pressure. In a typical system, incoming cold mains supply is heated either directly in the cylinder by an electric heater, or indirectly from your central heating boiler. When you open a tap, the hot water stored in the vessel is forced out by incoming mains cold water, hence you get hot water at mains pressure. This solves the problem of weedy flow rates to showers, but such systems need at least 2.5bar of mains water supply pressure to work well, and there is no back up storage tank in the event that your supply is cut off. Alternatively, you could free up some useful airing cupboard space by opting for an 'all-in-one' unvented pressurised HW system, such as the Potterton 'Powermax', which combines a gas condensing boiler and cylinder into one wall-mounted box, 550 wide x 600 deep x 1460 high.

Boilers

Adding extra radiators to a creaky old existing system may be the straw that breaks the camel's back. The old boiler may not be of sufficient capacity to cope with heating the extra rooms. As a rough guide, depending on how they're maintained, boilers may last no more than around 20

years, considerably less for some combination boilers. So renewal may be overdue anyway.

Boilers are rated according to the power they produce, measured in BTUs. One kilowatt is equivalent to 3,410 BTUs. As a rule of thumb, a 40,000 BTU boiler should be capable of heating seven radiators, as well as producing hot water. But, as noted above, you need to carry out a

'Powermax' combined boiler & hw cylinder

heat calculation for each room to accurately determine how much boiler power is needed.

Boilers are now awarded energy efficiency ratings, from A (90–94 per cent efficient) to G (50–70 per cent efficient). But as well as running costs, reliability is probably the single most important factor. The choice of available brands and models should be discussed with the contractor early on in the project, otherwise you may get lumbered with some obscure make for which spare parts are scarce.

Boilers are available that run on a wide variety of fuels as well as mains gas, such as oil, bottled gas (LPG/propane), and even solid fuel. A useful website to compare boilers is www.seduk.com.

Every household in the UK creates around six tonnes of carbon dioxide emissions a year. Looked at another way, a third of the nation's CO_2 emissions come from the energy used in our homes – which is why the Building Regs require that all new boilers are of the 'condensing' type. The secret of condensing boilers is their extra large heat exchangers, which make for a very efficient combustion process. Much of the waste heat pumped out in the exhaust gases is captured and recycled, so the exhaust temperatures can be as low as 50 degrees (compared to over 200 degrees on traditional boilers). This in turn means flues can be made of plastic, and accounts for the trademark ghostly 'plumes' of water vapour seen at flue terminals. Another distinctive feature is their propensity to emit quantities of mildly acidic condensation, which needs to be piped to an outside gulley, or into the soil stack.

If you're installing a new boiler to serve your freshly extended home, you may want to consider fitting a combination boiler (which are also condensing boilers). Combis currently account for around 50% of UK boiler sales. The great thing about them is they are very efficient at providing endless hot water instantly, as well as taking care of your space heating requirements. They are bulkier than ordinary boilers since they contain a built-in hot-water vessel, but crucially the need for separate water tanks and cylinders is dispensed with, as well as all that costly associated plumbing. So although dearer to buy, they are actually cheaper and easier to install. Their limitations have traditionally been their low flow rates, so look for ones than can achieve more than 1.5 litres per minute.

Modern wall-mounted boilers breathe through small circular balanced flues projecting through the wall. These are room-sealed, requiring no extra air vents to the room in which they're situated. They draw their air for combustion from outside (via the outer ring of the flue) and expel exhaust gases externally through the same flue (inner ring).

The rules governing location of

Wet UFH system placed over insulation awaiting screed.

balanced flue terminals are quite complex, but generally they should be at least 300mm away from gutters, windows, doors, eaves, airbricks etc. Fan-assisted flues can be closer and can also vent via extended flue ducts, which means greater flexibility in the boiler's positioning. Flues should obviously not discharge into enclosed areas, like side passages – they must have a free passage of air passing over them.

The preferred location for boilers is within garages, kitchens, or utility rooms. Locating them in bedrooms or bathrooms is normally discouraged, although it should still be possible with a room-sealed appliance. But boilers in such locations should be boxed-in (eg enclosed within a cupboard) and may need external wall vents unless they're of a type that can work safely at higher temperatures. On a small extension there may be no spare wall space available, so vertical flues that pass through a roof can sometimes be fitted.

Hanging with your posse anywhere below the emergency overflow pipe would not be cool, should a faulty boiler suddenly expel a high pressure stream of boiling water, so the regulations now require pipes to be safely directed downward to ground level along the outer wall surface.

Controls

Traditional room thermostats sense the air temperature in the room where they're installed. To work accurately they need to be positioned on a wall about 1.5m above floor level. The best arrangement is to have one main thermostat, in addition to adjustable thermostatic radiator valves (TRVs) fitted to each radiator, allowing a custom temperature to be set for each room.

You need to be able to control heating and water separately and most makes of boiler now have built-in clocks and programmers as well as a thermostat control that shuts off when the water gets to a certain temperature. Essentially, programmers are sophisticated on/off switches for the whole heating system, overriding other controls. Old systems relied on gravity and

convection to move water around, but modern boilers use integral pumps. Extending your existing system may therefore require an additional electronic slave pump to improve flow.

The task of wiring heating controls to boilers, programmers, pumps etc, is a bit of a grey area, and is often done by plumbers, but the electrician will need to position a fused spur socket nearby.

Underfloor heating (UFH)

After a slow start (it was invented by the Romans), underfloor heating is becoming increasingly popular in new properties, and is often installed in kitchens and conservatories. Although costlier than just extending your central heating system, it does add a touch of luxury, plus there's the added benefit of freeing up wall space with no bulky radiators to get in the way of your furniture.

There are two main types:

◾ Wet systems: Warm water is pumped at low pressure through concealed pipework buried in the floor screed which acts as a heat reservoir, rather like a storage heater.

◾ Dry systems: Electric heating elements, in the form of ultra-thin flexible mats, can be laid directly under floor coverings. Especially popular with ceramic tiles. An easier choice for upgrading an existing floor, with lower installation costs.

For new home extensions, wet systems are the more popular choice. These employ a series of narrow plastic water pipes run in loops embedded within the floor covering. They're normally laid within the screed or below a chipboard surface, placed above the insulation layer (obviously not below it) so the heat is released slowly and stays close to the floor. Most floor finishes are compatible, but they're especially effective when used with stone or tiled surfaces that would otherwise be cold. If you're worried about your dinner party guests complaining of scorched feet this shouldn't be a problem. Typical floor surface temperatures are a comfortable 26–29°C, and are temperature-controlled by room thermostats. Underfloor systems are actually highly energy efficient, since to heat an entire room they need only be set to relatively low room temperatures (10–15°) compared to radiator systems (18–30°). This suits modern condensing boilers, which are at their most efficient at lower temperatures.

UFH may be more expensive to install than standard rads, but with the increasing popularity of tiled and wooden floors it can provide good background heat with few cold spots. The only snag is the relatively slow response time, so this may not be ideal for people who pop briefly in and out of their homes, only occupying them for a few hours a day. That said, intelligent controls can be programmed to anticipate temperature changes, boosting warmth when needed. Many users find it best to leave them on continuously, just set at a lower temperature at night. The optimum arrangement is often to have UFH downstairs and radiators upstairs.

Alternative energy

You don't have to be an organic tofu eating activist to incorporate intelligent green ideas. 'Passive solar gain' means taking full advantage of the sun, by having more south-facing windows, and fewer on the north side. 'Active solar gain' is achieved by using the latest generation solar panels to heat your hot water. They can provide most of what you need in the summer but only around 15% in the winter. Photovoltaic cells which convert sunlight into electricity can manufacture a good deal of a home's electricity requirements. But at present solar power may only save 10% off your overall fuel bills and the payback period can be over 50 years.

If you prefer the idea of relieving the Government of lots of grant money, whilst at the same time doing your bit for global warming, then 'micro-generation' could be the thing for you. Turning your home into a mini-power station has until now been largely the preserve of the rich and famous, but times are changing. It's estimated that micro-generation could provide up to 40 per cent of the UK's electricity needs by 2050. New buildings, including home extensions, are increasingly expected to generate some of their own power to subsidise energy bills, so it may not be beyond the realms of possibility to consider fitting a state-subsidised wind turbine on your roof.

Planning permission should no longer be a major obstacle to installing renewable micro technologies like domestic wind turbines and solar panels. But since most of us live in urban areas with distinctly stunted windflow a better alternative may be fitting solar panels. As prices drop, payback periods are shortening, and with energy companies regularly hoiking their prices, solar and wind 'renewables' are inevitably becoming a serious option.

Main trades needed on site

- **Electricians:** Running cables and boxes.
- **Plumbers:** Running supply pipes, heating pipes and waste pipes. Fitting water tanks and CH systems.

www.home-extension.co.uk

14 PLASTERING, SCREED AND INTERNAL FINISHES

For many homeowners there's only one finish that looks right, and that's good honest plasterwork. Saving a few quid with a cheap and cheerful finish on your extension now could be a big mistake, and simply wouldn't do justice to all the hard work to date.

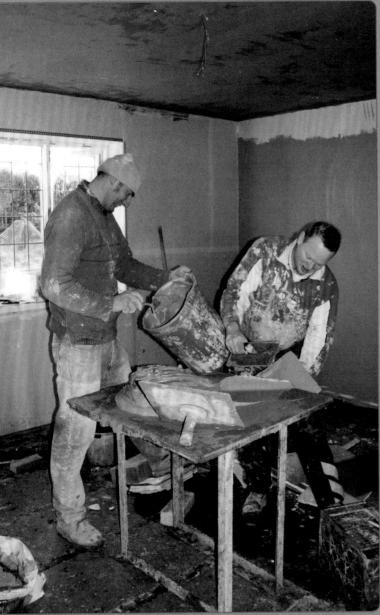

Psychologically, this is one of the big turning points in the entire project. A few days of *'bish, bash, bosh'* and the resulting pinky-brown veneer on your walls creates a profound and pleasing transformation. Suddenly your extension will start to feel like part of your home, albeit one in need of decoration and fitting out.

But this brief description of plastering doesn't really do justice to the skills involved. Many of us who pride ourselves at being able to turn our hand to tackling most jobs have had a bash at plastering at one time or another, only to retreat chastened by the unfortunate experience to assess the saggy, uneven results from a safe distance.

So revered were plasterers during the late 1980s housing boom that the legendary 'Loadsamoney' TV character was cast as a high-earning member of this select band. But the expense of employing tax-exile plasterers resulted in a number of alternative finishes being introduced, such as artex and brush-on 'textured' paints designed to disguise rough surfaces. Other alternatives included hanging thick vinyl wallpapers, polystyrene foam ceiling tiles, DIY easy-skim plaster, and skipping the plastering process altogether by painting directly onto plasterboard. Of these, only the last is now considered to be both desirable and technically feasible for large surface areas.

For most home extension projects the choice is whether to opt for a traditional hard plaster surface to masonry walls, or plasterboard dry-lining. Hard plaster requires at least one base coat (either sand/cement render or gypsum plaster), plus a single smooth plaster finishing coat. The advantage is that it's extremely durable. The main disadvantage is that it can put enormous amounts of water into the structure, requiring long drying-out times. In skilled hands, taped and jointed dry plasterboarding can provide a surface finish that once decorated looks indistinguishable from hard plaster.

There are some surfaces, however, that are better left naked. Where your extension joins the existing house there may be an old brick wall, the former outer wall surface. This can present an opportunity to create a stylish 'urban loft' look by leaving the brickwork exposed. Such 'feature brickwork' often looks the business, especially on fireplace chimney breasts, and should be finished by applying a masonry sealer. But be sure your intentions are clearly communicated to the plasterers or they'll automatically assume their mission is to obliterate every visible surface, and you'll get charged a second time for the extra labour involved in hacking it all off. Another alternative is Victorian pine matchboarding, fixed vertically between skirtings and dado rails, a useful device for hiding pipes and cable runs. But first, there are some key tasks that need to be done elsewhere.

Window boards

Once the windows have been installed the inside sills can be finished, by fixing the window boards in place. This can, of course, be done earlier in the build, but it's best left as late as possible to avoid damage. If your windows are of timber, and you're wondering what the horizontal grooves along the lower back are for, they're actually for the boards to be neatly rebated into. The boards are fitted level and flat, with the curved 'nosing' edge projecting into the room. They usually extend roughly 50mm wider than the window itself, beyond the plastered wall reveals.

It's easy to be wise after the event. After the plastering process is finished you might notice lots of mountainous blobs of indelible plaster all over your nice new window ledges – which is why covering them with protective sheets is advisable, thereby saving hours of laborious scraping and sanding.

Plasterboard

Plasterboard is an indispensable modern building material, providing a quick and easy way of covering large expanses

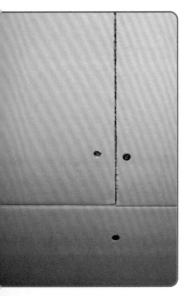

of wall and ceiling. Essentially it comprises a thick layer of compressed rigid gypsum plaster sandwiched between heavy-duty sheets of lining paper. It has been universally used for many years in mainstream construction, having finally superseding old lath and plaster in the 1930s.

Whilst you might have justifiable misgivings about ever truly mastering the art of plastering, lining walls with plasterboard should be within the capabilities of most seasoned DIYers. Having said that, neat and accurate fixing is crucial to the finished appearance of ceilings or walls.

Boards are commonly sold in thicknesses of 9.5mm and 12.5mm

and are normally fixed to ceiling joists or wall battens. They come in two main sheet sizes – giant economy size 2,400 x 1,200mm and the not quite so backbreaking 1,800 x 900mm size.

These dimensions perfectly suit studs or joists spaced at 600, 450 or 400mm centres, so you could be in for a nasty surprise if you've spaced your studs any differently. In such a situation either the edges of boards will be left unsupported (not a good idea) or the boards will have to be specially cut to fit.

When fixing boards, don't line them all up neatly next to each other. The joints should be staggered, to reduce the risk of cracking. The traditional use of clout nails to fix boards in place has today been superseded by screws, thanks to the invention of cordless power-screwdrivers.

Traditionally, boards had ivory-coloured paper on one side and a grey finish on the other. The ivory surface was for wallpapering onto directly, whereas the grey side would give a better bond when skimmed with a finishing plaster. Most plasterboard now comes with a grey surface suitable for either skimming or decorating.

It's now standard practice in mainstream housebuilding for the blockwork inner leaf of main walls to be dry-lined. This means the walls can be boarded ('tacked out') along with the ceilings. There are several advantages to decorating directly to the plasterboard, quite apart from the fact that it's a quick and easy way to provide a flat smooth surface. It cuts out the expense and hassle of wet plastering which would otherwise introduce damp into the building, and boosts the thermal insulation to help achieve good 'U' values.

If you want something a little more exciting than the standard variety, you could always fit thick thermally insulated board, or super fire-resistant plasterboard, or the foil-backed type that blocks condensation, or moisture-resistant board for use in steamy bathrooms. For beefed up sound insulation try gypsum fibre boards, which are not only more durable but are also strong enough to accept wall fixings directly.

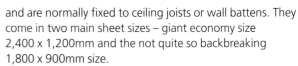

Decorating directly onto plasterboard

- ■ If you want to decorate direct to the surface without plastering it's best to use 'tapered-edge' boards rather than square-edged. These have thinner sides so that when they're butted together a shallow recess is formed either side of a joint.
- ■ The recess can be filled with jointing compound and then covered with joint tape (or a traditional cotton or hessian 'scrim').
- ■ When dry, it is then filled with two more coats of jointing compound, each one sanded down when dry. Each coat has a setting time of roughly 90 minutes.
- ■ Going over the edges with a damp sponge helps disguise the joint, leaving a smooth surface.
- ■ Finally, the surface can be sealed before receiving two coats of emulsion.

Photos: Lafarge Plasterboard.

Ceilings

Your choice of plasterboard will depend on how the joists are spaced. The thicker 12.5mm type is needed where ceiling joists are at 600mm centres, since 9.5mm board can only realistically cope with spans of up to 400mm between joists.

Where you're boarding a ceiling which has a cold space on the other side, such as a typical bedroom ceiling (below the loft), or when boarding direct onto the roof rafters, it's recommended that special foil-backed plasterboard is used. The foil helps prevent warm moist air from the house getting through and condensing into damp in the roof. Alternatively, a large polythene sheet can be fixed to the joists or rafters before boarding to act as a 'vapour check'. In some locations, you may need to place insulation between joists or rafters before plasterboarding.

Once fully 'tacked out' ceilings are normally skim plastered. But first the joints between boards are traditionally jointed with a scrim or tape, and jointing compound. The thin finishing coat of smooth plaster is applied by hand-held trowel, the plasterer standing on planks laid across small scaffold towers (or wearing stilts!). Any coving or decorative mouldings can be fitted afterwards.

There are about 60,000 house fires a year, with over 500 deaths – the vast majority of which are preventable with a few simple precautions. Fortunately, plasterboard is naturally fire-resistant and can normally protect the floor structure above for a minimum of half an hour. But despite being reassuringly non-combustible and inert, to be fully

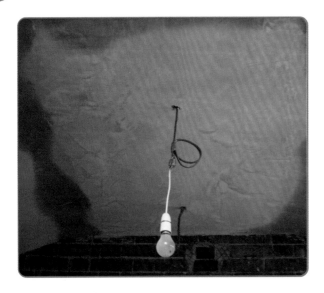

fireproof the surface needs to be skim plastered so that the paper lining doesn't get burnt and peel off. This is why ceilings and partition walls to integral garages must be plastered. In locations especially at risk from fire-spread plasterboard also needs to be laid to a double thickness.

In a typical house fire, flames will spread rapidly across the ceilings. It is at this juncture that some DIY enthusiasts have come to regret fitting highly combustible polystyrene foam tiles or timber cladding. If you really insist on having an Olde Worlde wooden-beamed ceiling in your extension, there are ways of doing it that still comply with the necessary half-hour fire-resistance standard. Applying special fire-retardant paint means it should be possible to achieve a 'Class 1 fire-spread rating'. If you're a little reluctant to paint your treasured timber beams, bear in mind that in the space of half an hour untreated softwood can burn through to a depth of at least 25mm, enough to weaken a timber structure sufficiently to bring about collapse.

Steel beams

The use of steel beams can permit designs that would otherwise be structurally impossible. Vast open roof spaces with cavernous ceilings, or sheet-glazed expanses of curtain walling are examples of the structural gymnastics afforded by RSJs. Tough though they undoubtedly are, as noted earlier, steels behave badly when confronted by fire, being prone to alarming degrees of buckling and twisting. This isn't what you want to see when your floors and walls are dependent on them for support. In short, they need protecting. Fortunately, the application of double layers of thick plasterboard with a skim plaster finish should keep Building Control happy. If, however, you favour the raw steel and bare brick 'warehouse look' in your extension, painting the exposed beams with special intumescent paint should do the trick (see Chapter 9).

Loft conversions

In the event of a house fire, you might have no option but to escape the burning inferno by jumping out of a first floor window. And there's every chance that you'd live to tell the tale. But making a similar dive from roof level means you might not be so lucky. So one of the main design challenges with loft conversions is trying to accommodate the far stricter fire regulations that apply to 'second-floor extensions', which includes any extensions built up above an existing part of the house. The regulations require that unless a suitable 'escape window' is provided, you need to create a fire-protected escape route through the house leading safely to an external door. Any existing doors leading off this escape route must be upgraded to a half-hour fire resistance standard with self-closers. Any timber stud walls along the way will also need special treatment (see below) and the door to the new loft room itself must meet the same 'FD30' standard.

Boarding internal walls

Back in Chapter 12 we left the freshly-built timber stud walls awaiting 'first fix'. This having now been done they are ready for plasterboarding. This job is made more challenging by the profusion of cables and pipes sprouting out of the walls and it's advisable to protect such services with clingfilm or tape since plastering by its nature can be a messy business.

For timber stud walls in locations that require better soundproofing or added resistance to the spread of fire, (such as those to integral garages), it's preferable to use the thicker 12.5mm boards, ideally in double layers.

Plastering

Modern gypsum plasters are far easier to use than old Victorian sand and lime wall finishes, being quicker to dry and less prone to cracking. However, that doesn't mean the finished job is guaranteed to be brilliant – far from it. The reality is that a lack of care on site means that a large percentage of the snagging issues that arise after completion often relate to plastering defects. Problems such as cracking or surface coats coming loose (due to shrinkage of backing coats) are not at all unusual.

Because most main walls are now dry-lined internally,

you can either choose to apply a skim finish over the plasterboard or decorate direct to its surface. However, many homeowners prefer the appeal of 'good solid' walls, so if your internal walls are of blockwork, or your main walls are not dry-lined, they'll require the hard plaster treatment (not an option for timber-framers).

Here, two coats of plaster will be needed, a base coat to cover the rough blocks, and a lightweight gypsum plaster coat for a smooth finish. This, of course, assumes the walls have been reasonably well built – no amount of 'dubbing out' can easily overcome an out-of-plumb wall, and no amount of paint or wallpapering will successfully cover bad plastering.

One of the secrets of successful plastering is to specify the right plaster for the job. The type of base coat to use will depend on the surface to be plastered. You may either choose a 'browning' or a 'bonding' plaster, or even a sand/cement render base coat. This 'floating coat', as it's known, is applied over the bare wall to a depth of about 8–16mm using a hawk and trowel. It is then 'scratched' to provide a key for the finish coat. The base coat is allowed to set for a couple of hours, but not to completely 'go off' and become too dry, otherwise it will need dampening before the smooth finishing coat can be applied. The skim coat is applied with a float, and a brush to flick water onto the surface to achieve a hard shiny finish (or a fine plant sprayer can come in useful). With modern plasters it should be possible to apply the base coat in the morning and the finish coat in the afternoon, or at least within 24 hours.

Photo: Savrow-stilts.com

Plasters of the world

There are many brands and varieties of plaster on the market, including some special-purpose plasters such as those designed to give protection from X-rays! But whatever the brand name, they can generally be classified as:

■ **Browning:** A lightweight gypsum plaster used for the base coat on normal surfaces such as blockwork. It's applied quite thickly to about 10mm to smooth any unevenness in the wall. Surfaces with high 'suction', such as aerated concrete blocks, may need a surface coat of PVA adhesive prior to plastering. Sets within about 2 hours.

■ **Bonding:** An alternative lightweight gypsum plaster backing coat for surfaces that have poor 'suction', *ie* that don't readily absorb moisture, such as engineering bricks and some dense concrete blocks. Never use two layers of bonding plaster as it can cause shrivelling and crazing in the top coat – instead apply a layer of browning plaster over a layer of bonding. Sets within about 2 hours.

■ **Sand/cement render:** So hard that it's normally used externally, render can also be used inside as a base coat. It's comparatively heavy and impact-resistant. Often used where there's some risk of damp, such as in basements or rooms prone to condensation. It needs to be 'scratched' and left to dry for a few days before the finish coat is applied.

■ **Finishing:** A surface coat is applied as a 'skim' direct to plasterboard or on top of the base coat once it has hardened, to a depth of about 2mm (no more than 5mm). Can be trowelled off to produce a smooth 'polished' surface where walls are to be emulsioned. If you intend skimming over existing plaster or previously painted surfaces, rather than direct to plasterboard, then a coat of diluted PVA bonding should be applied, otherwise the surface may crack. Sets within about 1.5 hours.

■ **One-coat:** Instead of requiring a day between coats of conventional plaster, one-coat plasters can allow the work to be carried out in one operation, but 'trowelling-off' takes more skill and patience.

Helpful tip: When mixing plaster, always add the plaster to the water, not the other way round.

The drying-out process with traditional two-coat plasterwork can mean having to wait anything between two and six weeks before decorating. A 'breathable' water-based paint should be used rather than vinyl emulsion, which can trap in any residual moisture. If your base coat is of sand/cement render, it may take even longer to fully dry out. The rule of thumb is to allow about one month per inch total thickness of plaster, but in reality the weather and localised conditions on site can significantly affect performance. Builders have been known to assist nature's drying out process by installing battalions of industrial sized heaters, roaring away like jet engines, but this can cause cracking in the plaster and create moisture and condensation elsewhere, which doesn't do the timbers much good. Too much heat from air dryers will suck moisture off the face of the plaster, leading to a 'crazy-paving' effect. Just providing good ventilation to the room is normally the best approach.

Modern plaster contains a retardant to delay premature setting and to extend its workability, but this becomes less efficient after a long storage period, so never use old plaster since it will dry too quickly. The shelf life for bags of new plaster may be no more than three to four months, and they should be stored on site within strong plastic

bags to prevent damp finding its way in and making the material useless.

Many months later, when you've happily moved in and the building work is but a distant memory, it's not unknown for a strange phenomenon to occur. The plastered interior of the main walls in some modern buildings have been known to develop a weird ghostly effect called 'pattern staining' where the shape of the concrete blocks can be made out, eerily appearing through coats of plaster and emulsion. This is normally down to the mortar joints becoming visible since they're less well insulated than the lightweight aerated blocks, and being colder they attract condensation from the air. This in turn allows more dust to stick, creating the pattern. The solution is to wash the wall or redecorate, ideally with darker colours which will show it less. In severe cases, dry-lining with plasterboard should solve the problem.

entire wall it can be divided up into manageable sections, or bays, using vertical wooden battens temporarily nailed into place. These are known as 'grounds' and provide a useful guide to the plaster's depth. They should be set out using a spirit level so that they're truly vertical.

Working upwards from the bottom right corner of each bay, the plaster is applied in parallel vertical strips. Once each bay is plastered with its floating coat (base coat), its surface can be smoothed by running a wide horizontal batten up from ground level running along the 'grounds' on either side, like railway lines. This is performed with a sawing motion and then any low spots are filled with more plaster. As each bay is completed, the right hand 'ground' can be repositioned to form a new bay ready for plastering. Once the plaster surface has been keyed, the final thin layer of finishing plaster will later be applied.

Plastering a wall

Plastering a wall requires considerable care and patience, as plaster is not the easiest of materials to work with. It may readily slip from the hawk or trowel, or may slump perilously down the wall.

First, check that internal door linings are in place and positioned to suit the required depth of plaster (say about 12mm). Similarly, metal boxes for electric sockets and switches should have been set into the masonry but left projecting so that when the plastering is completed they'll be flush with the surface. Check that any conduits and pipes are securely fixed, with no pipes touching each other, and that there's sufficient space for them to be buried within the plaster covering.

Corner beading of galvanised metal or plastic should be fitted to any outer corners of walls, door openings, and window reveals. These are set in dabs of plaster and carefully aligned using a spirit level (or they can be anchored with galvanised masonry nails).

To ensure the correct depth of plaster across the

Dry-lining

Most large housing developers today dry-line the main walls internally as an alternative to traditional plastering, but not just for the thermal efficiency benefits. Although dry-lining is actually more expensive than traditional

plastering, this is offset by big savings from decorating direct or skim plastering that requires considerably less time to dry out. Skimmed plasterboard walls and ceilings of only 2mm thickness dry out very swiftly and can normally be decorated within 24–48 hours.

Photo: Lafarge Plasterboard

Photo: Lafarge Plasterboard

Plasterboard sheets can be fixed to the walls with a timber framework of battens or by simply squashing them onto blobs of plaster known as 'dabs'. It's good practice to leave a tiny gap of about 2mm between the adjoining sides of boards. Once these board joints are taped they'll be ready for decoration or skimming. As with hard plastering, angle beads should first be fixed in place over corners before being skimmed over for a neat finish. To conceal joints the boards have tapered edges, so that where they meet and are screwed in place the recess can be filled with jointing compound, covered with joint tape and a final slurry finish. This hides any visible shrinkage that could result in cracks.

Where a new plasterboard-lined stud wall joins up with a brick or block wall there's always going to be a risk of the plaster surfaces cracking at the join between the different materials, due to their different rates of expansion. Fixing metal lath over the join before plastering should hide any such movement. Likewise, where timber lintels or wallplates etc need to be plastered, metal lath should be first put in place to carry the plaster surface over them and to protect the timber.

Floor screeding

So far the concrete ground floors have been left unfinished in order to minimise the risk of damaging the new surface. But now is the time to complete the job by applying a suitable finish upon which the carpets or floor-tiles etc can be laid.

Whether you've opted for a traditional concrete slab floor, or modern beam and block construction, the most popular method of finishing is to apply a fine sand and cement screed, which provides a smooth, flat floor finish. This is a job best carried out by the plasterers. However, there are alternatives to screeding, such as placing floorboarding over battens and a layer of polythene sheeting.

First, however, you'll normally need to insulate the floor with a layer of rigid foam insulation placed over the concrete slab or the beam and block structure, as described earlier. The only time this wouldn't be needed is when concrete slab floors have already been insulated beneath the slab, at the foundation stage. Here the sand/cement screed mix would be applied directly over the slab, the concrete having been dampened down with a bonding mixture. This 'grout' of water and cement is mixed to a creamy consistency with diluted PVA bonding and applied prior to laying the screed. But normally concrete floors must be insulated prior to screeding, using special flooring grade insulation panels. Then once the surface of the insulation is clean and dust-free, the 'floating screed' mix can be poured, ensuring that an insulated gap is left around the perimeter.

Screed is typically laid to a thickness of about 75mm over insulation panels (the minimum depth required is 65mm). However, if it's applied directly to a concrete slab it only needs to be 40mm thick since it should bond strongly with the surface of the concrete. Where the damp-proof membrane hasn't already been installed below a concrete slab, the plastic sheet DPM must be laid over the slab before the insulation layer.

If you plan to run pipes and cables through the screed, purpose-made plastic ducts should be

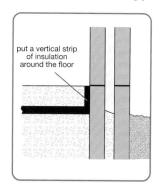

put a vertical strip of insulation around the floor

Floor insulated, awaiting screed. Photo: eddystoneselfbuild.co.

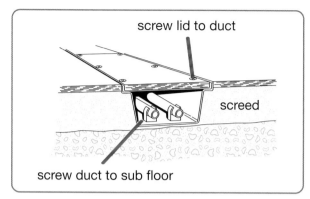

screw lid to duct

screed

screw duct to sub floor

Above: Difference in old & new floor levels allows for screed to extension.

embedded within it, with access covers for maintenance (since unprotected copper pipes in concrete floors will corrode within a few years). Here it's advisable to add a minimum extra 10mm depth of screed to reduce the risk of cracking.

As a precaution, pipe ducts and conduits should be located away from the edges of the room to avoid any risk of puncture from overenthusiastic carpet fitters later banging in sharp carpet-gripper nails. Screeds usually don't need reinforcement, but where the floor loadings are likely to be unusually heavy, then reinforcement mesh can be placed within the mix to reduce the risk of cracking.

The screeding mix should be quite dry, without too much water, and can be mixed on site from cement and sharp sand. A mix of 1:3 cement/sand is better for flexible floor coverings like vinyl, and 1:4 for a rigid tile floor. Or it can be delivered ready-mixed in truck-loads. To avoid sandy patches and hollow areas in the floor, the mortar must be well mixed.

Achieving a nice, smooth, perfectly level surface is more difficult than it sounds – some builders have been known to produce floors you could ski down. Obtaining a level floor finish is made easier by dividing the slab into oblong strips or 'bays', using thin wooden planks known as 'screeding rails' to act as depth guides. These must be perfectly level and placed across the floor about every 450mm, parallel to each other. Once poured, the screed can then easily be levelled by running a wide batten along the top of both rails. The final surface can be smoothed with a steel trowel, keeping the blade wet to lubricate it. Each batten can then be removed once the bays are filled, and each resulting narrow gap packed with screed and smoothed to match. Or the surface can be smoothed using a power float.

Once complete, the wet screed should be protected for the drying period by a layer of polythene, and then left to cure for at least three days before being walked on. As with plaster, extra time must be allowed for the newly laid screed to thoroughly dry out before covering with tiles, timber boarding, laminate etc. This normally means waiting at least another two weeks, which is why it makes sense to coincide the job with the plaster drying-out period.

In addition to 'plain vanilla' floor screeds, more

sophisticated specialist self-smoothing screeds are now available which cure within a few hours. These can be mixed and poured from a bucket, and then spread using a steel float. They are available in more exotic colours than the drab grey/green of the traditional sand/cement mix. Such self-levelling screeds are easier to use but more expensive.

Above: Freshly screeded floor.

Main trades needed on site

- **Carpenters:** Fitting timber window boards etc.
- **Plasterers:** Plastering walls and plasterboard, screeding concrete floors.
- **Labourers:** Fixing plasterboard sheets to ceilings and walls, laying insulation.

www.home-extension.co.uk

15 SECOND FIX

Once the walls are all nicely plastered, the electrician, plumber and joiner will need to return to complete their work. Whereas the first fix works are hidden away within the structure, the second fix items will be there for all to see. The bathroom sanitary fittings can now be installed, and the kitchen fittings connected up. But first, all the mess left behind by the 'wet trades' should be cleared and the site tidied.

Photo: InHouse kitchens

Although kitchens and bathrooms are one of the last areas to be completed, they depend on quite elaborate plumbing and electrical connections all being in the right place. It's therefore essential to carefully plan your requirements well in advance, to avoid the need for expensive alterations later.

Dream kitchens

During the 1990s, something happened to our relationships with our kitchens. The old design template of a kitchenette stuck on the back of the house as something of an afterthought was no longer adequate. The traditional small kitchen and separate dining room layout was pronounced dead. Instead, new houses boasted generous open-plan kitchen/diners, some incorporating bright integral conservatories. This sudden desire for spacious family kitchens is probably the most significant change in interior layouts for 50 years, somewhat ironically coinciding with the nation's insatiable desire for takeaways and microwave meals. Today, the kitchen is very often the focal point of the home and one of the busiest rooms in the house. Hence the need for many of us to extend.

Designing your new kitchen sounds like fun, but it's fun with a potentially massive price tag attached. Getting carried away is easy, squandering a king's ransom on fabulous hand-crafted bespoke units. But unless you live in a very pukka residence indeed you probably don't need to part with all that cash. The hard truth is, splashing out lavishly on custom fittings will probably make very little difference to the value of the average house when you finally come to sell. Obviously, if you insist on buying exclusive designer brand-name appliances your budget will evaporate more rapidly. But with a bit of thought it shouldn't be too hard to create an impression of opulence using relatively inexpensive units, perhaps set off with a good quality granite or hardwood worktop and some stylish fitted appliances.

Photo: Romanys EBKE

Kitchen planning

There's considerably more to designing the layout of a kitchen than first meets the eye, and woe betide those who fail to first consult the ladies. Having to change the position of fittings at a later date is likely to mean re-routing the electrics, the gas pipes, and the plumbing, which will be neither cheap nor easy. So it pays to mull over the proposed kitchen layout at some length well in advance.

Kitchen suppliers are normally happy to create a detailed 3D image of the room so you can easily visualise the new units in place before placing your order. If, however, you don't want to rely entirely on the (not unbiased) opinion of an in-store salesperson, it's not too difficult to conceive your own 'virtual kitchen' before making that purchase commitment. If you're not overly confident with IT and, like most of us, not terribly CAD-literate, invest instead in a pad of graph paper. Carefully draw a scale plan of the kitchen, starting with the main

walls, and then add all the window and door openings, marking the positions of radiators and sockets. Then draw an elevation view looking at each wall in turn as if standing in the room. It may sound a little Blue-Peter-ish, but cutting out scale shapes of units and appliances and sticking them on your grid-plan can prove extremely helpful, saving you from making grave errors later on site.

Fortunately, this is one part of the build where Lady Luck really is on your side. The great thing about building a purpose-made extension is that right from the start you can custom-design the room to suit the kitchen units and layout that you want. Need space for a king size wine rack? No problem, just make your extension 600mm bigger. It's far easier building it from scratch than trying to squeeze new kitchen units into an odd-shaped old room with bowed walls, minimal sockets and antique pipework.

Having said that, you still need to have your wits about you. It's scary how easily key design issues can get overlooked – for example, discovering at the last minute that there's a door just where you wanted to put the fridge. So it's important to carefully plan the hot and cold water supply routes, the wastes for sinks, washing machines, and dishwashers, and vents for dryers. Check the position of all the new electric power point sockets and light switches in relation to the new units and appliances. Also bear in mind the positions for fused isolator switches, oven master controls, cooker hood fans and extractor vent ducting, as well as any under-unit lighting. Not forgetting to check available power supplies for waste disposal units or water softeners etc.

Base units are normally 700mm high and 600mm deep. Wall units are also 700mm high but only 300mm deep. If

Photo: visionhouse-software.co.uk

there is a standard width it's the 'appliance friendly' 600mm unit, although 300, 400, 500, 1,000 units are also available. Laminate worktops are usually sold in 40mm thicknesses, but dearer hardwood beech or oak ones can be 26mm or 42mm. Beech is considerable cheaper than oak, and iroko is a popular mid priced alternative. Granite tends to be the most expensive choice.

Builders can normally buy kitchen units at discounts of 20–40% off the list price. If your builder both supplies and fits the units, there should be no doubt about who's responsible for fixing any snags like gaps and loose fittings. If you supply your own units this may not be so straightforward.

There's a lot of detail to get right when installing new kitchens, so before parting with your next interim payment check that all the units are well fixed to the walls or floors, that the doors operate freely, and that the worktop is the

Kitchen design

- **Internal room measurements** must be accurate and in metric (usually mm). Ensure your kitchen supplier visits the site to take his own measurements, so that he can't blame you later if things don't fit!
- **Check design restrictions** – *ie* the positions of boilers, doors, windows, supply pipes and waste pipes.
- **Mark the position** of hot and cold supply pipes and waste pipes.
- **Electric sockets and switches** must be well clear of hobs and sinks.
- **Note the internal heights** of window sills, and the available ceiling space.
- **Cookers** need a minimum 300mm of clear worktop space either side and should not be located next to a sink or beneath a window.
- **Wall units** must not be fixed directly above a hob/oven or above a sink.
- **Fridges or freezers** shouldn't be next to a cooker.
- **Door swing openings** for all base and wall units should be marked on your plan.

correct thickness and is neatly joined with a decent seal or upstand where it meets the walls. Check also that the finishes have not been damaged or units weakened by holes cut for pipes and cables.

Designer bathrooms

The modern bathroom is much more than just somewhere to wash. If there's one room that can lend itself to a spot of soothing mood creation, this is probably it. Indeed, many sales brochures no longer even refer to 'bathrooms' as such, instead promoting the virtues of 'aquatic rooms' – '*havens of relaxation that will help you wash away your day leaving you peaceful and calm*'.

It's hard to argue with that, but what style of fittings would best suit your vibrant new 'aquatic room'? Choose from a mouth-watering selection of spa bath tubs, concealed and counter-sunk units, repro Victorians and Edwardians, corner baths, walk-ins, whirlpools and jacuzzis, massage and steam tubs and baths for aqua aerobics and yoga. Available in a choice of ceramic, marble, granite or glass. And that's before you encounter the wonders of themed panels and decorative toilet seats.

It may help to focus on the original architecture of your house. For example, art deco style fittings should look good in 1920s and 1930s properties, whereas a post-modern glass and stainless steel bathroom won't do a lot for the average thatched cottage. Post-war houses generally allow more style-freedom and often suit the clean lines of modern designs.

Beyond the choice of sanitary fittings, there are other design issues to ponder, such as whether to install cupboards and bathroom furniture for storage space. If space permits, it's normally a good idea to have a separate shower cubicle within a bathroom rather than just a mixer over the bath. Or how about a Continental-style walk-in wet room, with fully-tiled waterproof floors and walls? Good tiling adds a vital water-resistant quality to walls and

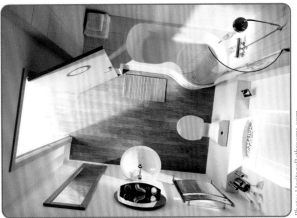

Photo: HeritageBathrooms.com

Photo: CPLraindance.com

floors as well as creating a pleasant Mediterranean theme. Finally, you may wish to keep your towels dry with an ingeniously sculpted artistic heated towel rail and enjoy a touch of the 'Tate Moderns' whilst 'washing away your day'.

On a more practical note, if the contractor is quoting to supply as well as to fit the bathroom, ask him to state the cost of the sanitary fittings separately. The contractor's price should be pretty close to the price you'd pay if buying them yourself. He'll get a trade discount that will cover his 'margin' and so shouldn't need to bump up the price.

When the job is done pay careful attention to the detailing at the edges of baths and shower trays. Probably the most common cause of leaks in bathrooms comes from the joints where they abut walls, particularly if using plastic fittings. Never rely on grout, but rather use purpose-made sealing trim strips, or a suitable silicone

mastic sealant. Many brown stains on downstairs ceilings are due to such minor defects, or from ill-fitting shower screens on baths.

Baths

Chocolate advertisements and shampoo commercials have a lot to answer for. Some have achieved considerably more sales of exotic roll-top Victorian baths than crumbly chocolate treats. But bubbly notions of fabulous antique cast iron baths gracing your dream bathroom may be swiftly discarded the moment you try to lift one. Even with the help of all your mates from the pub it may take the best part of an afternoon to install an original iron bath, before you notice it actually needs expensive re-enamelling. But the biggest problem is the miniscule claw feet, which transfer incredibly high loadings to the floor surface – as much in terms of pounds per square foot as a Challenger

Photo: Romanys Architectural Ironmongers

tank. A bit of chipboard floor panelling under the bath just isn't going to be up to the job, so if you don't want a moving experience when sitting in your bath be sure to first strengthen your floor.

Electrics

Your chosen electrical surface fittings can now be connected to all the loose cables and boxes that have lain dormant since first fix. The sudden appearance of socket covers, switches, ceiling roses, and light fittings throughout the extension lends it a homely aspect. As far as the lighting is concerned, Part L1B of the Building Regs requires that you install at least one energy-saving fluorescent or CF bulb for every three rooms, including hallways. The actual light fittings must exclusively accept these low energy bulbs (to stop you substituting them later with old cheapo ones). External lighting must also use energy efficient CF bulbs with sensors so they only operate occasionally. And bathroom light fittings must be concealed, such as sealed downlighters, to prevent any risk of direct contact with water.

Otherwise, the second fix electrics are normally a fairly straightforward process, assuming there are no last minute changes of plan. The various switches and socket covers are normally fitted before decoration, although any tiled wall surfaces should if possible be completed beforehand. The decorators will nevertheless later need to go round loosening the covers so as not to ruin their appearance by camouflaging them with artistic daubings (they will then regard it as someone else's job to screw them all back again). Any unfinished safety earth-bonding must be completed before appliances are connected. The consumer unit to the main house electrics may also need to be upgraded, so it's best to time this with when the family aren't all glued to their favourite TV soaps or computer games. Finally, a test should be carried out and a safety certificate issued.

Plumbing

Second fix for heating and plumbing is a little more arduous than for the electrics. All the pipework tails will need connecting up to the various new kitchen and sanitary fittings. Dishwashers and washing machines should be connected and checked that they work properly – something often left for the client to struggle with. One other thing sometimes overlooked is the testing of new boilers, which should be jointly carried out by the electrician

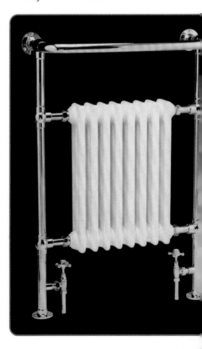

and plumber. In an ideal world the new plumbing system would be leak-free from the word go, but in reality a loose connection here or an unsoldered joint there isn't unusual. Just make sure the plumber hasn't disappeared without trace at the crucial moment. Small leaks usually manifest themselves within the first couple of days.

One job that you may prefer to leave until after the walls are decorated is the fixing in place of the radiators, because trying to paint behind them once fitted isn't much fun. When all the plumbing is complete and all the sinks, basins, baths, WCs and showers are fully connected up, Building Control may want to carry out checks, such as ensuring non-return valves are in place to the various water supply pipes. They'll want to be sure that waste water discharges fluently, and that all the above-ground plumbing has been tested as fully watertight, which means the system being capable of holding water or air under pressure for at least three minutes.

Floor finishes

Beautiful flooring can give real character to even the plainest of rooms. But as anyone who's ever owned a plain beige carpet will tell you, floor coverings need above all to be practical.

Your choice of floor coverings is very much down to personal taste. In recent years, the British love affair with wall-to-wall carpets has been on the wane, perhaps because laminate and timber flooring seems to make even the smallest rooms appear cavernous. Ceramic tiles and limestone floors need careful laying, but the results can be stunning, with the added benefits of easy cleaning and low maintenance. Traditionally found only in kitchens, bathrooms, and some hallways, their quality and durability means that they're now becoming popular in reception rooms and even bedrooms.

Internal joinery

The job isn't over until all your skirting boards, doors and architraves are in place. But this can't happen until your final floor levels are known and any floor tiles laid. Second fix carpentry is a bit of a mixed bag of different joinery jobs, and there may be other outstanding items, such as fitting staircase balustrades, boxing in pipes, fixing mouldings, dado and picture rails, and finishing off the kitchen units. The desired style of joinery, such as traditional Victorian ogee or modern plain chamfered, needs to be consistent throughout the new rooms, if possible matching the joinery in the main house.

The quality of finish is very important as it's the one thing most people notice above all. A lot of snagging items are concerned with getting the detail right – ensuring joinery is securely fixed with joins neatly mitred, and that any pipe ducts have screwed access panels.

Medium density fibreboard

Good old MDF. It made the career of 'Handy Andy' and other television DIY heroes! There's not much in the way of internal joinery that you can't buy in MDF – picture rails, dado rails, architraves, skirting. Unlike real wood, it doesn't warp, split or shrink, nor does it suffer from the inconvenience of knots that need priming. But unlike timber its raw appearance isn't attractive and it needs to be painted, which is why it comes pre-undercoated, ready for the topcoat, saving time and money. Once painted it's virtually impossible to tell apart visually from the real thing. Unfortunately, however, there's a potential health issue when cutting and drilling the stuff. Ultra-fine dust particles emitted when cutting with electric saws can cause irritation to skin, eyes, and lungs, so it's essential to wear a suitable dust mask.

Internal doors

As noted earlier, one of the joys of a newbuild project is that you don't have to muck about trying to squeeze standard-sized new doors into hideously warped old frames. Instead, your new doors should slide fluidly into their new frames. Most internal doors are hinged to a frame made of timber liners screwed to the studwork or blockwork wall. Only once the liners have been fitted, the plastering completed, and the final floor levels known should the internal doors be hung. Obviously a little consideration is first required as to whether the door is to open inwards or outwards, and which side of the frame you want the hinges to hang from.

When it comes to selecting internal doors, the choice is essentially between hollow or solid. The majority of factory-made internal doors are of the hollow, lightweight variety. These comprise a simple timber frame with a honeycomb cardboard core, clad on both sides with moulded panelled surface covers. But before hanging hollow doors be aware that the timber frame on the side that is to be hinged is often slightly thicker to accommodate the screws, which is why it should be marked '*hinge side*'. You also need to locate the solid wood block that will house the door latch (the metal tube that is embedded inside the door).

Solid doors are normally made of pine or similar softwood and have a more expensive feel, giving a more pleasing chunky sound when they shut. Timber internal doors are either stainable or paint-only grade. Paint-only ones are often remarkably good value being made from cheaper timber, but this may contain dead knots, which can work loose. Stainable solid softwood doors can be twice as expensive, but don't cost anything like as much as

solid hardwood oak or meranti doors. Hardwood veneer can be a less expensive compromise.

Fitting latches and locks in solid doors should be relatively straightforward. If your heart is set on having door knobs, rather than handles, they need to be set further in from the edge so that you don't scrape your knuckles on the frame every time you open the door. Because the hole in the latch determines how close the handle will be to the edge of the door, you need to use a longer 75mm latch rather than the standard 63mm size (or 95mm for external doors).

Fitting external doors inside the house is not a good idea, as their moisture content of around 18 per cent is way too high, so they tend to twist and warp. The moisture content of internal doors should ideally be about 10 per cent or lower.

It's unlikely that you will need fire-check doors in a typical home extension, unless it's three or more storeys high or you're building a self contained 'granny flat' dwelling (the plans won't have been passed by Building Control without fire-doors being specified where appropriate).

Most internal doors can be supported by a pair of butt hinges – brass ones are preferable, especially in moist kitchens and bathrooms since they won't rust. As with exterior doors, upper hinges are positioned about 150mm from the top and lower ones 200–225mm from the bottom. Fire doors may require a third hinge as well as self-closers and thicker doorstops.

From a design viewpoint, part-glazed doors are a useful way to boost the amount of light in a room. You may want to create a sweeping entrance to a room with a pair of glazed double doors, but note that any glazed lower door panels need to be fitted with safety glass.

Your choice may be influenced by the doors in the rest of the house, unless you're replacing the whole lot. In terms of styles, there are plenty of options – such as

smooth, modern flush doors, traditional four-panelled Victorian, six-panelled Georgian, 'one over three' panelled 1930s, or 'ledge and brace' cottage style.

Standard internal door sizes are 1,981mm high by either 762 or 686mm wide and are normally 35mm thick. Although door liners are sold in sizes designed to accept doors of standard heights and widths, builders sometimes construct them from scratch. If you know this in advance it may be a good opportunity to make a bold architectural statement by fitting some unusual or super-wide 838mm doors (which comply with the accessibility and mobility requirements of the Building Regs Part M). Or if you're feeling courageous, why not conjure up some quaint, curiously-dimensioned doors from the local salvage yard? As long as it's all planned in good time, well before the internal walls are built, this may not cost a great deal more than fitting ordinary doors, and is a great way to add some real style. Reclamation yards are great places to source all kinds of weird and wonderful objects – perhaps you'll unearth an intricately carved *Grinling Gibbons* masterpiece.

It always pays to chew things over carefully before buying. Warped doors can rarely be much improved, and most over-large doors can only be trimmed by a small amount before it affects their strength.

Door furniture should match the age and style of the property – for example, lever handles aren't architecturally suited to most pre-1950s houses, where knobs were often

the order of the day. Salvage yards may once again stock some weird and wonderful original handles.

Doorstops and architraves

Once the new door is swinging smoothly on its hinges and the catch clicks satisfyingly into place, the frame can be completed by fixing the doorstops in position. These are the long strips of 30 x 12mm softwood that are fitted up the middle of the liners, literally stopping the door from swinging through the frame. Each doorstop can be nailed into position on the liner using small 'lost-head' oval nails, their heads punched and buried below the surface ready for filling. Fire doors will need special treatment, with beefed up doorstops, or with an intumescent strip as described earlier. Which just leaves one problem – what to do about the ugly joint between the door liner framework and the plaster.

Architraves are the time-honoured solution. These long strips of decorative moulded timber are fixed around the sides of the doorframe, neatly covering rough gaps. You can fix them in place using lost-head nails driven into the liner at an angle. Or if you believe the claims made by glue manufacturers, nails may not be required at all. The architraves are normally set back about 6mm from the inner edge of the door liner. At their top corners they're mitred and pinned together, and at their feet they may project out slightly, being a little thicker than the adjoining skirting boards. The architraves can then be skew-nailed into the skirting boards.

Skirting, dado and picture rails

The purpose of the humble skirting board is traditionally to disguise unseemly gaps where the plastering on the walls comes face-to-face with the floor. For the Victorians, the secondary purpose was to protect expensive wallpaper from damage, a task shared by the dado rails higher up the wall at waist level. Skirting is by no means essential, and is sometimes absent in properties where the detailing is neat enough to be left exposed, or in Mediterranean holiday homes with rendered walls that merge seamlessly with concrete floors.

However, skirting is an extremely handy device for covering the expansion gaps that must be left at the edges of various types of floor coverings, such as laminates. Skirting may be screwed, glued or nailed to the walls. The accuracy of mitring and fitting is more important when the wood is left exposed and varnished or stained, whereas a small amount of filler is permissible when it's to be painted.

Main trades needed on site
- **Electricians:** Second fix wiring.
- **Plumbers:** Second fix and fit bathroom and kitchen.
- **Heating engineers:** Fitting radiators, boilers and finishing heating systems.
- **Joiners:** Internal joinery and kitchen units.
- **Tilers:** Wall and floor tiling.
- **Labourers:** Humping heavy bath and kitchen fittings etc.

www.home-extension.co.uk

Picture rails are slim horizontal moulded timber strips traditionally placed along walls about a foot below ceiling level. It's unlikely that you'd want to fit them other than where your new rooms need to match the style of a pre-war or period house. Dado rails situated roughly halfway up the wall have, on the other hand, made a bit of a comeback in recent years, allowing an appealing two-tone decorative regime to be applied to the walls.

Apples and pears

If, back in Chapter 12, your extension was one of the few requiring a new staircase to be installed, you'll now be glad that you took the precaution of protecting the staircase joinery. Dustsheets covering the treads, risers and strings will by now be hidden beneath a thick film of grime. It shows the sense of waiting until now before fitting the delicate handrail and balusters (spindles).

Finishing

Victory is now so close that you can almost touch the completion certificate shimmering tantalisingly on the horizon. But it's not over until the decorators have done their stuff.

This is when you may notice some rather ugly pieces of work left exposed, such as bathroom waste pipes, central heating pipes and cables under boilers. Surely these should have all been neatly boxed in? Regrettably, unless clearly specified these are items commonly charged as 'extras'. And it's amazing how expensive a bit of 'two-by-one' covered with plywood can suddenly be.

Although your project may be getting very near its end, it's important to remember that a lot of trades will still need to come and go, ferrying tools and materials through the house. There remains real potential for your priceless Louis Vuitton cut-glass light shades to get accidentally smashed and for those beautifully mitred worktops and expensively veneered floors to get cracked, scratched, and sprayed with paint. If it can be damaged, it probably will be, so don't be too hasty whipping away those covers.

16 FINISHING THE JOB

Until now you may have been perfectly happy to stand back and let the professionals get on with the job of creating your new dream home. But if your budget is starting to wear a bit thin it might be worth considering tackling some of the finishing work yourself. Most of us are not averse to a spot of emulsioning, so perhaps doing a little decorating could help breathe some life back into the bank account.

Photo: Sadolin

Internal finishing

You may have been planning to get your hands dirty with a bit of DIY input right from the start, but if not, any such change of plan now could constitute a change in the contract and must be discussed. If your builder is willing to accept your proposal, he'll first need to formally agree to this in writing, with the contract sum reduced accordingly for savings in labour and materials.

But far from being crestfallen at the prospect of losing a profitable part of the job, it's not unusual for contractors to actually be quite happy to oblige. They'll know from bitter experience that it's now, at the decoration stage, that clients often feel confident enough to start changing their minds about colour schemes and generally interfering. This is also the phase where the contractor's sights are firmly set on the next job, and their prior enthusiasm for your project is rapidly wearing off. Seduced by the aroma of big bucks wafting over the fence, they might be only too keen to have everything wrapped up as swiftly as possible. So bringing forward the completion date and allowing them to get their hands on the final payment and some of the retention money could be a tempting proposition.

But taking such a shortcut could be counterproductive unless you're very confident in your own abilities. For many house buyers the quality of the finish is everything, and cutting corners with streaky, dripping and patchy decoration will spoil the job.

Decorating

People easily forget what a skilled job this is, because anyone can buy a can of emulsion and a roller and start slapping paint on a wall. But in reality achieving good results requires not just skill but a lot of hard graft. The old cliché is still very true – decoration can only be as good as the preparation. Which means plenty of perspiration. Laborious rubbing down, followed by filling and then rubbing down again, before going anywhere near a can of paint.

Bad paintwork will manifest itself in the form of runs, bubbles, streaks and gaps. There'll be rough lumpy surfaces and trapped dust. Poor varnishing will appear patchy and after the first few months may start to blister and peel off. Good decoration, on the other hand, can hide a multitude of sins, although obviously there are limits. Because this is the final finished surface that the client sees, decorators are sometimes unjustly put in the firing line for everybody else's rubbish work. Even the best spray paint job can't completely hide a rusty wreck underneath.

Within reason, it's the decorator's job to 'snag' the previous finishing trades – such as repairing around any holes cut by plumbers or electricians and filling edges of panelling and boxing that the carpenter has constructed. It's obviously important that no paint is applied until the dust in the air has settled and the immediate environment is clean, so a good decorator will avoid working where there are piles of rubbish or where other trades are still active.

The decorating trade is usually carried out on a labour only basis. Decorators normally supply their own brushes, filler and sandpaper etc, but the paint will be supplied by the main contractor, or by the client if the trades are being employed directly.

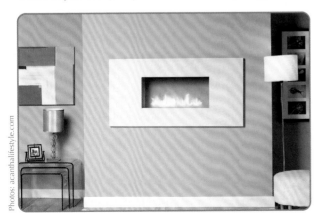

Photos: acanthalifestyle.com

Photo: capitalfireplaces.co.uk

Preparation

New timber surfaces should be rubbed down to a smooth finish before the first coat, using medium to fine paper of about 120 grade, and then rubbed down again between coats.

After initial sanding there may be small indentations, such as from nail heads, which need to be filled. It's a bit of a DIY myth that paint alone can fill holes; you really need to apply a suitable filler. For surfaces to be varnished, a wood filler should be used which matches the colour of the wood as closely as possible. There may be larger gaps where skirting and architraves meet the walls, which can be filled using flexible filler or decorators' caulking from a sealant gun.

Painting softwood

Time was when all the visually important internal joinery – the doors, skirting, architraves etc – was universally finished in good old gloss white. Today preserving the natural beauty of the wood using a stain, wax or varnish finish is a popular alternative. A matt white or soft sheen cream finish can also add an element of charm to the interior design.

Where bare timber is to be painted (as opposed to stained or varnished) it will typically require one or two coats of primer, after any knots have been treated. It should then be undercoated before the final coat of gloss, silk or matt paint is applied.

Knotting solution is used on resinous areas to prevent resin leaking and discolouring the subsequent layers of paint. Aggressive resins can even force the paint surface to separate entirely from the timber. Knotting solution takes approximately three hours to dry. Alternatively, a 'self-knotting' primer can be used.

Wood primer is a thin paint which soaks into the grain taking some of the porosity out of the new timber. This seals the surface to prevent further coats of paint soaking in. If you skip this and apply an undercoat or topcoat directly to bare wood the moisture is sucked out of it too quickly and the paint dries on the surface but is poorly bonded, and may quickly peel.

Painting new softwood

- Rub down with glasspaper to get a smooth finish over the entire surface.
- Apply knotting solution to any knots.
- Apply a coat of wood primer or universal primer.
- Fill any voids with a suitable filler and smooth using glasspaper.
- Brush off all dust.
- Touch up any exposed knots.
- Apply undercoat.
- Apply at least one top coat.

Varnish and wood stain

Applying boring old gloss paint may not do justice to all that expensive new joinery. You may instead prefer a transparent varnish, stain or waxed finish that enhances the timber rather than hides it. But this means any faults and blemishes in the joinery will stand out, so extra careful preparation is needed to achieve a good, natural finish. Varnish is popular for joinery and timber floors as it protects the wood and highlights the beauty of the grain. It is often applied before the walls are decorated, since careless emulsioning could leave visible marks showing through on the finished product. Varnish combines polyurethane with wood stain, so that the stain effectively sits on the surface of the timber rather than being absorbed into it. If you want to modify the colour of the joinery to blend in with other woods, coloured varnishes can be used, for example giving softwood the appearance of oak.

Preparation is similar to that for painting, but the sanding process needs to be more thorough, finishing off with a fine grade of paper. Note that sanding across the grain can leave scratches which may later become exaggerated. Varnish is applied in layers of two to four thin coats. To achieve a durable finish, the bare wood should first be sealed with a thinned coat of varnish diluted with about ten per cent solvent to key into the timber. Allow to dry and apply a further two coats of undiluted varnish. Remember that each coat applied will darken the wood, so once the desired shade has been achieved, subsequent coats of clear varnish can be applied. It's important to apply an even film to avoid patchy colours and brush marks, and to not double-coat the varnish (or wood stain) where it overlaps.

Wood stains are easy to use and resistant to fading. They consist of dyes which are spirit or water-based. The technique for applying wood stain is different from painting since the dye is much more fluid than paint and will dry very quickly into the wood. It can be applied quickly and evenly using a clean rag after the surfaces have first been sanded. Note that water-based dyes can cause the grain of the wood to temporarily swell when applied, so the wood should not be sanded directly after it's been dyed.

Paint safety

Gloss paints and spirit stains contain chemical cocktails known as VOCs (volatile organic compounds). From a health risk point of view, as well as an ecological perspective, it's better to specify low VOC paints, or water-based gloss paint. Water-based acrylics are more user-friendly and make washing out your brushes dead easy. Despite some trade prejudice against them, they perform as well as oil-based paints, but won't give a highly shiny gloss finish (but then silk or matt is often preferred).

When the job's done, flammable or polluting materials such as white spirit and paint should not be chucked away down drains – councils provide special waste disposal facilities.

Emulsioning

As noted earlier, you can't just slap paint onto a freshly plastered wall surface. If you do, it will shrink, crack and peel. Fresh plaster normally needs to be left for a few weeks before painting, until it's dry to the touch. The best guide is to ask the plasterers about recommended drying-out times. Fortunately, there is a short cut. Skimmed plasterboard surfaces can normally be decorated within a day or two.

If patience isn't your strongest quality, don't bank on wallpapering your extension any time soon. You'll need to allow several months for the surface to completely dry out prior to wallpapering, so that any shrinkage cracks can be filled and sanded. Even then the surface must first be 'sized' with a coat of diluted wallpaper paste. Wallpapering over plasterboard without first sealing it, will cause trouble in future when you want to remove the wallpaper, since it may be impossible to strip without also tearing away chunks of the plasterboard.

Emulsioning plastered walls

- ■ Rub down with fine glasspaper.
- ■ Brush off to remove all dust and particles.
- ■ Apply one coat of thinned emulsion paint (one part paint to three parts water) as primer.
- ■ Apply two coats of non-vinyl emulsion.

Once dried out, newly plastered walls, are normally decorated with emulsion, but not with vinyl emulsion, which prevents walls from breathing and traps any residual moisture. If you intend to decorate the plasterboard directly, it helps to prime the surface to make the paper less absorbent. For emulsion, use a diluted coat first to prime; for oil paints and wallpapering use an all-purpose primer.

Colour therapy

It's well established that the colours around us can affect our moods. So interior designers don't just pick a colour they like as much as one that will set the atmosphere for the room – to induce the right mood. And with your bank balance by now on life-support, creating a soothing, otherworldly ambience with some pastel-colours might be just the thing to help regain your sanity. So don't be deterred from creating a cool and inspired decorative vibe. True, estate agents routinely advise playing safe and sticking to neutral colours, and property developers rarely venture beyond the safer shades of magnolia, but hey, this is *your* home, so why not try something more original? A little feng shui colour therapy could be just what the doctor ordered after months of coping with builders on site.

Ceramic tiling

Wall and floor tiles come in a bewildering variety of shapes, sizes, colours, textures and patterns. Yet nothing seems to date quicker than last year's tile styles. Indeed, you can often date the age of a house fairly accurately from its wall tiles alone. But don't let that put you off. Wall tiling should be well within most DIYers' capabilities. Fortunately, you'll be off to a flying start working with smooth new wall surfaces rather then having to stick reluctant tiles to flaking plaster on old bowed walls.

Photo: designer-radiators.com

Wall tiling is normally carried out after the plastering is completed and fully dried out. It typically takes a tiler about an hour to fix a square metre of tiles plus another 10 minutes to grout them. The use of the correct tile spacers is important to help even out any inconsistencies in tile shapes. If timber panelled surfaces or boxed-in pipes are to be tiled, they are best made from water resistant plywood.

Flooring of ceramic, quarry or stone tiles is usually laid onto a screed, but can be laid on timber floating floors as long as the correct flexible adhesive is used and the surface is as rigid as possible. Even with a screed floor there may be some initial movement due to shrinkage, so using a flexible adhesive is still advisable. Finally, it's a wise precaution to buy at least a half a dozen more tiles than you need – if breakages or cracks occur in future, the colour of new tiles from different batches may not match.

Eco-design

If you want to go the extra mile creating a stunning, seductive interior that will amaze your friends, then you need to raise your shopping game further than the local DIY store. Going one step beyond the conventional means considering unusual alternatives and materials – such as polished concrete floors and creative use of LED lights in floors and walls. 'Eco-design' is currently very topical, focusing on using recycled and natural materials, such as non-toxic paints, recycled hardwood or slate flooring, and reclaimed wood worktops etc.

Insulating the roof space

What's the worst job you've ever had? Whatever the answer, it was probably a whole lot better than crawling around in hot cramped roof voids laying rolls of itchy glassfibre or mineral wool insulation, a job traditionally given to the new boys on site. This job is often carried out soon after the roof has been constructed and the ceilings fitted, although the stage at which it's done isn't critical. But builders can sometimes be prone to overlooking this task, so it is always worth taking a quick glance up there prior to completion.

Insulation is not an optional extra. The Building Control Officer will not pass the project without the work having been done satisfactorily. Out of all the things you can do to insulate your home, laying loft insulation is one of the most cost-effective and efficient. Normally about 150mm depth of insulation is laid between the ceiling joists and then another 100–150mm laid at right angles over the top (which will hide the joists from view, so watch where you tread). Fitting special plastic 'roof ventilator' trays at the eaves allows a clear passageway for air whilst letting you pack insulation into the eaves – a thermal weak-point. Talking of which, don't forget to insulate the loft hatch and ensure it sits snugly at the edges, so that howling draughts don't make a mockery of all your careful insulation efforts.

Whilst there's no scientifically proven evidence to date of associated health risks from loft insulation, common sense would suggest that snorting in lots of fine, airborne fibres over time isn't likely to do your lungs a tremendous amount of good. So if you're going to lay your own loft insulation, be sure to wear eye protectors and a facemask, and when the job's done thoroughly hose yourself down and vacuum all the bits off your clothes. It's better to use 'clean' loft quilt that comes ready-encased in polythene sheeting. Sheep's wool is nicer to work with as it isn't itchy like synthetic fibreglass or mineral wool, but it's about five times the price.

External finishing

Now for the finishing touches on the outside that will make your new home the envy of all who see it.

Painting

You need to be something of a natural optimist to be an outdoor painter in Britain, as well as being blessed with large reserves of patience and a generally philosophical attitude to life. If it's not raining, the weather is often too cold to achieve a sound finish. That's when it's not too windy, too humid, or even too hot. Damp or humid surfaces can prevent paint from sticking properly, leading to peeling. For a good result with external decoration, you ideally need weather that's calm, dry, and reasonably warm. A generous degree of flexibility needs to be built into your work programme so that you can wait for the right weather conditions to come along and then crack on with the job.

Fortunately, painters no longer need to be daredevils. Thanks to health and safety legislation the days of being sent on dangerous missions up impossibly high ladders are gone. Modern scaffold towers are easily erected and considerably safer.

External timbers

The traditional way of finishing external timbers is with oil-based gloss paint, applied in three coats – primer, undercoat and gloss. But today, new timber windows and doors should arrive on site ready-primed with a honey coloured stain basecoat, just awaiting their finish coats of stain or paint. If you want a painted finish it can save time and money to specify joinery ready primed with paint (rather than the standard stain basecoat). However, any bare timbers such as at roof level, will need the full treatment - which means knotting and priming (or a stain basecoat). Primer should be carefully brush into all the corners and joints, working along the grain. Once dry, it can be rubbed down, and then the undercoat applied. This in turn is allowed to dry and is then sanded down. Finally,

the surface coats of gloss paint are applied. The key to cutting decorating costs is reducing the number of coats needed to get a good quality finish, *eg* by using 'one coat' paints that let you dispense with the undercoat.

The main alternative to paint is woodstain – varnish is not now widely used externally as it can be prone to flaking or blistering. Stains are dearer to buy than paint, but quicker to apply and modern stains should let you dispense with the traditional third coat. Because stain soaks into the timber it is far less prone to peeling than paint or varnish. The thicker stains are classed as 'medium build' and have a light treacly consistency. The thinner 'low-build' variety are used on sawn timber, which can guzzle a surprising amount of the stuff. Traditionally, stains have been spirit-based, but like paint they are now available as water-based acrylics and normally contain a fungicide to inhibit mould growth.

So far so good. The only snag with having immaculate, gleaming new paintwork tastefully adorning your extension is that it might make the old house look a bit shabby in comparison. Nowhere is this more obvious than at eaves level where the new fascia boards meet the flaking paintwork of the old ones. This is why many home extenders decide to grasp the nettle and give the old timbers a good rub down and a lick of paint whilst the scaffold towers (and decorators) are at hand. But apart from the well-known risks of working at height, there are other potential dangers lurking here. Using a flame gun or hot-air burner on old paintwork can release particles of poisonous lead from old lead paint, which was widely used up until the 1960s. Worse, it's not unknown for a momentary lapse of concentration to cause tinder-dry eaves and rafter feet to become engulfed in flames.

Tile hanging

At the design stage you may have opted to partially clad the outside walls in a traditional architectural style that

dates back centuries – vertically hung tiles or slates. The use of patterned ornamental tiles can create a decorative feature to spruce up an otherwise plain-looking wall. Tiles are not only a good way of visually breaking up a large expanse of brickwork, but they're also extremely practical – they can help insulate an external wall whilst still allowing it to breathe. Tiling also requires

very little maintenance, which may account for its enduring popularity.

Plain tiles are typically sized 265 x 165mm and each tile is hung on a batten and double nailed in place. A layer of underfelt is first laid below the preservative-treated battens, which are normally fixed to the blockwork. The felt should be of 'breather-quality', *ie* not polythene. Above the tiles there should be a horizontal strip of lead apron (min. Code 4 lead) placed under windowsills and dressed over the tile course below by about 100mm, in order to make the joint watertight.

Weatherboarding

You don't have to live exclusively in East Anglia or Kent, the natural homes of 'clapboarding', to justify using traditional barn-style timber cladding on your house. This is a popular way of giving an instant character boost to otherwise conventional buildings. Currently, weatherboarding is rather in vogue, especially when painted pale colours rather than the traditional black.

It can also provide a handy method for disguising ugly old 1970s brick walls, whilst upping your insulation into the bargain. But this will have already been chewed over at some length, at the time when your extension was a mere glint in its designer's eye.

From a pure design perspective, this is one of the few wall treatments that seems to produce harmonious results, almost regardless of the style of existing house that the extension is bolted on to. Its amazing versatility means you can mix and match, perhaps applying it on just one small part of the extension. It is often seen adding colour to upper walls, contrasting with brickwork or render down below. Because it's fairly lightweight, particularly when combined with timber frame wall construction, it may provide a useful technical solution where loadings can't be too great, such as building over an existing single-storey extension with relatively shallow foundations.

However, there is a downside. It's not maintenance-free, so expect to spend a bit of time up your ladders wielding a brush every few years. It is good practice to apply at least one coat of stain or paint before fixing, to avoid the risk of bare

strips peeping out at you between courses when the timber inevitably shrinks. Roughsawn timber drinks woodstain and needs a re-application about every seven years, but the amount of time required for keeping up appearances can be reduced by using special low maintenance wood stain or microporous paint or varnish. To protect against rot, all wood should be pre-treated with preservative, ideally arriving on site already pressure impregnated. Otherwise it will need liberal coats of preservative brushed well in, especially to the grain at cut ends.

If you prefer a maintenance-free lifestyle, some of the more expensive 'fit & forget' timbers such as cedar or heat treated redwood may be worth investigating. Other cheaper options are cladding made from fibre cement board or UPVC, which is available in a range of different colours. Now whether UPVC cladding makes a suitable alternative to the real thing is really a matter of personal taste and depends on the type of house you're extending. It may be just the job for matching extensions to some 1960s or 1970s houses. Call us old-fashioned, but with traditional architecture it has to be said that UPVC doesn't quite 'float the boat'. You can't beat real wood for style and quality.

Timber cladding normally needs to be fixed to a timber sub-frame of battens, over the underlying blockwork. Laying the boards over a sheet of roofing felt will give greater weather protection. Special annular shank nails or purpose-made galvanised nails are recommended for fixing boards because they grip the wood very well, and the lost-head variety can be punched below the surface and concealed with filler.

There are different styles of timber cladding. Traditional 'barn' cladding comprises roughsawn feather-edged horizontal planks of boarding, typically fixed with a 30mm overlap. Boards should not be nailed through the point where they overlap since it can cause splitting by restricting their ability to move with temperature changes.

A well-known planed timber alternative style is rebated shiplap cladding, which is equally weather-resistant, although being laid completely flush arguably means it loses something of the 'period house' feel. If you want to invigorate your cladding, try fitting the boards diagonally, perhaps set within panels. Vertical boards can look good in some cases (laid to shiplap style rather than feather-edge).

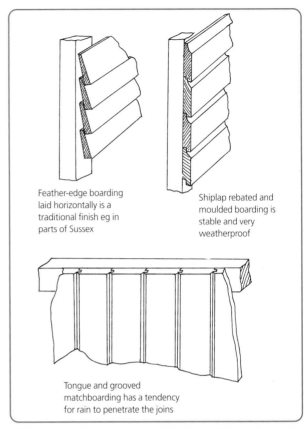

Feather-edge boarding laid horizontally is a traditional finish eg in parts of Sussex

Shiplap rebated and moulded boarding is stable and very weatherproof

Tongue and grooved matchboarding has a tendency for rain to penetrate the joins

Different types of boarding are available for cladding, and a good timber merchant should be able to supply a variety to choose from.

Rendering

In exposed locations where wild weather is no stranger, outer wall treatments often traditionally comprised of coatings of protective render. In order to enhance its weather-resistance, lumpy pebbledash or roughcast would commonly be applied, since these finishes are even better at deflecting rainwater than smooth sand/cement render – hence its popularity in stormy coastal areas such as parts of Scotland and Cornwall.

It's usually the plasterer's job to render the outside of the building. Render is normally applied to blockwork in two coats, a base coat about 10–12mm thick followed by a finishing coat of about 8–10mm. For a smooth finish the final coat is rubbed down with a float or trowel. Pebbledash is created by thickening the final coat and then throwing ('dashing') dry pea shingle against it so that the pebbles stick, and then pushing them home with a trowel. 'Roughcast' contains bigger lumps of shingle mixed into the final coat which is then thrown on and left rough. A modern variation on the theme is 'Tyrolean render', which is created by a hand-held 'snow machine' that sprays a mix of render and pebbles onto the render base coat. Or you might fancy a spot of traditional Olde-Worlde (or 1930s) 'half timbering' on your gables, comprising 50 x 125mm timbers fixed to the blockwork, infilled with render or herringbone pattern brickwork.

To successfully disperse rainwater, rendered wall surfaces should project outwards at their base just above DPC level in the form of a 'bellmouth drip'. Below this, the wall may be brickwork or blockwork painted with a black bituminous band of paint to keep damp at bay.

As with most cement-based materials, care should be taken to avoid applying render in frosty conditions, otherwise cracking can occur.

Plain render and roughcast are normally painted. White tends to be the colour of choice unless you happen to live in 'Balamorey' or a quaint fishing village where rainbow colours make welcome relief from the constant drizzle. Render is therefore not maintenance free, requiring decoration every five years or so (although some paints claim up to 15 years before needing recoating). Masonry paint comprises special water-based emulsion with anti bacterial properties, incorporating reinforcement for strength, and can be applied by roller, brush, or sometimes spray. However, before painting newly cement rendered walls, the underlying surface must first be allowed to fully dry out, which can take ages if the weather isn't clement. Once dry, the render can be sealed with a stabilising solution before painting, to bind the surface and make it less absorbent. But if you've already taken the scaffolding down, painting the walls will take twice as long.

Tidying up

Now that all the building works are largely complete, it's tidy-up time. You may notice a marked lack of enthusiasm amongst site-personnel by this stage, and if you want to know the true meaning of words like 'reluctant' or 'grudging', asking builders to clear up around the site at the end of the job is about as close as you're ever going to get. But a good contractor will see the job through to the bitter end, which not only means tidying up but also cleaning all the dust and debris both indoors and out, and generally leaving the place ready for occupation. Any brickwork that's been splashed with mortar should be cleaned and sticky labels removed from new glazing. Splashes of paint or plaster over indoor joinery and fittings must be cleaned off. Lastly that industrial-sized Dyson must be put through its paces. Then, with hands all a tremble, the protective covers can finally be whisked away, including those to smoke alarms and lights.

Landscaping

Landscaping works may be required as a condition of your planning consent. Or you might just have the urge to let rip and embark on some serious mulching. Either way, garden design has come a long way in recent years, with inspirational TV programmes spurring us into horticultural action. It's worth taking a bit of time to jazz up your own private slice of green belt, since creating the perfect patio with some stylish decking and a few shrubs can transform your erstwhile building site into a mini paradise. But there are some practical considerations to consider.

Photo: acanthalifestyle.com

If you recall all the trouble we took during the build to deter damp from the walls, it would be daft to now encourage damp problems by piling earth up against the walls, or to allow rain to splash and dampen the brickwork. Patios are notorious for raising external ground levels excessively. The ground should be a minimum of 150mm below DPC level and if for any reason this can't be achieved, the next best option is to cut back the hard ground surface next to the walls of the house and create a shallow gravel-filled trench around them. This will allow any damp to evaporate and disperse safely. Paths and hard surfaces near the house should slope gently away to expel rainwater. If you prefer timber decking, select FSC-accredited timber bearing the mark of the Forestry Stewardship Council (so you can't be held personally responsible for destruction of the rainforests).

Access

The requirements for disabled access in Part M of the Building Regulations may have some influence on the design of your immediate garden area. Although they don't strictly apply to home extensions, it may be worth incorporating some of these features as they can make life easier for lots of people, including young children, pram pushers and wheely bin operatives. Or you may need to accommodate a family member with special needs. This means the pathways approaching the house should facilitate wheelchair access with shallow gradients leading up to external doors and ramps instead of steps where possible. On entering the house there should be level thresholds, especially to the main entrance door. Whilst there's no obligation to upgrade your old house for disabled access and usability, your new extension must not adversely affect the existing building.

Planning your defences

There's always the risk that your stunning new extension might attract the wrong sort of attention – neighbourhood scumbags looking for rich pickings. It pays to think like a burglar in order to design-out opportunities for crime. Flat roofs and nearby trees can provide tempting pathways to upstairs windows. Easy ground cover from hedges and shrubs along with a swift escape route can also make your property an appealing target. All the evidence confirms that intruders are deterred by the sight of alarms and

CCTV cameras, and good old-fashioned guard dogs are still a serious turn-off for opportunist thieves.

One thing to avoid, however, is indiscriminate use of PIR security lights, flooding the neighbourhood in dazzling white light every time a dog scratches its rear quarters, with the result that everyone ignores them,

including the intruders. There should be an indoor override control switch for outdoor lighting. Similarly, oversensitive house alarms that sound-off routinely will inevitably be ignored the one time your home is in mortal danger.

Defensive planting

One well-kept secret that's not often mentioned by TV gardeners is the deterrent value of 'defensive shrubs' – a little strategic planting of naturally sharp thorny species such as hawthorn, pyracantha ('firethorn'), blackberry, holly and rambling rose may be all you need to repel intruders.

Whilst on the subject of planting, if you want to live in peace with your neighbours it's best to avoid the notorious fast growing leylandii (cypresses), which can grow to an incredible three times the height of your house. Instead, try planting low water demand species such as holly, yews, silver birches, box, brooms, dwarf pines and privets.

Completion

The job is not officially done until you've notified Building Control and the final inspection has been carried out to their satisfaction. You'll then need to formally request that a completion certificate is issued. The completion inspection should always be carried out before the contract with the builders has terminated and they've vanished off site. Failing this, any remedial work required will be your responsibility to complete.

NOTIFY BUILDING CONTROL 8
Final inspection – two days' notice

Unless already inspected at a previous stage, the Building Control Officer may want to check that the necessary thermal insulation has been installed, that all the plumbing is connected up and works satisfactorily, and that the necessary fire or sound protection is in place. They may also check that external ground levels are no higher than the prescribed 150mm below DPC level.

But what Building Control consider complete, and what you regard as complete, can be two very different things. For example, they won't be terribly interested in all the cosmetic stuff, like whether the decorations have been done or the skirting boards are secure. Remember, the Building Regulations are only the minimum standard acceptable for health and safety purposes. They aren't a guarantee that the builders have finished everything they were supposed to have done. That's where snagging comes in. Which is pretty much down to you.

Snagging

The objective of the snagging inspection is to draw up a list of all remaining defects. These are normally very minor things, like paint blemishes, sticking doors and windows, loose joinery, missing mastic to joints, messy tile grouting and wonky wall sockets – in fact anything that doesn't look too clever. It's always best to go round the building unaccompanied as you write out your list, so you can concentrate and methodically inspect each room and component of the building in turn. Surveyors have a trained eye and are the best people to do this job, but if none are available ask a friend or colleague to take an independent look, in addition to making your own inspection.

You'll then need to provide the contractor with a copy and, together, take a long hard walk around the building to agree all the points. Later, when the work is done, check off all the snagging items that have been satisfactorily completed.

Practical completion and final payments

You may recall that useful 'builder-motivating device' known as a retention. If you don't, the builders certainly will, since you'll have kept back some of the money owed to them. But now is the day of reckoning. It's at this stage – known as 'Practical Completion' – that in accordance with the contract you'll be required to release half of the retained money. This can be paid together with the builder's final payment.

If you've employed an architect or surveyor to manage the project, they should be able to issue and sign the certificate of practical completion once you're happy the snagging has been substantially completed. This will formally trigger the release of funds.

However, the final totting up process can be quite complex, since any change instructions and extras will need to be taken into account. It's not unusual for there to be small differences of opinion, often due to fading memories, so some degree of compromise may be needed on both sides. After all, everyone now wants to get on with their lives rather than bickering over the last 99p.

There then follows a period known as the 'defects liability period', normally three or six months depending on the contract. It's during this period that any latent defects that appear (typically things like minor shrinkage cracks to plasterwork and small leaks) should be made good, with the help of a final snagging list. The architect or surveyor can then issue and sign the appropriate certificate triggering the release of the remaining retention money due to the contractor.

Insurance

Just to put a dampener on things, if your house suddenly burned down right now the insurance company could conceivably wriggle out of paying the full amount. Why?

Because you've just massively added to the value of your home, and your house insurance has not been increased to reflect it. Calculating the rebuild insurance cost shouldn't be too hard, since it would normally equate approximately to the total amount you've paid for the build (or see website for insurance calculator). Simply tot up all those cheques that you've handed over to the builders and then add the retention and VAT.

Oh, and those nice people at the Council may have clocked your increased property value and are right now busy upping your council tax band.

How to celebrate

You don't need a Haynes manual to tell you how to celebrate, but you deserve warm congratulations for seeing the job through. There's no such thing as a stress-free building project. There will always be challenging moments and potential for minor disputes. So if you've survived the job reasonably unscathed – well done! Hopefully, all the expense, hassle, noise, dust and dirt will have been worth it. Not just in terms of added property values and improved lifestyle but in terms of experience gained and one or two new friends made.

As we noted at the beginning, the skills required to do what you've just achieved are essentially no less than those needed for building your own house from scratch. Just be sure to give yourself a well-earned break before embarking on your next grand design!

Main trades needed on site
- **Decorators:** Decorating walls and joinery, tiling.
- **Labourers:** Tidying up, cleaning, insulating lofts, landscaping.
- **Carpenters:** Weatherboarding.
- **Tilers:** Tile hanging.
- **Plasterers:** Rendering.

www.home-extension.co.uk

INDEX

Author	Ian Alistair Rock MRICS
Technical consultants	Colin K. Dale FRICS
	Michael Haslam MSc FRICS
	Basil Parylo, Building Control Leeds City Council
Photography	David Davies, Basil Parylo,
	Richard Woodroofe MRICS
Project Manager	Louise McIntyre
Copy Editor	Ian Heath
Page Build	James Robertson